Network+™ Exam Notes™

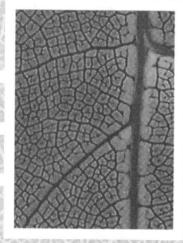

David Groth
Ben Bergersen

San Francisco • Paris • Düsseldorf • Soest • London

Associate Publisher: Guy Hart-Davis
Contracts and Licensing Manager: Kristine O'Callaghan
Acquisitions Editor: Neil Edde
Developmental Editor: Linda Lee
Editor: Jeff Gammon
Technical Editor: Mark Kovach
Book Designer: Bill Gibson
Graphic Illustrator: Tony Jonick
Electronic Publishing Specialist: Franz Baumhackl
Project Team Leader: Teresa Trego
Proofreaders: Susan Berge, Rich Ganis
Indexer: Marilyn Smith
Cover Designer: Archer Design
Cover Illustrator/Photographer: FPG International

To my little naches. May you be happy and healthy.

—David Groth

To Tina, who means the world to me.

—Ben Bergersen

Acknowledgments

As with any book, it took many people to put the *Exam Notes* together. First off, I would like to thank my co-author, Ben. We had fun at the Network+ exam writing sessions and also had fun writing this book together. Ben is MCSE, MCT, CNA, CTT, and A+ certified, as well as being an IEE Computer Society member. He is a systems engineer and faculty member at SUNY Monroe Community College in Rochester, NY. He has also recently become engaged. (Way to go, Ben!)

This book would not exist if not for Linda Lee, my developmental editor at Sybex. Thank you for putting up with all of my phone calls and neurotic e-mails (and for not blasting me with a phaser when you had the chance). Additionally, thanks go out to Sybex editor Jeff Gammon for turning my collection of chicken-scratchings into a cohesive, useful study guide.

I would also like to acknowledge my wife, family, and friends. My wife Linda tirelessly wrote and edited the Appendices and kept me on the right track. She was a real trouper because she did it while being pregnant and sometimes sick. Thank you to my family and friends who understood when I couldn't go out because I had to work on the book; I really appreciate your understanding.

Finally, thank you, the reader, for purchasing this book. I know that it has all of the information necessary to help you pass the test. If you have questions about Network+ or this book, feel free to e-mail me at dgroth@corpcomm.net. Ben can be contacted by writing to ben@bergersen.org.

Ben and I worked very hard on this book to make it the best Network+ exam notes available. I hope you feel the same.

—David Groth

Thanks to David Groth for getting me involved and for our long conversation late one night.

Thanks to Neil Edde for giving me a chance.

Thanks to Linda Lee for being a tiger in editing and teaching me a lot.

Thanks to Jeff Gammon for understanding.

—Ben Bergersen

Contents at a Glance

Table of Contents

Introduction

If you've purchased this book, you are probably chasing after Network+ certification. This is a great goal, and it is also a great career builder. Newspaper Help Wanted ads are always looking for qualified employees in today's network engineering market, and Network+ certification indicates that you have network skills. Obtaining Network+ certification means that you know something about the product, but, more importantly, it also means that you have the proven ability, determination, and focus to *learn*—the greatest skill any employee can have!

The *Network+ Exam Notes* has been developed to give you the knowledge and skills you will need for the Network+ exam. This book provides a solid introduction to Network+ and will help you on your way to obtaining the sought-after CompTIA Network+ certfication.

Is This Book for You?

The *Network+ Exam Notes* was designed to be a succinct, portable exam review guide that can be used either in conjunction with a more complete study program (book, CBT courseware, classroom/lab environment) or as an exam review for those who don't feel the need for more extensive test preparation. The goal of this book isn't to "give the answers away." Instead, the Exam Notes aims to both identify the topics on which you can expect to be tested and to provide sufficient coverage of those topics.

Perhaps you've been working with networking technologies for years now. The thought of paying lots of money for a specialized Network+ exam preparation course probably doesn't sound too appealing. What can they teach you that you don't already know, right? Be careful, though. Many experienced network administrators have walked confidently into test centers only to walk sheepishly out of them after failing an exam. After you've finished reading through this book, you should have a clear idea of how your understanding of the technologies involved matches up with the expectations of the Network+ test makers.

Or perhaps you're relatively new to the world of networking, drawn to it by the promise of challenging work and higher salaries. You've just waded through an 800-page study guide or taken a class at a local training center. Lots of information to keep track of, isn't it? Well, by organizing the *Exam Notes* according to the Network+ exam objectives, and by breaking up the information into concise, manageable pieces, we've created what we think is the handiest exam review guide available. Throw it into your briefcase and carry it to work with you. As you read through the book, you'll be able to quickly identify the areas that you know best as well as those that will require a more in-depth review.

NOTE The goal of the *Exam Notes* is to help Network+ candidates to familiarize themselves with the subjects on which they can expect to be tested during the Network+ exam. For complete, in-depth coverage of the technologies and topics involved, we recommend the *Network+ Study Guide* from Sybex.

How Is This Book Organized?

As mentioned previously, the *Exam Notes* is organized according to the official exam objectives list that has been prepared by CompTIA for the Network+ exam. The chapters coincide to the broad objectives groupings. The exam objectives are distributed throughout the book, and specific objectives are addressed in each chapter. In turn, objective sections are divided, as detailed in the following paragraphs, according to the type of information being presented.

Critical Information

This section presents the most detailed, relevant information about the objective in question. This is the place to start if you're unfamiliar with, or uncertain about, the technical issues related to an objective.

Exam Essentials

This section is comprised of a concise list of the most crucial subject areas that you'll need to fully comprehend prior to taking the Network+ exam. This section can help you to identify the topics that might require more study on your part.

Key Terms and Concepts

A mini-glossary has been compiled to list the most important terms and concepts relating to each specific objective. You'll understand what all of those technical words mean within the context of the subject matter being discussed.

Sample Questions

Questions similar to those that you'll encounter on the actual Network+ exam are included for each objective. Answers and explanations are provided so you can gain some insight into the test-taking process.

NOTE For a more comprehensive collection of exam review questions, check out the Network+ Test Success book, also published by Sybex.

How Do You Become Network+ Certified?

Becoming a Network+ certified technician is actually very simple. You only need to pass the Network+ exam, which has been developed by CompTIA and its partners and is administrated by Sylvan Prometric.

Where Do You Take the Exams?

You can take the Network+ exam at any Sylvan Prometric authorized testing center. Call Sylvan (1-888-895-6116) or visit the registration Web site (http://www.2test.com) to locate your nearest testing center.

Most major cities in North America have at least one authorized testing center.

What the Network+ Exam Measures

The Network+ exam measures your ability to understand both the fundamental networking concepts involved in networks today and your ability to implement and troubleshoot a network. The test was designed to test network professionals who have 18–24 months of experience implementing networks.

Tips for Taking Your Network+ Exam

Here are some general tips for successfully taking your exam:

- Arrive early at the exam center so you can relax and review your study materials, particularly tables and lists of exam-related information.

- Read the questions carefully. Don't be tempted to jump to an early conclusion. Make sure you know *exactly* what the question is asking.

- Don't leave any unanswered questions. They count against you.

- When answering multiple-choice questions that you're not sure about, use a process of elimination to get rid of the obviously incorrect questions first. This will improve your odds in case you need to make an educated guess.

- Because the hard questions will eat up the most time, save them for last. (You can move forward and backward through the exam.)

- This test has many exhibits (pictures). It can be difficult, if not impossible, to view both the questions and the exhibit simulation on the 14-inch and 15-inch screens usually found at the testing centers. Call around to each center to see if it has 17-inch monitors available. If it doesn't, perhaps you can arrange to bring in your own. Failing this, some participants have found it useful to quickly draw a question's diagram on scratch paper (provided by the testing center) and then to use the monitor to view just the question.

- Many participants run out of time before they are able to complete the test. If you are unsure of the answer to a question, you may want to choose one of the answers, mark the question, and go on; an unanswered question does not help you. Once your time is up, you cannot go on to another question. However, you can remain on some questions indefinitely, so, when you are almost out of time, go to a question you feel you can figure out—given enough time—and work until you feel you have got it.

- You are allowed to use the Windows calculator during your test. However, it may be better to memorize a table of the subnet addresses and to write it down on the scratch paper supplied by the testing center before you start the test.

Once you have completed your exam, you will be given immediate online notification of your pass or fail status. Also, the test administrator will give you a printed Examination Score Report indicating your pass or fail status and your exam results by section. Test scores are automatically forwarded to CompTIA within five working days after you take the test. You do not need to send your score to CompTIA. If you pass the exam, you will receive confirmation from CompTIA, typically within two to four weeks.

Contact Information

To find out more about Network+ materials and programs, to register with Sylvan Prometric, or to get other useful information, check out the following resources.

CompTIA Network+ Web site—http://www.comptia.org/networkplus/index.htm

As it seems, this is CompTIA's Network+ Web site. It contains all of the information you need to know about Network+, including test objectives, registration information, test sponsors, and sample test questions. Check this source for the most up-to-date information about Network+ certification and the exam.

Sylvan Prometric testing centers—800-755-EXAM

Contact Sylvan to register to take the Network+ exam at any of more than 800 Sylvan Prometric testing centers around the world.

Sylvan Internet Registration—http://www.2test.com

This Web site can be used to register for any exam that is administered by Sylvan. CompTIA has announced that you can register for the Network+ exam via this Web site as well.

How to Contact the Authors

The authors of this book can be reached by e-mailing dgroth@corpcomm.net. We appreciate any comments you may have about your success with the Network+ exam and this book's part in obtaining your certification.

How to Contact the Publisher

Sybex welcomes reader feedback on all of its titles. Visit the Sybex Web site at www.sybex.com for book updates and additional certification information. You'll also find online forms for submitting comments or suggestions regarding this or any other Sybex book.

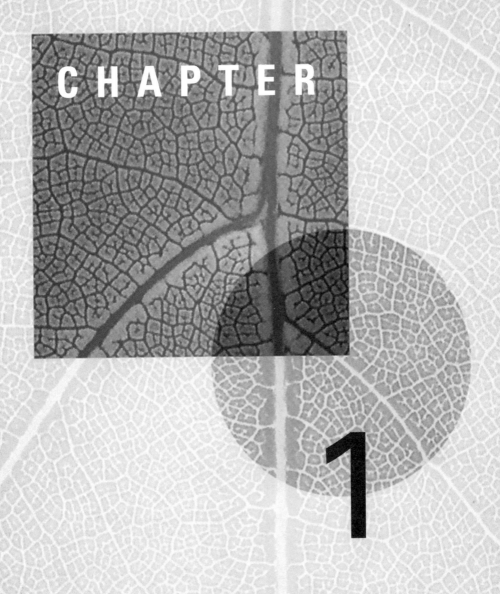

CHAPTER

1

Basic Knowledge

Network+ Exam Objectives Covered in This Chapter:

Demonstrate understanding of basic network structure, including: *(pages 4 – 17)*

- The characteristics of star, bus, mesh, and ring topologies, their advantages and disadvantages
- The characteristics of segments and backbones

Identify the following: *(pages 17 – 34)*

- The major network operating systems, including Microsoft Windows NT, Novell NetWare, and Unix
- The clients that best serve specific network operating systems and their resources
- The directory services of the major network operating systems

Associate IPX, IP, and NetBEUI with their functions. *(pages 34 – 43)*

Define the following terms and explain how each relates to fault tolerance or high availability: *(pages 44 – 53)*

- Mirroring
- Duplexing
- Striping (with and without parity)
- Volumes
- Tape backup

Define the layers of the OSI model and identify the protocols, services, and functions that pertain to each layer. *(pages 53 – 60)*

Recognize and describe the following characteristics of networking media and connectors: *(pages 61 – 71)*

- The advantages and disadvantages of coax, Cat 3, Cat 5, fiber optic, UTP, and STP, and the conditions under which they are appropriate
- The length and speed of 10Base2, 10BaseT, and 100BaseT
- The length and speed of 10Base5, 100Base VGAnyLan, and 100Base TX
- The visual appearance of RJ-45 and BNC, and how they are crimped

Identify the basic attributes, purpose, and function of the following network elements: *(pages 72 – 83)*

- Full- and half-duplexing
- WAN and LAN
- Server, workstation, and host
- Server-based networking and peer-to-peer networking
- Cable, NIC, and router
- Broadband and baseband
- Gateway, as both a default IP router and as a method to connect dissimilar systems or protocols

The basic goal of networking is to share information and resources. However, making a network function properly requires a lot of specialized knowledge. This chapter provides the fundamental networking background that you will need to understand the rest of the information in this book and to pass the Network+ exam. (The Network+ exam starts out with basic networking knowledge.)

Computer networks are either run on wires (known as cabling) or are wireless. Wire-based networks are easier and cheaper, and they comprise the overwhelming majority of networks throughout the world. This section will review star, bus, mesh, and ring cabling topologies.

To pass the exam, you will need to be familiar with the three most common network operating systems, which, in the corporate environment, are Microsoft Windows NT, Novell NetWare, and Unix. Each of these operating systems needs to talk on the wire in a particular language, or protocol. Interoperability between networks is paramount. Companies are not throwing out their old servers when a migration occurs. Rather, all of the different operating systems are applied where they are most efficient. The proper use of protocols allows different operating systems to talk to each other. (TCP/IP, IPX/SPX, and NetBEUI/NetBIOS protocols are most often used.)

Protocols can only work if there are devices present to do the transmissions. Devices on the network include servers, workstations, hosts, routers, and gateways. Typically, servers are specialized machines that provide a service—hence the name. Web, file, print, fax, e-mail, and database servers all constitute the mainstream support of users on a network. The data on these servers is critical to the smooth operations of a company. Data is so important that redundant disk arrays are used in case a hard drive fails. Users, on the other hand, rarely sit down and access their data directly from the server console. From a workstation, users access their data over the network. Workstations are less critical because you can replace them inexpensively. This does not mean a user's machine is unimportant; it just means that tens of thousands of dollars are not spent on fault tolerance for each workstation.

Workstations, servers, and remote users need the network in order to communicate with each other. The number of wide area networks (WAN) and local area networks (LAN) seems to be exploding every day. The largest WAN in the world is the Internet. Today, you can buy books, CDs, cars, and so much more over computer networks. College courses, music, and video are transmitted from large networks to home PCs. All networks, including their data and devices, need to be managed. The Network+ certification will help you to take advantage of this exciting time in computer networking.

Demonstrate understanding of basic network structure, including:

- The characteristics of star, bus, mesh, and ring topologies, their advantages and disadvantages
- The characteristics of segments and backbones

A fundamental part of a network is its *topology*–the design and layout of the networked devices, and the cabling that connects those devices. Knowing the cost, advantages, and disadvantages of each cable type allows you to select the appropriate wire for a particular job.

Stars, buses, meshes, and rings are cable layout designs. Stars and rings can use central hub devices. Buses and meshes can have computers directly connected to each other on the same segment without any additional devices. When your network gets larger than one cable can accommodate or needs to connect different areas, you will begin utilizing segments. A *segment* is a logical, physical grouping of computers that are all connected by the same set of wires. The top-level wire is known as the *backbone* and allows different parts of your network to communicate with each other. The exam will test your knowledge of backbones and their purpose.

In the real world, networks can use any of these types of topologies. Because networks have many different types, the Network+ exam tests your knowledge of the different types of topologies that are used when implementing a network.

Critical Information

The star, bus, mesh, and ring topologies are used to lay out the cabling for your network. A bus layout is advisable for small offices with tight budgets because it is the simplest and least expensive cable design to implement. Every computer connects directly to one long cable, or bus. If you can spend a little more money, then go for the star design (with a star layout). Many bus networks can go down when someone damages any single portion of the central cable. But with a star network, each computer node is connected to a central hub like spokes connected to the hub of a wheel. If any single connection goes down, a node uses an alternate route to communicate. These same kinds of comparisons can be made between all types of network topologies. The Network+ exam will test your ability to describe and identify all four types of physical topologies.

Physical Topologies

Physical topologies are the designs by which cables and devices are laid out. Star, bus, mesh, and ring are the four types of physical topologies. Each design has different features, design complexity, cost, capacity to change and to troubleshoot, fault tolerance, and maximum number of nodes. The Network+ exam tests your knowledge of these features, and you need to know whether each feature is an advantage, disadvantage, or just a general feature.

Star Topology

The most common layout of network cabling in offices today is the star topology. A star topology has cables that start at a central hub and radiate out to each computer node. (Remember the analogy of a wheel hub with cables going out like spokes to the perimeter and connecting to computers.) This means that there are only two nodes connected to each cable—the computer and the hub. A failure along any single point affects only one computer, thus isolating the effects of a cable failure. This design, however, does not provide redundancy. There is only one cable connecting each computer to the hub. If that cable fails, that node loses network connectivity.

Typically, the hub and wire connections are secured in a wiring closet. Computer network equipment usually shares space in the wiring closet with telecommunications equipment. As shown in Figure 1.1, computers are connected to each other via cabling and the central hub.

FIGURE 1.1: Star topology

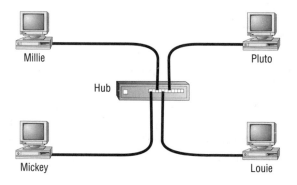

The key features, advantages, and disadvantages of a star topology are outlined below.

Advantages

Cost The cost is moderate compared to other topologies. Every machine must have a cable going from it to a central hub, so star topologies are more expensive than buses, but they are cheaper than meshes.

Design complexity The complexity of designing a star is average compared to other topologies. Each computer has a cable connecting it to a central hub. A line drawing looks like a star where lines project out from a center dot to each remote computer.

Fault tolerance A single failure will not cause a loss of service for all computers; the failure is isolated to a single cable and, hence, a single node.

Reconfiguration You can easily change the configuration of a star. A hub is used to centrally connect all computers. To add a computer, you just plug an additional cable into the hub.

Troubleshooting Cabling problems can be quickly resolved. A single computer going down points to a particular cable as the culprit.

Disadvantages

Installation complexity Because of the number of cables involved (one for every single network device) it is more complex to install than other network topologies.

General Features

Maximum nodes One network device is connected to one end of each cable. The other end of the cable directly connects the device to the hub.

TIP The maximum number of nodes relates the to the total number of computers connected to a single cable. A star topology does not limit the number of computers on the network. Hub configurations and cable communication methods limit totals with this design.

Bus Topology

A bus topology operates by connecting all computer nodes to a single cable called the bus. Since each computer connects directly to the main cable, central hubs are not used. With just one cable running the entire network, any damage to the cable causes the entire segment to lose network connectivity. This topology is best suited for connecting terminals on multiple floors of a building and should be housed in protected shafts in the walls.

When the bus (or single cable) is used in an office or laboratory, problems can arise. For example, a loose connection to a single computer disconnects all computers from that segment. However, bus networks are still common even with their lack of fault tolerance. This is because they are the least expensive network design. Therefore, you may inherit such a cabling infrastructure.

The bus topology allows up to five segments to be connected to each other by repeaters. A *repeater* is a network device that regenerates (amplifies) an electrical signal from one physical segment to another and allows you to overcome cable length limitations. A bus topology can support a maximum of four repeaters. A length of cable between repeaters or at the end of a repeater is known as a physical segment. A total of five segments can exist on a single bus network, with four repeaters between them and three populated segments. (This is known as the 5-4-3 rule and does not restrict the number of computers allowed on a single segment.) Three segments can have computers connected to them. And at the end of each bus, you either have a repeater or a terminator. Without termination, you will get signal bounce-back.

Figure 1.2 shows a bus topology. Notice that all of the network devices connect to a single cable and that the cable runs more or less in a straight line from the first device to the last.

The key features, advantages and disadvantages of a bus topology are outlined below.

Advantages

Cost   Because of their simplicity, bus topologies are often the cheapest topology for companies to implement.

Design complexity   A bus topology is simple to design and install. Each computer connects to a single cable.

Disadvantages

Fault tolerance   A bus topology cable fault causes all computers on the segment to lose connectivity. (This is compared to limiting the effects of failure to one node in a star network, and no loss of connectivity at all in a mesh network.)

FIGURE 1.2: Bus topology

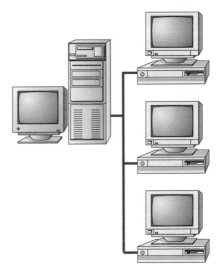

Troubleshooting   Cabling problems are difficult to isolate; a loose connection anywhere brings down the entire segment and all attached computers. No visible clues tell you which computer might have an improper connection.

Reconfiguration   Since a single cable is used to connect all computers, any disruption of the cable will sever connectivity for the entire segment. T-connectors, terminators, and barrel connectors can become loosened from the main cable by pulling on them. When any piece of hardware becomes loose, network connectivity is affected.

General Features

Maximum nodes   Remember the 5-4-3 rule, which governs the maximum number of repeaters and segments that can be populated with nodes. Five segments are allowed per bus network. A maximum of four repeaters connect each segment, and three segments maximum can be populated with nodes. The number of nodes is limited only by the performance of the network. The more nodes that are added, the more traffic that is generated.

Mesh Topology

In a mesh topology, every computer in a network is individually connected to all other computers. Two computers are connected to each cable, but several cables are now connected to a single computer. To figure out the maximum number of connections, and hence the number of cables used, use the formula $x(x-1)/2$, where x is the number of nodes. For example, four computers in Figure 1.3 would have $4(4-1)/2$, or 10 cables connecting every computer via a direct cable to every other computer.

This high number of connections makes the system redundant, but it's also the most expensive topology to install. While costly, multiple connections attached to a single computer can go down but the node still won't lose network connectivity.

TIP The Internet is designed in a partial mesh layout. Not every node has a dedicated connection to every other node.

FIGURE 1.3: Mesh topology

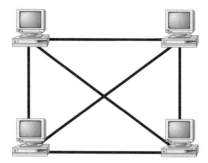

The key features, advantages, and disadvantages of a mesh topology are outlined below.

Advantages

Fault tolerance   Every computer has multiple communication paths. Communication is assured even if several connections fail.

Disadvantages

Cost   Cable costs rise as the number of computers increases. For example, when there are two computers, two cables are needed; when there are six computers—all interconnected—fifteen lines are needed.

Design complexity   Every computer has a cable connected to every other computer. There is no central communications device (such as a hub) or central communication cable (as in a bus). Organization and maintenance quickly become complex as communication lines overlap each other.

Reconfiguration   The high number of cables going to each computer makes installation complicated. You will need to be very careful to keep track of the destination of each cable.

Troubleshooting   You may not even know a cable has failed. Many possible communication paths will exist between two computers alone, and each cable must be individually checked.

General Features

Maximum nodes   A computer is connected to multiple other nodes by attaching additional cables. If you add n computers to a mesh topology, then the number of cables will be $n(n-1)$ divided by 2. So, for five stations there will be $5(4)/2$, or 10 cables. With 10 computers, that number goes up to 45 cables.

Ring Topology

The ring topology connects computer nodes with a cable laid out in a loop. Each computer is connected to two other computers. A failure with a single cable within a physical ring causes the ring to go down and is detrimental to its fault tolerance. Physical ring topologies are not seen very often in today's networks because of the high cost and complexity in installing them.

It is important to note that this is *not* a Token Ring. Developed by IBM, Token Rings use a logical ring layout, but also a physical star layout. This means that even though the cables are laid out in a star topology the signals travel to each station, in order, in a ring.

F I G U R E 1.4: Ring topology

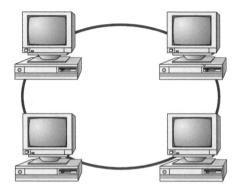

Notice how all of the computer nodes are connected in a circle in Figure 1.4. This is an example of a physical ring topology.

The key features, advantages, and disadvantages of a ring topology are outlined below.

Advantages

Accessibility   Every computer has equal access to the network. The use of a token assures that all nodes equally enjoy the speed of a low-utilization network (but they also may encounter the pain of a slow, busy network).

Fault tolerance   A single cable break can be sustained without communication loss to any computer when using a physical ring topology. With a logical ring topology, a cable failure will only affect the single computer to which it is attached.

Disadvantages

Cost   This topology requires special equipment, which is expensive.

Reconfiguration, physical ring   Reconfiguration is difficult. A ring was not meant to be broken. The ring will reseal itself after one break, but network connectivity goes down for the segment after a second break.

Troubleshooting   Proprietary equipment and the use of a token makes troubleshooting difficult.

General Features

Maximum nodes per segment   The total number of nodes varies with a physical ring. For a logical ring, you can only have two nodes per cable—one for the hub and one for the computer.

Network Superstructure

A network superstructure is a way of categorizing the different parts and functions of the network. The superstructure includes all of the cables and subnetworks that make up the network. Basically, the superstructure consists of the different cable segments on the network and how they are classified.

One main cable segment connects all of the other cable segments in the network together. This main segment is known as the backbone. The backbone connects all of the different segments in a network together. These segments are subdivisions, or subnetworks, of a larger network. Each segment has its own cabling and transmission setup.

Segment

As subdivisions of a large local area network, segments can be divided by special network equipment such as routers. Segmentation—the creation of segments—is used to reduce network traffic. For instance, if your Accounting Department connects to a database server and your Research Department connects to a newsgroup server, you have a good reason to segment the network. With one large network, all users' computers share a single wire. But you can minimize network congestion by separating the paths to different departmental servers.

NOTE   Routers are discussed later in this chapter as well as in the *Network+ Study Guide* (Sybex, 1999).

Backbone

The backbone is the top level of a segmented network. This level allows communications between all nodes in different segments. Multiple locations, such as cities, campuses, or buildings, can be connected by the backbone. In a LAN, the backbone will have a high speed.

Exam Essentials

Be prepared to describe and identify the different types of network topologies. You should also know the specifics of each type of typology, as well as the maximum length and other restrictions for each.

Know how to identify different network topologies. A single cable with computers attached to it is a bus. A central hub with cables radiating out to computers is a star. Crisscrossed, redundant connections to all computers is a mesh. An outer loop connecting all computers is a ring.

Know how to select a network topology based on its advantages. If redundancy is the key criteria, a ring provides a medium level of redundancy, while a mesh offers high redundancy. When you have a limited budget, consider selecting a bus, the most inexpensive design. The star design easily isolates problems and allows for prompt and effective troubleshooting. Be aware that no single design has all the advantages.

Know how to configure a bus topology. A bus must have a terminator or repeater at each end. A ground is recommended but not required. Use the 5-4-3 rule to determine computer node placement and maximum number of components. You can have five segments, four repeaters, and three populated segments.

Know how to calculate the number of cables in a mesh topology. Mesh topologies have a separate dedicated connection from each computer to all computers in the network. The formula for the total number of connections is $(x * (x-1)) / 2$, where x is the number of nodes. If you have five nodes, then you need 10 cables. With 10 nodes, you need 45 cables.

Know how to configure a ring topology. Computers are connected to an outer loop, with the loop sealed in the form of a ring. Special equipment is needed to accommodate rings. Realize that there are two types of rings—physical and logical.

Know how to identify a network segment and backbone. A backbone is the main communications path to which all subsections, or segments, connect. The backbone should be the highest-speed connection in a local network. Segments help reduce network traffic by providing access to specific servers for particular groups or departments.

Key Terms and Concepts

Backbone   The main communication cable for a network.

Bus topology   A network design where all computer nodes are connected to a main cable called a bus. Messages are transmitted along the cable for all nodes to receive. Each end must be terminated; otherwise, the signal will bounce back and corrupt other packets being sent through the cable.

Hub   An electrically powered device that allows multiple cable-connected nodes to communicate with each other. A hub has multiple ports to accommodate connections.

Mesh topology   A network design where every computer is connected to all other computers. Each computer has multiple cables connecting it to the other computers. (To calculate the total number of links, use the formula $(x * (x-1)) / 2$, where x is the number of computers.)

Node   A device that communicates via a network interface card and is attached to the network. A node is commonly a computer but can also be some other device, such as a printer directly connected to the network (instead of a computer).

Repeater   A device that regenerates an electrical signal. Repeaters are used to extend a network when the maximum length of a cable has been reached.

Ring topology   A network design where all computers connect to a communications loop. A token is needed to communicate on the ring and thus ensure equal access to the bandwidth of the wire. Physical rings connect computers directly to each other. Logical rings attach to a special device that recreates the actions of a physical ring by sending the data to each computer in turn.

Segment   A subdivision of a larger network.

Star topology   A network design where nodes connect to a central network device. A star network can be likened to spokes connected to the central hub of a wheel.

Wiring closet   A room where hubs and other network equipment are stored. Cables run from the external nodes back to the central wiring closet and connect to the hubs.

Sample Questions

1. Which of the following is a feature of a mesh network?

   A. Minimal cable costs

   B. Improved reliability

   C. Fire code requirement

   D. Token needed to operate

   Answer: B—Mesh networks have additional lines that connect computer equipment to each other. These additional lines provide improved reliability by alternating communication paths when the main links are down. (Cable costs are actually increased when implementing a mesh network because of the multiple links to each node. Tokens are not required in a mesh network.)

2. If you have six computers, how many cables do you need for complete fault tolerance in a mesh network?

   A. 6

   B. 10

   C. 15

   D. 18

   E. 30

   Answer: C—The formula $(x * (x-1)) / 2$ is used, where x is the number of computer nodes. $(6 * (6-1)) / 2 = 15$.

3. What is the least expensive network topology?

   A. Bus

   B. Star

   C. Mesh

   D. Ring

   E. Hybrid

Answer: A—Bus topologies, generally speaking, have the lowest-cost cabling and use the least amount of equipment. (Stars have medium-cost cabling and use a separate cable for each node. With fully redundant cabling routes, mesh topologies are the most expensive. And rings use proprietary equipment, which makes them expensive. A hybrid network will always be more costly than a single type of network topology.)

4. What is the maximum number of repeaters that can be used in a single bus network?

   A. 2

   B. 3

   C. 4

   D. 5

   E. 6

Answer: C—Four repeaters can connect up to five cable sections in a bus network.

Identify the following:

- The major network operating systems, including Microsoft Windows NT, Novell NetWare, and Unix
- The clients that best serve specific network operating systems and their resources
- The directory services of the major network operating systems

Network operating systems (NOS) are used to manage files and to provide services to users on a network. The NOS is the software that manages all functions of a network and the server that it runs on. Microsoft Windows NT, Novell NetWare, and the various flavors of Unix are all examples of network operating systems.

This objective is designed to test your ability to identify the major network operating systems and the appropriate clients that will allow a workstation to use the services of each NOS. Additionally, each NOS has some kind of repository for information about users, printers, computers, and network services. These repositories are commonly called directory services, and each is maintained by the network operating system. The Network+ exam will test you on your understanding of the basic directory services of each major NOS.

Critical Information

There are several basic facts to know about the leading network operating software. The predominant network operating systems each enable workstations running several different software clients to connect to the network and its servers. Once connected, users are able to use the directory services offered by their NOS to access network resources.

Major Network Operating Systems

Although there are many network operating systems in use, only three so far have achieved widespread use across many industries. These major NOS platforms are Microsoft Windows NT, Novell NetWare, and Unix. They have all been improved and advanced in recent years, and each has its particular strengths. Windows NT is the easiest to learn initially because the interface in version 4 is similar to Windows 9.x (the most commonly installed computer operating system). NetWare 5 now has TCP/IP as its primary protocol, along with a Java-based console. Unix is available and certified on the Intel Pentium platform by many different vendors. All systems can communicate with each other and run Internet services by using the TCP/IP protocol.

Microsoft Windows NT

Microsoft Windows NT has become the predominant general-purpose server for many industries. Its versatility and familiar graphical user interface belie its complexity. Using TCP/IP and other protocols, Windows NT can communicate with NetWare and Unix servers. Windows NT was released in the mid-1990s, with versions 3.5 and 3.51. NT did not become popular until version 4, which switched from the GUI interface of Windows 3.11 to the GUI interface of Windows 95.

NOTE Windows 2000 is based on NT technology and will be the current version of Microsoft Windows when it is released.

Interface   Windows NT Workstation and Server both utilize the Windows GUI interface made popular by Windows 95. You can do remote administration with Windows-based graphical utilities on Windows 9.*x* and Windows NT machines. Though rarely used, there are command-line versions of many Windows NT utilities.

Relevant versions   The Network+ exam will test you on Windows NT Server 4 and Windows NT Workstation 4.

Server role   NT Servers can act as both workstations and servers. Be aware that only administrators or those who are granted access are able to log in to the console.

The hardware requirements and recommendations for Windows NT 4 are listed in Table 1.1.

TABLE 1.1: Windows NT Server 4 Hardware Requirements and Recommendations

Hardware	Minimum	Recommended
Processor	Intel 80486 or higher (I386 architecture) or a supported RISC processor (MIPS R4x00, Alpha AXP, or PowerPC)	Pentium 90Mhz or higher (the faster the better)

TABLE 1.1: Windows NT Server 4 Hardware Requirements and Recommendations *(cont.)*

Hardware	Minimum	Recommended
Display	VGA	SVGA
Hard disk space	120MB free	300MB free
Memory	12MB (Workstation); 16MB (Server)	32MB (or greater)
Network card	At least one that matches the topology of your network	At least one that matches the topology of your network
CD-ROM	None	8x (or greater)
Mouse	Required	Required

Novell NetWare

Novell NetWare is a powerful network operating system that first became popular in the 1980s. Companies wanted to connect their Microsoft MS-DOS and Windows computers but could not afford the jump to a minicomputer or mainframe computer. NetWare filled the gap between PCs and minicomputer networking by being able to run server software on inexpensive PC-sized computers. The current version of NetWare is 5, but the company still supports NetWare 3.*x* and 4.*x*. Unlike its predecessors, NetWare 5 offers a choice of three interfaces. There is a command-line–based console, menu-based utilities, and a new Java-based graphical interface. The latter interface is based on the Unix X-Windows standard.

Common features of Novell NetWare include:

> **Interface** NetWare 3.*x* has local administration through a command line interface and menu-driven utilities. Remote administration is through separate Windows 9.*x* and Windows for Workgroups utilities. NetWare 4.*x* includes the Windows 9.*x* and NT NetWare

Administrator remote utilities. NetWare 5 has all of the earlier features, with a Java- and X-Windows–based console added locally.

Relevant versions The Network+ exam will test you on several versions of NetWare. NetWare 3.*x* servers are stand-alone servers, while 4.*x* servers operate within a directory services called an NDS Tree. NetWare 5 servers operate within an NDS Tree and have a Java- and X-Windows–based console.

Server role A NetWare server can only operate as a server. There is no capability to log in to the console and use the machine as a workstation.

The hardware requirements of Novell NetWare 5 are listed in Table 1.2.

T A B L E 1.2:   NetWare 5 Hardware Requirements and Recommendations

Hardware	Minimum	Recommended
Processor	Pentium 100Mhz	Pentium 133MHz (or faster)
Display	VGA	SVGA
Hard disk space	350MB	1GB or more
Memory	64MB (128MB if running Java applications)	128MB or more
Network card	At least one	As many as required
CD-ROM	Required	8x (or greater)
Mouse	Not required	If using graphical interface; PS/2 style is the best choice

Unix

Unix began as a command line system in engineering and academic environments. Unix was designed for networking from the ground up; office applications and a graphical user interface came later. There are no specific server or workstation versions of Unix; all versions can perform all tasks related to both. (The shareware counterpart to Unix is Linux.) Today, there are many machines that run Unix with a fully functional graphical user interface.

Several vendors exist for Unix. Sun Microsystems, Hewlett Packard, IBM, and many other companies offer commercial products. RedHat, Caldera, and other vendors offer a Linux version that is based on an Intel implementation of Unix that was originally written by Linus Torvalds.

NOTE MIT researchers invented X-Windows as a graphical user interface (GUI) for Unix. Today, companies package various GUIs along with the text-based operating system.

Interface The command line was originally the primary interface for Unix, but X-Windows and its various flavors have since added a graphical user interface (GUI) to Unix.

Relevant versions The original versions of Unix derived from Berkeley Systems Distribution (BSD) (from the University of California at Berkeley) and System V (from AT&T Bell Labs). All new Unix versions originate from one or both of these. (Linux is a shareware version of Unix that is available for many platforms in either free or commercial versions.)

Server role Unix boxes can simultaneously function as both workstations and servers. Dedicated Unix servers are commonly used as routers. In the workstation role, Unix machines are used as desktop computers.

Table 1.3 lists the hardware requirements for RedHat Linux 5.1, a widely distributed version of Unix for the Intel platform.

TIP Unix hardware requirements vary from vendor to vendor. As such, they are not currently covered by the exam.

TABLE 1.3: RedHat 5.1 Linux Hardware Requirements and Recommendations

Hardware	Minimum	Recommended
Processor	Intel 80386 or higher (I386 architecture), 680x0, or a supported RISC processor (MIPS, AP1000+, Alpha AXP, SPARC, or PowerPC)	Pentium 90Mhz or higher (the faster the better)
Display	VGA	SVGA
Hard disk space	500MB free	1GB free
Memory	16MB	32MB (or greater)
Network card	None	At least one that matches the topology of your network
CD-ROM	None	8x (or greater)
Mouse	Required	Required

Clients That Best Serve Each NOS

A *client* is a piece of software that allows a workstation to communicate with a particular network operating system. The client for Microsoft-based networks comes with Windows 9.*x*. NetWare clients need to be downloaded or installed from a Novell CD. Unix clients are usually developed by third parties and allow Windows 9.*x* and NT computers to talk to Unix servers. If you select the wrong client, network resources will not always be available.

Although each network operating system can accept a wide variety of clients, not all provide full functionality. When a partially compatible client is used to communicate on a network, not all resources will necessarily show up. Your best solution (or prevention) is to use the NOS vendor's client. When you run a Novell NetWare network, use the Novell client; when you run a Microsoft Windows NT network, use the Microsoft client. However, Unix environments have third-party clients, which you will need to independently test.

Microsoft Network Clients

The client for Microsoft Networks needs to be installed to allow a client Windows 9.*x* computer to see any Microsoft-based computers on the network. This is regardless of the operating system for the client; Windows for Workgroups, Windows 9.*x*, and Windows NT machines all require the Microsoft client in order to communicate.

Novell NetWare Clients

The Novell NetWare client is the primary client used for connecting to NetWare servers. The Microsoft Client for NetWare Networks, which is also listed in the client installation list, should not be installed. The Microsoft client for NetWare is an acceptable implementation for general users. When using a machine for network administration and the NetWare Administrator utility, be sure the Novell-brand client is the only NetWare client installed.

WARNING Stay away from Netx and NetWare 3.*x* clients. They will not provide you with full connectivity to NetWare 4.*x* and 5 servers. (The exam asks questions specific to NetWare 4.*x* and later.)

Unix Clients

The generic term for a Unix client is Client for NFS. (Several companies, such as Sun, NetManage, and others provide Client for NFS software.) A Unix client allows non-Unix workstations to connect to Unix servers. Specifically, Windows 9.*x* and NT machines will connect to the Unix Network File Systems (NFS). NFS allows you to map directories from remote computers to your own directory structure. With a Unix client, the directories are mapped in as subdirectories; with a Windows 9.*x* computer, the remote Unix directories are mapped to drive letters.

TIP For the Network+ exam, you do not need to know specific vendors, just the Unix client name and its use.

Selecting a Primary Client

Most computer networks are comprised of servers from several different networks. To access each of the servers, multiple clients need to be loaded onto the workstations. One client needs to be loaded for each network—Microsoft, Novell, or Unix—that you want to access.

After you have installed all of the clients on the workstation, you need to select a primary client. The primary client will load first when Windows 9.*x* starts up. You will also see computers in the Network Neighborhood first that are part of the same network. So, if you set the Microsoft Client first, you will initially see Microsoft computers upon opening the Network Neighborhood.

WARNING Do not add multiple copies of clients designed for the same network. For instance, you can load a client for Microsoft Networks and a Novell NetWare client, but do not add the Microsoft Client for NetWare Networks. The workstation would then have duplicate NetWare clients installed; one client would uninstall the other, or both would end up having problems.

NOS Directory Services

Directory services are organizations or resources on the network. These resources include usernames, passwords, groups, shares to directories, and pretty much everything else. Directory services manage everything from one central database instead of separately on each server.

It is important for you to understand and differentiate between stand-alone servers and network directory services–based networks. A stand-alone server manages its own set of usernames, passwords, and groups. A directory services–based network has a centralized repository for the username and group information. The reason this is important is that, with stand-alone servers, you must manage each server's user and account database separately (i.e., create a user ten times on ten separate servers), whereas, with true directory services, you only create the user once. Every server will grant or deny access to networks based on the information contained in the directory services database. Network operating systems have different directory services depending on the vendor.

NOTE The Lightweight Directory Access Protocol (LDAP) is a vendor-independent directory service that is gaining in popularity. Many vendors can look up user information about other vendor's products by using LDAP.

Microsoft Windows NT

Windows NT servers use workgroups in the stand-alone mode and NT domains when acting as part of Microsoft's directory services. NT Directory Services (NTDS) is Microsoft's first implementation of directory services. NTDS manages usernames, passwords, and groups. To a limited degree, printers and shared directories can also be managed.

Stand-Alone Workgroups Loosely associated computers in Microsoft networks are grouped together in workgroups. These computers maintain their own databases of usernames, passwords, and groups. Windows for Workgroups 3.11 is the first operating system to use workgroups. Windows 9.*x* and NT computers have the ability to be configured either as part of a workgroup in a stand-alone mode or a network-based environment by using directory services.

Network-Based NT Directory Services Windows NT 4 servers and workstations can operate using NT Directory Services. When they are part of NTDS, they are more commonly referred to as being in a domain. A server can play three different roles in NTDS. First, a Primary Domain Controller (PDC) is an NT server that holds the master list of usernames and passwords in the SAM database; every domain must have a single PDC. Second, a Backup Domain Controller (BDC) holds a copy of the PDC's database. BDCs authenticate users and allow them access to network resources by giving tokens to the user. When a username or password is changed, the PDC is updated; BDCs then get an updated copy from the PDC. And the third role of a server in NTDS is that of member server. Member servers are in the domain and utilize the accounts in the SAM database to regulate access to its resources. The member server does not play a role in maintaining the accounts. Web servers are commonly made member servers to separate the security accounts from general Web pages. File, print, e-mail, and other network tasks are commonly run as member servers. NT Workstations also act similarly in an NT domain.

Windows NT 4 workstations and servers can operate in a workgroup or in a domain. If they are in a workgroup, then each maintains locally on each machine a separate list of usernames and passwords in their SAM database. If the computers are in a domain, then they use a nearby BDC or the PDC to authenticate logins. Examine how the BDCs in Figure 1.5 have a copy of the SAM database from their domain PDC using NTDS.

TIP   Notice the features that make Microsoft's directory services different from offerings by Novell and Unix.

FIGURE 1.5: An NTDS network

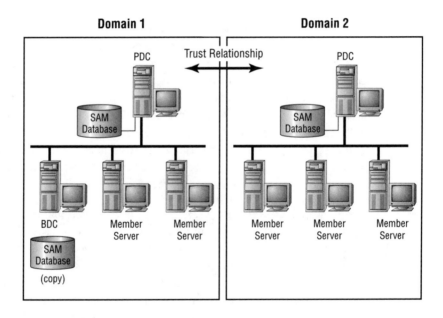

Novell NetWare

Novell has two versions of its network operating system that use directory services—NetWare 4.*x* and NetWare 5. The directory services are stored in a hierarchical structure (called an NDS Tree) and are known as Novell Directory Services (NDS). An NDS Tree is a graphical representation of the Novell NDS network database except that it is upside down. The root of the NDS Tree is at the top of the network, with branches and leaves spreading out and down. Each device, account, service, program, etc. is a leaf in NDS.

Stand-Alone Bindery in 3.x   Stand-alone NetWare 3.x and earlier servers maintain a bindery, which is a simple database of users, groups, and security information that resides on a particular server. Its use is limited to versions of NetWare before version 4.

A user may use the same username on different servers, but the accounts that are represented by the username on each server are still separate. When a single account gets a password change, the must remember that the accounts on other servers are not affected. Users will have to connect to each server individually and change their password.

Network-Based NDS in 4.x and 5   The most distinctive feature of NetWare 4.x (and later) is its directory service, Novell Directory Services. NDS is a service that provides access to a global, hierarchical database of network entities (called objects) that can be centrally managed. Based on the X.500 global directory standard, this database-called the Directory, with a capital *D* (not to be confused with a DOS directory) is distributed and replicated to all of the NetWare servers on the network. Each server contains a part of the directory database. Additionally, all servers know about each other and the directory information contained on each.

One of the major advantages NDS has over the bindery is that NetWare organizes the entire network into a hierarchical structure called an NDS Tree, which is a logical representation of a network. As shown in Figure 1.6, the NDS Tree includes objects that represent the users, servers, printers, and other resources of that network. On the other hand, the bindery only contains user information for that server. NDS is described as a *network-centric* directory service, whereas the bindery is *server-centric*.

Unix

Unix boxes were originally designed to operate as stand-alone servers. Each server had independent username and password lists. To access files on different servers, users had to log in separately to each machine.

FIGURE 1.6: A sample NDS Tree

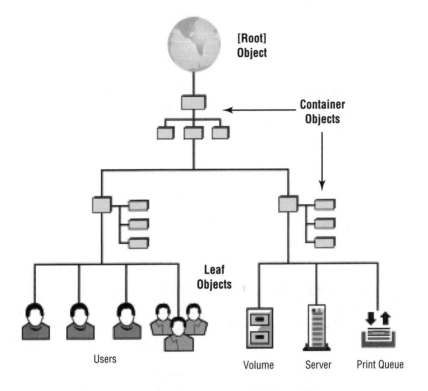

Network-based Unix computers now use a single username and password file maintained by a network information service (NIS and NIS+) server. The network information service is Unix's implementation of a directory service. NIS is used to copy the *passwd* file, which contains user and group information, to all computers.

Exam Essentials

You will need to be able to identify and differentiate between the directory services for each operating system.

Know how to identify a workgroup. A workgroup is a collection of stand-alone computers running various operating systems ranging from Microsoft Windows for Workgroups 3.11 to Windows 9.*x* and Windows NT. Each computer retains its own list of usernames and passwords that is not shared with other account databases. Windows NT computers utilize usernames and passwords while earlier network operating systems in the workgroup structure just use share-level passwords.

Know how to identify NTDS. Windows NT servers can run a network-based structure called a domain. NT Directory Services are incorporated into Microsoft's NT Server 4 domains. Windows NT workstations, NT member servers, Windows for Workgroups, and Windows 9.*x* clients can use a BDC or PDC to authenticate into the domain.

WARNING Do not confuse NTDS with NDS. Think of NTDS as NT "space" DS. NT is a Microsoft product. NDS is a Novell product.

Know how to identify NDS. Novell Directory Services is a global hierarchical directory service that is based on the X.500 specifications. NDS has a tree with subordinate objects called organizational units, containers, and leaves. NetWare 4.*x* and later servers support NDS.

WARNING Do not confuse X.500 with X.400. X.500 is a directory structure. X.400 applies to e-mail.

Know how to identify NIS and NIS+. Unix servers use Network Information Service (NIS and NIS+) servers for their directory services. An NIS server replicates the *passwd* file to every computer; users can then be authenticated using the local copy of the *passwd* file.

Key Terms and Concepts

Authenticate The process of logging onto a network and having your identity verified by a username and password.

BDC (Backup Domain Controller)   Windows NT 4 domains use BDCs to offload user login authentication from the PDC. The main copy of the database is on the PDC (see below), but BDCs authenticate logins. An NT domain can have multiple BDCs.

Bindery   Novell Servers 3.*x* and earlier use a bindery database to store user account and password information for a single server.

Client   Software that allows a workstation to properly communicate to specific network operating systems and servers.

Domain   A group of computers, using Windows NT, that have their usernames, groups, and passwords managed by a network-based directory server on the PDC. A user can log in at any machine using the same username and password.

Linux   A shareware version of Unix, written by Linus Torvalds, that now has many vendors and is available on many platforms.

NetWare   Novell's network operating system. Versions 1.*x* through 3.*x* use single servers with independent databases of usernames and passwords. Versions 4.*x* and 5 are network centric.

NDS (NetWare Directory Services)   Novell's directory service, which assigns every network resource (i.e. user, printer, server) an object in a global directory (called a tree) that has containers and leaf objects. Everything from printers to users are listed and, regardless of location, have corresponding objects in the NDS Tree.

NFS (Network File System)   The system by which directories are shared between computers in Unix.

NIS and NIS+ (Network Information Service)   Unix servers that maintain a network-based file of usernames, groups, and passwords. NIS servers copy the *passwd* file out to Unix computers.

NTDS (NT Directory Services)   Microsoft network directory services that are implemented in a network-based system when NT domains are slected. PDCs or BDCs authenticate user login requests.

PDC (Primary Domain Controller)   Used by Windows NT 4 domains to maintain the master database of usernames, passwords, and groups. Every domain requires and is limited to one PDC.

Server   A computer that provides services such as, but not limited to, network authentication, file sharing, printer sharing, e-mail, Web services, and database access.

Tree   The basis for Novell's global hierarchical directory services (in NetWare 4.*x* and later). Subordinate components in a tree are called objects; common objects include containers, organizational units, and leaves.

Unix   A command-line-based network operating system that originated in scientific and academic circles. Unix uses X-Windows for its GUI. It is now available for several CPUs and is usable on home computers, although supported applications are still limited.

Windows NT   Microsoft's network operating system, available in Workstation, Server, and Enterprise Server versions. These NOSs have the same popular GUI used by Windows 9.*x*, and they can be stand-alone, in a workgroup, or network-based in a domain.

Workgroup   A loose collection of computers (Microsoft Windows 9.*x* or NT) for searching convenience in the Network Neighborhood. Workgroup computers are single-server based and, as such, have separate, unrelated databases of users, groups, and passwords.

Workstation   A desktop computer, which is typically a high-end PC with a lot of RAM and a fast CPU to support sophisticated business applications. Microsoft has incorporated the term into NT Workstation; do not assume that a workstation is NT-based unless it is specified as such.

X.400   Specifications created by the International Telecommunications Union (ITU), a division of the United Nations, to define a global standard for e-mail services. X.400 works well with X.500 directory services.

X.500   Specifications created by the International Telecommunications Union (ITU), a division of the United Nations, to define a global standard for directory services. Novell's NDS is based on the X.500 specifications.

Sample Questions

1. What are the directory services used by NetWare?

   A. NTDS

   B. NDS

   C. NFS

   D. NIS

   E. NIS+

   Answer: B—NDS stands for Novell Directory Services.

2. Microsoft uses what naming convention to designate a collection of stand-alone systems?

   A. Domain

   B. PDC

   C. BDC

   D. Workgroup

   E. Member server

   Answer: D—A workgroup is a loose collection of computers with separate user databases. (A domain uses directory services. Both a PDC and BDC operate as part of a domain. And a member server is a Windows NT server that utilizes the directory services provided by PDCs and BDCs.)

3. A tree is used to represent the directory services of which operating system?

   A. NetWare

   B. Windows NT

   C. Unix

   D. Linux

   Answer: A—In Novell NetWare 4.x and later, a tree represents directory services. (Windows NT uses domains. Unix and Linux utilize NIS or NIS+.)

4. Unix utilizes what technology to share directories on servers?

A. NIS

B. NIS+

C. NFS

D. NDS

E. NTDS

Answer: C—The Network File System (NFS) mounts shared server directories to a local workstation. (NIS and NIS+ are used to authenticate Unix users via a single login. NDS is Novell's directory services, and NTDS is Microsoft's directory services.)

Associate IPX, IP, and NetBEUI with their functions

As has already been discussed, a protocol is the language used by computers to talk on a network. Each protocol has its own set of features that suit it for a particular purpose. Internetwork Packet Exchange (IPX) and Internet Protocol (IP) are designed to operate on the enterprise level and are part of protocol suites; IPX/SPX and TCP/IP are considered protocol suites because they encompass multiple components and traverse multiple layers of the Open Systems Interconnection (OSI) model. NetBIOS Extended User Interface (NetBEUI) is a self-configuring, non-routable protocol used in Microsoft networks. When implementing a network, it is important to understand the various protocols and the implications involved in implementing them on your network.

Critical Information

The three protocols covered on the Network+ exam are IPX, IP, and NetBEUI. Each one of these is commonly found on corporate networks today (sometimes these protocols are used together).

IPX is part of the IPX/SPX protocol suite, and IP is part of the TCP/IP protocol suite. You need to realize that a protocol suite crosses over several layers of the OSI reference model. TCP and SPX operate on the Transport layer while IP and IPX work on the Network layer. Net-BEUI is not a part of a suite; rather, NetBEUI is the default transport for the NetBIOS protocol (although NetBIOS can use any transport, including IPX and TCP/IP).

Internetwork Packet Exchange Protocol

The Internetwork Packet Exchange was developed by Novell and is based on the Xerox Network System (XNS) protocol. IPX scales well to the enterprise and needs very little hand-tuning. As a Network layer protocol, IPX uses a unique address for each computer node to facilitate communications. IPX is also a routable protocol. This means that IPX packets are directed on the network (OSI model layer three) based on their destination address.

There are a few IPX settings that can be manually configured. The frame type refers to how the packets are formatted. The default installation of IPX for a Windows 9.*x* computer is to auto-detect the type. This does not tell the whole story, however. You will avoid problems if you manually set one of the five frame types: raw, 802.2, 802.3, Ethernet_II, and Ethernet_Snap. (The computer node is automatically created for you.) The last two settings are the internal and external IPX network address.

IPX addresses are hexadecimal and can be up to 24 digits long. Figure 1.7 shows a sample IPX address.

FIGURE 1.7: A sample IPX address

Some features of the IPX protocol are:

Name   Internetwork Packet Exchange.

Auto-configuration   A workstation's IPX address is automatically assigned. The frame type can be manually configured or set to auto-detect.

WARNING Do not set frame-type to auto-detect. If you do, the correct frame type may not be found, and your machines will experience unreliable connectivity. Always manually configure IPX settings.

Current NOS usage Windows 9.*x*, Windows NT, NetWare, Unix.

First application To connect NetWare servers and their clients.

Frame type Frame types are a kind of network packet. The five IPX frame types are:

- 802.2
- 802.3
- RAW
- Ethernet_II
- Ethernet_Snap

History Based on the Xerox Network System protocol.

IPX Internal Network Number Uniquely identifies a single server.

IPX External Network Number Uniquely identifies an entire network and all of its servers.

WARNING Be careful when you assign an IPX External Network Number or you may end up with the servers of other companies or the military appearing in your browse list.

Scalability IPX scales well to enterprise-wide global communication. However, it is not commonly used for communication between different companies.

Summary IPX is a connectionless Network layer protocol. Sequenced Packet Exchange is a connection-guaranteed Transport layer protocol. Together, they make up the IPX/SPX protocol suite.

Workstation Network Address A unique number for a workstation that is set by a combination of the MAC address and the IPX External Network Number.

IPX packets are directed to their destination via Network layer-three routing. These packets do not arrive in any guaranteed order and receive little error checking; SPX, the second half of the IPX/SPX protocol suite, provides these functions. As noted earlier, the Sequenced Packet Exchange protocol operates on the Transport layer, and SPX provides guaranteed delivery, error checking, and packet sequencing.

As you will see in Figure 1.8, the Novell family of protocols function across several OSI layers.

F I G U R E 1.8: The IPX family and its relationship to the OSI model

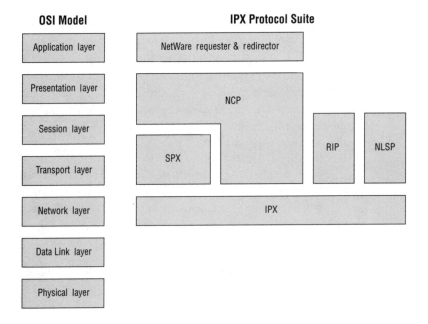

Internet Protocol

The Internet Protocol is a protocol developed by the U.S. Department of Defense (DOD) as the primary protocol for carrying data on the Internet. The IP protocol uses a four-decimal numbering scheme to address computer nodes. This generic method of labeling and routing allows IP to be used all over the Internet. IP operates on Network layer three, so it is routable, connectionless, and does not worry about packet sequencing. Network operating systems currently use IP version 4 (IPv4). (IP version 6 will be used in the future and will be based on six hexadecimal numbers, similar to the MAC address burned into network interface cards.) In Figure 1.9, note the four decimal numbers separated by periods in the sample IP address.

F I G U R E 1.9: A sample IP address

199.217.67.34   IP Address

255.255.255.0   Subnet Mask

In addition to the IP address, computers are assigned a subnet mask. This *subnet mask* is another set of four decimal numbers separated by periods. When a computer sends out a packet, the source IP address, subnet mask, and destination address are used to determine whether the destination computer is on the local segment. If the destination node is not local, the packet is forwarded to the destination network segment via a router. (Routers direct packets from one network to another on layer three of the OSI model.)

The Transmission Control Protocol comprises the upper half of the TCP/IP protocol suite. Similar to SPX, TCP operates on the Transport layer and offers packet sequencing, error correction, and a guaranteed connection. If a message is especially important, care should be taken to use TCP instead of IP.

Some features of the IP protocol are:

Name   Internet Protocol.

Summary   IP operates on the Network layer (layer three) of the OSI model. As such, it is connectionless, and packets are not ordered during transmission. TCP operates on the Transport layer (layer four) of the OSI model, and TCP has guaranteed connections, sequenced packets, and error correction.

History   Based on U.S. Department of Defense specifications.

First application   To connect Unix servers and their clients.

Current NOS usage Windows 9.*x*, Windows NT, NetWare, Unix.

Subnet Subnets are small divisions of a larger network.

Subnet mask A number used to determine whether a packet stays in a local network or is routed elsewhere. It is a grouping of four decimal numbers separated by periods. A machine decides if a packet is local to its subnet or is remote by applying this mask to its own IP address. The format is xxx.xxx.xxx.xxx, where *xxx* is any number between zero and 255.

IP address A number that uniquely identifies a single computer node on an IP-based network.

Auto configuration A computer's IP settings are automatically assigned by using a Dynamic Host Configuration Protocol (DHCP) server. (Manual configuration is also possible.)

Scalability IP scales well to enterprise-wide global communication. It can also be used on the Internet to have different companies communicate with each other.

IP is part of the TCP/IP protocol suite as shown in Figure 1.10 below.

F I G U R E 1.10: The TCP/IP protocol suite

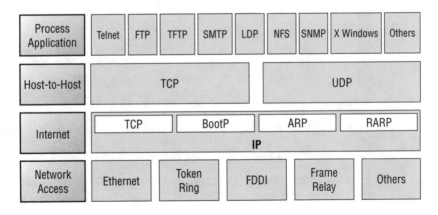

NetBIOS Extended User Interface Protocol

The NetBIOS Extended User Interface (NetBEUI) is a protocol based on IBM's NetBIOS protocol, which is designed to communicate with IBM mainframes. But you should realize that they are not the same. NetBEUI is the transport protocol for NetBIOS, and NetBIOS is a Session layer interface, not a transport protocol.

NetBEUI has been around since Microsoft's first network offering, MS-NET. The beauty of NetBEUI is that it is small, fast, and self-tuning. There is nothing to configure with NetBEUI. For very small networks, it is simply unbeatable in speed. With nothing to configure, NetBEUI's only disadvantage is that it is not routable.

NetBEUI is also broadcast-based, which means every computer must listen to the output of every other computer. Though not an issue in very small networks, this can quickly result in huge amounts of network chatter as a small network grows larger.

NetBEUI requires little configuration, apart from the installation of the protocol and the configuration of a workstation name. This is the reason that NetBEUI is the choice for Windows networks running on a small LAN.

Some features of the NetBEUI protocol are:

Name   NetBIOS Extended User Interface.

Summary   NetBEUI is the default transport protocol for NetBIOS. It operates primarily at the Transport layer of the OSI model.

History   Based on work done by IBM and Microsoft.

First application   To connect Windows servers and their clients.

Current NOS usage   Windows 9.x, Windows NT.

Auto configuration   The protocol will automatically configure all addresses and parameters for itself once it is installed on the workstation.

Scalability   NetBEUI has a great deal of overhead (required for self-configuration). It is also not routable, so it makes a poor choice for WANs and enterprise networks.

Exam Essentials

You will need to know the uses and features of IPX, IP, and NetBEUI. Realize that each network operating system can use several protocols. The key is to realize the differences.

Know how to identify the features and uses of IPX.   IPX is most commonly used in NetWare networks. Frame types, internal network numbers, external network numbers, and workstation network numbers need to be set on computers in an IPX-based network.

Know how to identify the feature and uses of IP.   IP is most commonly used to connect different network operating systems and to communicate on the Internet. IP addresses and subnet masks need to be configured on computers in an IP-based network.

Know how to identify the features and uses of NetBEUI.   NetBEUI is used to connect small Microsoft networks. This protocol is not routable, and there is nothing to configure. NetBEUI is small, efficient, and simple to install.

Key Terms and Concepts

Connectionless   A communication without the verification of packets being sent and received. There is no active link maintained between the sender and the receiver

Connection-oriented   A communication that maintains an active link between the sender and receiver. Packets are verified as being sent and received.

Frame type   IPX has five common packet types, or frame types. These are 802.2, 802.3, Ethernet_II, Snap, and RAW.

IP (Internet Protocol)   The connectionless component of the U.S. Department of Defense's TCP/IP protocol suite.

IPX (Internetwork Packet Exchange)   A connectionless protocol based on XNS. IPX originated on Novell NetWare networks but is now available on many vendors' operating systems.

IPX External Network Number   The number manually assigned to an entire network that uses the IPX protocol.

IPX Internal Network Number   The number manually assigned to a server on an IPX network.

NetBEUI (NetBIOS Extended User Interface)   A small, efficient, nonroutable protocol from Microsoft that was based on IBM's NetBIOS.

Network Basic Input Output System (NetBIOS)   Invented by IBM to communicate between IBM clients and their servers. NetBIOS can be implemented over many protocols such as NetBEUI and TCP/IP.

SPX (Sequenced Packet Exchange)   A connection-oriented protocol that is part of Novell's IPX/SPX protocol suite.

Subnet   A network subdivision.

Subnet mask   A four-decimal number in the form of xxx.xxx .xxx.xxx that is used to determine whether an IP address is on a local network or a remote one.

TCP (Transmission Control Protocol)   A guaranteed-connection oriented protocol that operates on the fourth layer of the OSI model (the Transport layer). Error checking and packet sequencing are part of TCP since these are also features of the Transport layer.

Sample Questions

1. What protocol has different frame types and is primarily used to communicate on Novell networks?

   A. NetBIOS

   B. IPX

   C. TCP

   D. IP

   E. NetBEUI

   Answer: B—IPX is Novell's protocol that has been adopted from Xerox's XNS protocol. (NetBIOS is IBM's protocol that has been adopted as part of Microsoft's NetBEUI. TCP and IP are vendor-independent protocols that were both created by the U.S Department of Defense as part of the TCP/IP protocol suite. And NetBEUI is Microsoft's small, efficient, nonroutable protocol.)

2. Which of the following is a correct example of a valid IP address for a single computer node?

   A. 0.34.1.2 *not valid*

   B. 12.34.23.256.2 *not valid*

   C. 3D:F4:12:90:23:A2 *MAC add*

   D. 206.100.29.83

   E. 255.255.255.0 *Subnet*

   Answer: D—With four decimal numbers between 1 and 254 that are seperated by periods, 206.100.29.83 is a valid IP address. (Valid addresses do not start with a zero. Numbers above 254 are not valid. Hexadecimal numbers are for MAC addresses, not IP addresses. And 255.255.255.0 is a subnet mask.

3. What kind of number is applied to a source IP address to determine whether destination addresses are within or outside of the same network?

   A. Subnet

   B. Subnet mask

   C. IP address

   D. IPX address

   E. MAC address

   Answer: B—Subnet masks are applied to source addresses and determine if packets need to be sent to local addresses or through a router to remote destinations. (Subnets are small divisions of larger networks that are linked by routers. IP addresses are unique identifiers for computer nodes using the IP protocol. IPX addresses are unique identifiers for computer nodes using the IPX protocol. And MAC addresses are unique identifiers for computer nodes on the Data Link layer (layer two) of the OSI reference model.

Define the following terms and explain how each relates to fault tolerance or high availability:

- Mirroring
- Duplexing
- Striping (with and without parity)
- Volumes
- Tape backup

Fault tolerance and disaster recovery are important issues in maintaining your network. This is the first thing that you should ensure when planning a network. To that end, mirrors and duplexes constitute a duplicate copy of your data on a second hard disk; striping and volumes are methods to span data over several disks. These methods are used to provide continued operation in the event of hardware damage, ensuring fault tolerance and high availability. But if a user deletes a file, it is gone; duplicate disks are seen as one logical unit, so all copies get deleted. This is where backups and restores come in. To handle a user file restore, tape backups need to be done.

Critical Information

The Network+ exam tests your basic understanding of disk configurations and tape backup. Redundant array of independent disks (RAID) technology is one of the more important disk management technologies. RAID enables a hard disk to fail without losing data. (This is known as fault tolerance.) Other disk management technologies on the Network+ exam include tape backup and restore. Changed data may undergo anywhere from a full backup to a partial backup. When data is copied to tape, it can be stored offsite to be protected from a disaster. If the computer becomes damaged, the remote tape is retrieved and then copied onto replacement computer equipment.

Disk Management

Even though hard disks increase in capacity and decrease in cost every year, data storage requirements also increase every time software upgrades are released. To handle this information overload, drive letters can span multiple disks, as in volumes. Multiple disks can also be fault tolerant, as in RAID systems. Or the same data can be stored on two different disks, as in mirroring and duplexing.

RAID

Redundant array of independent (or inexpensive) disks levels 0, 1, 3, and 5 are the most common, but a range of RAID levels are described below:

RAID 0 (common)   Known as volumes. Data is spread across several disks but appears to the operating system as one logical hard drive. This method provides no fault tolerance. There is no error checking, duplicate data, or parity stored. Multiple read and write heads are used simultaneously on each hard drive as data is spread over them. This is the fastest RAID level because all read/write heads are constantly being used without the burden of parity or duplicate data being written.

RAID 1 (common)   Commonly known as a mirror. Two hard drives compromise a mirror and provide a level of RAID 1 fault tolerance. No parity or error-checking information is stored. Each drive has duplicate information of the other hard drive. If a drive is damaged, data is not lost. However, a reboot of the computer with a replacement disk might be necessary to recreate the mirror.

RAID 2   Data is striped across multiple disks. Some disks carry error-checking information. This is not a commonly used implementation of RAID.

RAID 3 (common)   Data is striped across a minimum of three hard drives. One drive is dedicated to error checking and parity data. If a disk is lost, the system continues to operate without losing data.

RAID 4   Large stripes are implemented to facilitate fast reads from one drive. A parity drive is used, so there is still some loss of speed during write operations. If a disk is lost, the system continues to operate without a loss of data.

RAID 5 (common) The fastest system that provides fault tolerance. If a disk fails, the system continues to operate without losing data. The data and parity are striped across several drives, which allows for fast writes and reads. A minimum of three hard disks are required; most often, five or more disks are implemented.

RAID 6 A second parity scheme is added to the setup of RAID 5 to achieve RAID 6 status. The additional parity information gives the data a higher level of fault tolerance.

RAID 7 An operating system is embedded in a high-speed controller and uses a fast bus to manage the disks.

RAID 10 An array of stripes is used; each stripe is two drives in a RAID 1 array. This exceptionally high level of data integrity is very expensive.

RAID 5/3 An array of stripes is used, with each stripe an array of RAID 3 disks. Ultra-high fault tolerance is coupled with similarly high costs.

Mirroring

Mirrored hard drives (RAID level 1) consist of two drives that contain identical information. A single controller card controls both drives. This is the slowest RAID configuration because both drives write the same information and are powered by a single controller. The second drive is a duplicate, or mirror, of the first drive. The mirror drive is held in reserve for when the primary drive dies. The second drive provides fault tolerance since no data is lost during a single disk failure. Figure 1.11 shows two drives connected to a single controller card in a computer.

Duplexing

Duplexed hard drives (RAID level 1) consist of two drives that both contain identical information. A dedicated controller card controls each drive. This is the second slowest RAID configuration because the same data is still written to both drives. But duplexing is faster than mirroring since two controllers split the read/write work in a duplex. Duplexing is similar to mirroring in most other respects. This type of RAID provides fault tolerance because a single drive failure can be sustained and the data is still available. Figure 1.12 shows two drives that are each connected to their own dedicated controller card in a computer.

FIGURE 1.11: Mirrors

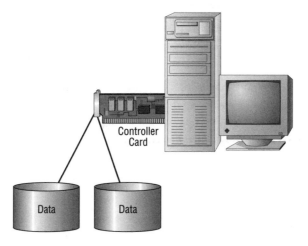

FIGURE 1.12: Duplexes

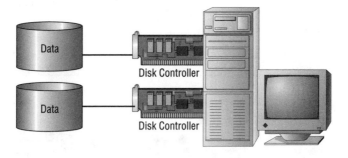

Striping (with and without Parity)

Simultaneously writing information to all disks in small portions is called striping. These portions, called stripes, maximize use by constantly working all of the of read/write heads. Duplicate information is not stored as it is in mirroring and duplexing, but separate information goes onto each disk instead.

With RAID 0, striping without parity, there is no fault tolerance. All of the drives read and write quickly, without any protection.

RAID 3 has a parity drive, which provides the benefit of simultaneous drive writing, along with a dedicated drive for parity. You can lose one disk—even the parity disk—without a hiccup. RAID 3 even allows you to pull a hot-pluggable drive out and still continue to operate. No matter how many drives you have, one is dedicated to parity.

The data and parity of RAID 5 arrays is striped through all of the drives, which speeds up the reads and writes. Also, all drives are equally secure because each one has data and parity stripes. Figure 1.13 shows an array of RAID 5-level hard disks.

FIGURE 1.13: RAID 5, striping with parity

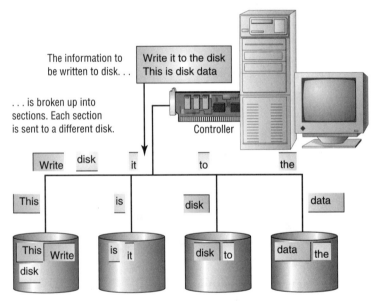

The information to be written to disk...
Write it to the disk This is disk data

...is broken up into sections. Each section is sent to a different disk.

Controller

Write disk it to the
This is disk data
This Write is it disk to data the
disk

Each disk holds a piece of the original information.

Volumes

A volume is a logical drive partition that spans several hard disks. The operating system sees only a single drive even though the configuration actually consists of several drives grouped as one. Figure 1.14 shows a D drive stretched across several disks as a volume. Most operating systems do not allow you to extend the volume of the partition with the operating system—the C drive in this case.

FIGURE 1.14: Volumes

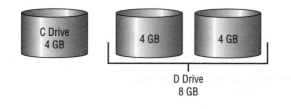

C Drive
4 GB

4 GB

4 GB

D Drive
8 GB

NOTE When disks are grouped as a logical unit without any RAID intelligence, each disk is filled before the next one is used. This is known as a volume.

NOTE A RAID 0 implementation is known as striping without parity. Since all read/write heads are operating simultaneously, all disks achieve high speeds. Neither type of disk setup provides any fault tolerance.

Tape Backup

Data is copied from the server to tape cartridges for disaster recovery. When data on a hard disk is accidentally deleted or is damaged, it can be restored from the tape cartridges. Tapes, however, do not provide fault tolerance. When a disk fails or data is destroyed, business continuity is lost, and the data on the tape is not automatically available for users to access. Therefore, tape backups complement RAID systems; neither one can protect your data alone.

NOTE Data can be copied to tape in a full backup, differential backup, or incremental backup session. (Tape backup procedures are covered in depth in Chapter 12.)

Exam Essentials

For the Network+ exam, you must know some basic definitions and distinctions of common disk fault-tolerance methods. Those concepts include some of the following:

Know how to identify the commonly used levels of RAID.   RAID levels 0–5 are most commonly used in the industry. RAID 0 provides no fault tolerance but has the fastest read/write access times. RAID 1 is fault tolerant but is also slow because all information must be simultaneously copied to both the prime and mirror drives. RAID 3 provides fast reads since the data is striped across multiple drives; however, writing is moderately fast because a dedicated parity drive slows down the process. Like RAID 3, RAID 5 uses a minimum of three drives but has fast writes because the parity is also striped.

Know how to differentiate between mirroring and duplexing. Mirroring and duplexing are both associated with RAID level 1. A mirror has a redundant, second hard drive that mirrors the data on the primary drive. Like a mirror, a duplex has two hard drives, but each drive has a separate controller. Mirrors only have one controller.

Know how to select a hard disk configuration based on your business needs and available equipment.   When speed is needed but fault tolerance is not, select RAID 0, striping without parity. When you only have two disks, fault tolerance is required, and speed is not a concern, choose RAID 1, mirrors or duplexes. The best of both worlds consists of speed and fault tolerance, which are provided by RAID 5, striping with parity.

Know how to provide for disaster recovery.   When your data is accidentally deleted or your equipment is ruined, you have a disaster on your hands. To prepare for such an event, data should be copied to tape each night. The tapes then need to be stored onsite in a fireproof safe as well as in a remote location.

Key Terms and Concepts

Duplexing When two hard drives have separate controllers and contain duplicate information.

Logical drive Multiple drives are grouped together and the operating system sees them as a single drive (e.g., three 2GB drives look like one 6GB D drive).

Mirroring A duplicate image of the primary hard disk is kept on a mirror disk. A single controller manages both drives.

RAID Redundant array of independent (or inexpensive) disks are hard drives that have data spread across them for fault tolerance or speed enhancements.

Striping (with parity) Data is spread across multiple disks in small portions. Parity information is also spread out and is used to rebuild data that is lost if a drive fails.

Striping (without parity) Data is spread across multiple disks in small portions. Parity information is not recorded. All drives read and write at the same time. With all drives working and no parity, this is the fastest type of system storage. There is no fault tolerance to handle a drive failure.

Tape backup Data is copied to tape cartridges for disaster recovery. When data is accidentally deleted or is damaged on a hard disk, it can be restored from tape cartridges.

Volumes A logical division, such as a drive letter, spreads across several hard disks via volumes. The first drive is filled up before data is recorded on subsequent drives. There is no increase in speed and no fault tolerance.

Sample Questions

1. What is RAID level 1 more commonly known as?

   A. Striping

   B. Striping with parity

   C. Duplicating

   D. Mirroring

   E. Master/slave

   Answer: D—Mirrors are defined in RAID 1. (Striping is RAID 0, and striping with parity is RAID level 4 and 5. Master/slave and duplicating are not part of any RAID level.)

2. What is the hard disk configuration that has the fastest reads and writes?

   A. Duplexes

   B. Volumes

   C. Striping without parity

   D. Striping with parity

   E. Mirrors

   Answer: C—Striping without parity is the fastest implementation. All read/write heads on all disks simultaneously transfer different data to storage. (Duplexes and mirrors duplicate information on two hard drives, which makes them slow. Volumes use multiple disks as one logical disk but operate each independently; the first disk in a volume is filled up before the other disks are used. And striping with parity is the second fastest system because error checking and recovery data—parity data—is also written.)

3. Which RAID level has a dedicated parity drive?

   A. 0

   B. 1

   C. 3

   D. 5

Answer: C—RAID 3 has a dedicated parity drive. (RAID 0 and RAID 1 don't have parity storage. RAID 5 has parity information spread across multiple drives.)

4. What method of preserving data will allow you to sustain damage to an entire site?

   A. RAID 3

   B. RAID 5

   C. Volumes

   D. Folder replication

   E. Tape backup

   Answer: E—Tape backups allow you to relocate tape cartridges and to store them in a fireproof safe. (RAID cannot help you if all of your hard disks are destroyed. Volumes only group disks together. Folder replication merely copies data from one disk to another. And fault tolerance and disaster recovery are not provided by either volumes or folder replication.)

Define the layers of the OSI model and identify the protocols, services, and functions that pertain to each layer.

The Open Systems Interconnection reference model was created by the International Standards Organization. The OSI model is a guide used to describe the various network protocols used in network communications. There are seven layers to the OSI model. Each layer provides different services during network communications between two network entities. Programmers write applications to communicate by using protocols at the various OSI layers. Each layer has a set of methods that are used to talk to the layers above and below it. When an update occurs, developers only need to replace one section of their program. This is because the method of communication between layers stays the same. People use the OSI Reference Model every day and do not know it. Network+ certified technicians can administer existing networks and need to know the basic function of each of the seven layers for the Network+ exam.

Critical Information

The OSI layers are stacked on top of each other. Each layer describes a specific function that a communications protocol stack can provide. At the top of the OSI model is the Application layer. Above the Application layer is the operating system and user interface. At the bottom of the OSI model is the Physical layer. Below the Physical layer is the network cable. Between the user and the network cable are the individual OSI layers. Each layer manipulates the data being communicated as it is transmitted between two users. The data in a communication will travel from the user down the protocol stack to the physical media where it travels to the destination. When the data reaches the destination, it travels up the protocol stack to the user. In Figure 1.15, notice how the OSI layers are stacked on top of each other.

F I G U R E 1.15: The Open Systems Interconnection reference model

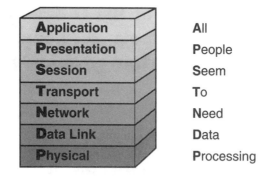

Application	All
Presentation	People
Session	Seem
Transport	To
Network	Need
Data Link	Data
Physical	Processing

TIP Some people use mnemonic devices to help them remember the order of the OSI model layers: APSTNDP (from top to bottom). A popular mnemonic for this arrangement is All People Seem To Need Data Processing.

Application Layer (OSI Layer Seven)

Layer seven, the top level of the OSI model, is called the Application layer. This does not refer to applications, such as word processing software. It does refer to items such as network access, file transfers, and e-mail delivery and routing. It may also support error recovery.

Some examples of some network protocols that operate at the Application layer include: X.400 e-mail services (see earlier section), X-Windows, HTTP, FTP, Telnet, SMTP, DHCP, NFS, NIS, NIS+, lpr, DNS, SNMP, NTDS, NDS, SMB, and SNA.

Presentation Layer (OSI Layer Six)

Layer six, the Presentation layer, is responsible for formatting data exchange. Graphic commands, conversion of character sets, and data encryption most often occur on this level. This layer may also be where data compression is handled to reduce the amount of data transmitted. The Presentation layer includes protocols and standards like SNA, ASCII, and EBCDIC.

Session Layer (OSI Layer Five)

Layer five, the Session layer, defines how two computers establish, use, and end a session. Practical functions such as security authentication and network naming are required for applications to occur here. LDAP, Remote Procedure Call (RPC), NetBEUI, and XNS are some examples of protocols that function at this layer.

Transport Layer (OSI Layer Four)

Layer four, the Transport layer, checks to ensure that data packets created in the Session layer are actually received without error. Layer four also divides long messages into smaller ones and, conversely, bundles a series of short data packets into one longer packet.

Packet sequencing and guaranteed delivery occur on layer four. Protocols on this layer are commonly (but not always) connection oriented and, therefore, guarantee the delivery of data. An active link between the sender and receiver is maintained. When a packet is sent from the receiver, an acknowledgement that the data has been received is then sent back to the original sender. You will frequently see this referred to as an ACK, which is shorthand for ACKnowledgement. This layer is responsible for the majority of error and flow control in network communications.

The TCP, User Datagram Protocol (UDP), SPX, and NetBEUI protocols operate at this layer.

Network Layer (OSI Layer Three)

Layer three, the Network layer, is responsible for logical addressing and the translation of logical names into physical addresses. A little-known function of the Network layer is data prioritization. Not all data has equal importance. For instance, it wouldn't hurt anybody if an e-mail is delayed a fraction of a second, but delaying audio or video data a fraction of a second could be disastrous to the message. This prioritization is known as *quality of service* (QoS).

Other functions of the Network layer include controlling congestion, routing data from source to destination, as well as building and tearing down packets. Most routed protocols, including SLIP, IP, IPX, and RIP, function at this layer.

Data Link Layer (OSI Layer Two)

Layer two, the Data Link layer, takes raw data from the Physical layer and gives it a logical structure. Two sub-layers exist within the Data Link layer—Logical Link Control (LLC) and Media Access Control (MAC). The logic used on the Data Link layer includes where data is meant to go, which computer sent the data, and checking the overall validity of the bytes sent. In most situations, after a data frame has been sent, the data link sends a frame and then waits for a positive ACK. If one is not received, or if the frame was damaged, it will send another one.

The Data Link layer also controls functions of logical network topologies and physical addressing. The MAC address sub-layer—the physical address of the computer node—manages access to a specific computer from the Physical layer. It is not either an Internet domain name or an IP decimal number assigned by the node's company association. 802.2, 802.3, Ethernet_II, Raw, and Ethernet_SNAP packets are created on layer two. Also, low-end logical networks are maintained on the Data Link layer.

OSI layers cannot normally be skipped. However, with the help of the LLC sub-layer, sections can be skipped. The LLC provides a jumping point for going directly to upper levels in the OSI model. But the common method of packet communication is still to move up through the layers one at a time.

PPP and ISDN allow remote access to a network through the Data Link layer. These communication mediums are discussed in detail in a later chapter. ISDN, Ethernet, CSMA/CD, Token Ring, FDDI, 802.2, 802.3, 802.5, PPP, PPTP, ATM, and SONET operate at layer two.

Physical Layer (OSI Layer 1)

Layer one, the Physical layer, controls the functional interface. Cable specifications are outlined in the Physical layer, and it determines whether you are on fiber, coax, wireless, unshielded twisted pair, or some other medium. Transmission technique, pin layout, connector types, and everything dealing with the physical medium is covered in OSI layer one. Also, ISDN, 10BaseT, 10Base5, 10Base2, 10BaseF, 100BaseT, 100BaseX, UTP, STP, fiber optic, and modem standards are defined in layer one.

Exam Essentials

For the Network+ exam, you must know the details of the various layers of the OSI models. Additionally, you must be able to distinguish between the functions that each layer defines.

Know the order and definitions of the seven layers of the OSI model. Application (layer seven), Presentation (layer six), Session (layer five), Transport (layer four), Network (layer three), Data Link (layer two), and Physical (layer one) are the seven layers of the OSI model. See the preceding Critical Information section for definitions.

Know how to identify which protocols and communication media are used at each layer. Do not merely memorize abbreviations here. Rather, understand what each item and layer does. Then you will be able to match them up with comprehension instead of just a list of abbreviations.

  1. **Physical**   ISDN, 10BaseT, 10Base5, 10Base2, 10BaseF, 100BaseT, 100BaseX, UTP, STP, fiber optic, modem standards (V.32, V.42, V.90, and all others)

2. Data Link ISDN, Ethernet, CSMA/CD, Token Ring, FDDI, 802.2, 802.3, 802.5, PPP, PPTP, ATM, SONET

3. Network SLIP, IP, IPX

4. Transport TCP, UDP, SPX, NetBEUI

5. Session LDAP, RPC, NetBEUI, XNS

6. Presentation NCP, NetBIOS, XNS

7. Application Mostly services and programs (see Note below)

NOTE All of these protocols and mediums are explained in detail in other sections and chapters. This part of the exam only requires that you be able to match them to an OSI layer.

Know how to identify services and programs at different layers of the OSI reference model. Due to their complex nature, services and programs primarily populate the upper levels of the OSI reference model. But these programs and services mainly reside at the Application layer.

7. Application X-Windows, HTTP, FTP, Telnet, SMTP, DHCP, NFS, NIS, NIS+, lpr, DNS, SNMP, NTDS, NDS, SMB, SNA

Key Terms and Concepts

Application layer (OSI layer seven) Programs and enduser interfaces operate on layer seven.

Data Link layer (OSI layer two) Frames packets and assigns a specific computer node address, or Media Access Control (MAC) address. The logical link control (LLC) is the upper sub-layer and can be used to jump to upper layers.

ISO (International Standards Organization) Creates specifications for everything from film speed to network protocol classification.

Network layer (OSI layer three) Network packets are given another address and routed to various networks on layer three.

OSI reference model Common reference for the Open Systems Interconnection reference model, which was developed by the ISO to divide network communication into manageable layers from the wire up to higher-level programs.

Packet A group of bytes organized according to a specific protocol.

Physical layer (OSI layer one) Communicates between the medium (commonly cabling) and network devices. Electrical and mechanical specifications are handled.

Presentation layer (OSI layer six) Accommodates data encryption, decryption, compression, and graphical representation of data.

Routing Directing packets from one computer to another and from one network to another via the Network layer.

Session layer (OSI layer five) Protocols that operate at this layer perform practical functions such as security authentication and network naming.

Sample Questions

1. Which layer of the OSI model is responsible for translating the data from upper-layer protocols into electrical signals and then placing them on the network media?

   A. Physical

   B. Transport

   C. Data Link

   D. Network

   E. Session

   Answer: A—The Physical layer specifies methods of electrical and mechanical communication between the network card and the cabling or wireless media. Of all the layers listed, the Physical layer is the only one that performs this function.

2. What OSI layer handles connection-oriented links?

   A. 1

   B. 2

   C. 3

   D. 4 *(TRANSPORT)*

   E. 5 *(NETWORK)*

   Answer: D—Layer four sequences packets and handles connection-oriented links. (Layer one handles electrical and mechanical conversions. Layer two frames packets. Layer three directs packets by routing them to computer node addressees. And layer five handles packet milestones and network resource naming.)

3. From the top down, what is the proper order of the OSI layers?

   A. Physical, Data Link, Network, Transport, Session, Presentation, Application

   B. Physical, Application, Presentation, Session, Network, Transport, Data Link

   C. Session, Application, Presentation, Transport, Network, Data Link, Physical

   D. Application, Data Link, Session, Transport, Network, Physical, Presentation

   E. Application, Presentation, Session, Transport, Network, Data Link, Physical

   Answer: E—Application, Presentation, Session, Transport, Network, Data Link, Physical

4. FTP, Telnet, and SMTP operate on what layer of the OSI model?

   A. 7

   B. 6

   C. 5

   D. 4

   E. 3

   Answer: A—Programs are offered on the Application layer (layer seven).

Recognize and describe the following characteristics of networking media and connectors:

- The advantages and disadvantages of coax, Cat 3, Cat 5, fiber optic, UTP, and STP, and the conditions under which they are appropriate
- The length and speed of 10Base2, 10BaseT, and 100BaseT
- The length and speed of 10Base5, 100Base VGAnyLan, 100Base TX
- The visual appearance of RJ-45 and BNC, and how they are crimped

It is important to know the types of cabling commonly used for network implementation. Each cabling specification has its own advantages and disadvantages, which are discussed in this section. These types include coaxial cable and unshielded twisted pair (UTP) cables. Coaxial cables primarily use BNC connectors. UTP cables, on the other hand, use RJ-45 connector modules, which make it the easiest cabling to manipulate.

Critical Information

To pass the exam, you need to know the various specifications for each cabling system. Specifications for cable types include maximum cable lengths, their speeds, and the naming conventions for each type. Naming conventions are primarily used for Ethernet cabling standards (which the Network+ exam tests you on). The naming convention of Ethernet cabling is #BaseN where # refers to the speed in megabits per second, *Base* refers to the entire cable being used for one communication channel (baseband), and *N* refers to the type of cable. When looking at 10BaseT, for example:

10   Stands for a maximum speed of ten megabits per seconds (Mbps).

Base   Short for baseband, which means the entire bandwidth of the cable is used for one communication channel.

T   Stands for twisted pair, which means it can go 100 meters. (Be careful; the last part of a cable designation is not always an exact abbreviation.)

Fiber Optic

Fiber optic cable is a clear plastic or glass shaft that transmits network signals in the form of light. Light transmissions over fiber optics go the farthest of any cabling medium. Since fiber optic cable transmits light rather than electricity, it is immune to the villains of electromagnetic interference (EMI) and radio frequency interference (RFI). You will see a complete discussion of these terms in Chapter 6, but you should know at this point that both can affect network performance. Anyone who has seen UTP cable for a network run down an elevator shaft (a great source of multiple types of interference) would no doubt appreciate this aspect of fiber.

Light signals are carried on either a glass or plastic core. Glass can carry the signal a greater distance, but plastic costs less. Regardless of which core is used, there is a shield wrapped around it. Two cores are then mated—one for transmission and the other for receiving—and wrapped up in an armor coating, which is typically Kevlar. Figure 1.16 shows the fiber optic connectors known as FDDI and SMA. FDDI is the Fiber Distributed Data Interface. SMA, the most popular connector in fiber optics today, is also known by its technical name, which is Field-Installable Subminiature Assembly (FSNA).

NOTE   Ethernet, running at 10Mbps over fiber, is normally designated 10BaseF; the 100Mbps version of this implementation is 100BaseF.

FIGURE 1.16: Examples of fiber optic connectors FDDI and SMA

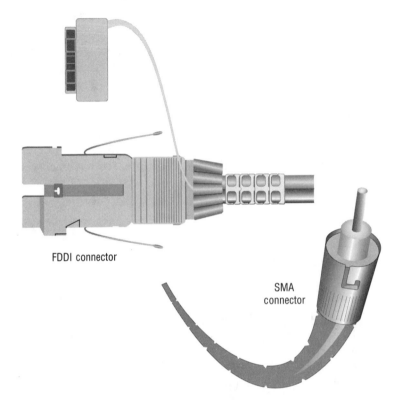

FDDI connector

SMA
connector

Pros and Cons
While it sounds like fiber optic cable can solve many problems, it does have its drawbacks; some pros and cons are listed below.

Pros
- Completely immune to radio or electrical interference

- Transmission up to 4 kilometers

Cons
- Most difficult installation

- More costly investment in installation and materials

UTP and STP

Unshielded twisted pair (UTP) and shielded twisted pair (STP) sheathing types are used for Category 3 and Category 5 wires. A connection is made by using a registered jack (RJ). You are probably already familiar with RJs; most telephones connect with an RJ-11. While the RJ-11 has four wires (or two pairs), the network connector, RJ-45, has eight wires (or four pairs).

The most common use for twisted pair cable (specifically UTP) is Ethernet. There are four major implementations of Ethernet over twisted pair, one of which runs at 10Mbps, and the others run at 100Mbps. The implementations are:

- 10BaseT
- 100Base VGAnyLan
- 100BaseT4
- 100BaseTX

10BaseT

10BaseT is probably the most common implementation of Ethernet in use today. It enjoys broad vendor support and is a mature standard. 10BaseT, as its name suggests, operates at 10Mbps, uses baseband signaling, and uses UTP as its cabling media.

Common name   Ethernet

Type   UTP four wire pairs (eight total wires); three twists per foot

Speed   10Mbps

Wire usage   Baseband

Length   100 meters, or 328 feet

Node connection   RJ-45

Resistance   50 ohm

Special equipment   A punch-down block, repeater, or hub is required to connect more than two computers to each other.

Cost   Moderate

100Base VGAnyLan

Hewlett Packard (HP) created their own specification for 100Mbps UTP cabling. HP's specification was among the first developed for high-speed networks. Their cabling also touted collision avoidance. However, 100Base VG failed to become the industry standard.

Common name   VG LAN, VGAnyLAN, AnyLAN

Type   UTP four wire pairs (eight total wires)

Speed   100Mbps

Wire usage   Baseband

Length   100 meters, or 328 feet

Node connections   RJ-45

Special equipment   A punch-down block, repeater, or hub is required to connect more than two computers to each other.

Cost   Moderate

100BaseT4

100BaseT4 is one of the 100 megabit "Fast Ethernet" standards. Its unique spin on the Fast Ethernet concept is that it uses all four pairs of a Category 3, 4, or 5 UTP cable.

Common name   Fast Ethernet

Type   UTP four wire pairs; three twists per foot

Speed   100Mbps

Wire usage   Baseband

Length   100 meters, or 328 feet

Node connections   RJ-45

Special equipment   A punch-down block, repeater, or hub is required to connect more than two computers to each other.

Cost   Moderate

100BaseTX

100BaseTX is the industry standard for 100Mbps networks. It uses two pairs of a Category 5 UTP cable. NICs that can autosense between 10Mbps and 100Mbps are known as 10/100BaseTX cards.

Common name   Fast Ethernet, 100BaseTX

Type   UTP four wire pairs (eight total wires, but only two pairs— or four wires, are used); three twists per foot

Speed   100Mbps

Wire usage   Baseband

Length   100 meters, or 328 feet

Node connections   RJ-45

Special equipment   A punch-down block, repeater, or hub is required to connect more than two computers to each other.

Cost   Moderate

RJ-45

The U.S Federal Communications Commission (FCC) specifies cable connector standards as registered jack (RJ) connections. An RJ-45 connector is attached to the end of a UTP or STP cable. The clear plastic module houses four wire pairs, or eight total wires. This looks similar to the RJ-11 phone wire module, except RJ-11 only has four wires, or two wire pairs.

TIP   An RJ-45 data module is twice as wide as an RJ-11 telephone module.

Category 3

Category 3 cabling is a data grade physical medium. It consists of four twisted pairs, with three twists per foot. It is rated up to 10Mbps. This has been installed in a lot of existing buildings. Be careful if you come across a preexisting installation and are asked to use it as a LAN. Check the category of the cabling because today's networks run at 100Mbps and gigabit Ethernet.

NOTE   Category 1 is voice grade (not rated for data communications), and the oldest UTP. It is frequently referred to as POTS (Plain Old Telephone Service). Prior to 1983, this was the standard cable used throughout the North American telephone system. POTS cable still exists in parts of the PSTN (Public Switched Telephone Network). You may have Category 1 or Category 3 already in your walls.

Category 5

Category 5 cabling is the current standard of wire that is run from wire closets to desktops. It consists of four twisted pairs and is rated for up to 100Mbps.

Coaxial Cable

Coaxial cable is thick cabling that is commonly housed in a black sheath. The thinner version, 10Base2, is commonly mistaken for television cable, due to its similar appearance. Both 10Base2 and 10Base5 are limited to the number of segments (5), repeaters (4), and populated segments (3) that can be situated on a network. This is known as the 5-4-3 rule.

WARNING   Do not confuse the number of segments that are listed with the number of nodes allowed on a network. This rule concerns populated segments, not the number of computers on a network.

10Base2
10Base2 is an Ethernet standard that uses a 10Mbps signaling rate, baseband signaling, and has a maximum distance of 185 meters (around 200 meters, which is what the 2 stands for).

Common name   Thinnet, Thin Ethernet

Type   3/16-inch coaxial stranded copper

Speed   10Mbps

Wire usage   Baseband

Length   185 meters, or 607 feet

Node connection   DIX Transceiver, BNC, or T-connector

Resistance   50 ohm

Special equipment   Terminator needed at each end of a segment. A ground is suggested on each segment.

WARNING   CATV television cable has a different resistance and looks similar to coaxial computer cable. They are not the same thing, so be sure you have the correct computer-grade cabling and terminators.

Fault tolerance   None. All computers on a segment are disconnected from the network if cable fails.

Cost   Low. This is the least expensive cable media.

10Base5

Common name   Thicknet, Thick Ethernet

Type   3/8-coaxial solid copper (not very flexible; difficult to handle or install)

Speed   10Mbps

Wire usage   Baseband

Length   500 meters, or 1,640 feet

Node connection   Vampire Tap, N-connector

Resistance   50 ohm

Special equipment   Terminator needed at each end of a segment. A ground is suggested on each segment.

Cost   Moderate

BNC

A BNC (Bayonet Neil-Concelman) connector is used to attach a network interface card to a 10Base2 network. Figure 1.17 shows the BNC connector.

FIGURE 1.17: A male and female BNC connector

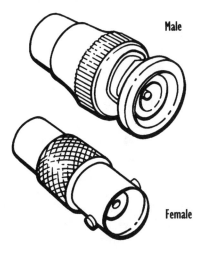

Male

Female

Exam Essentials

Know how to decipher the different portions of a cable name.
The naming convention of cabling is #BaseN, where # refers to the speed in megabits per second, *Base* refers to the entire cable being used for one communication channel (baseband), and *N* refers to the type of cable.

Know the length limitations of each cable type.

- 10Base2 can extend 185 meters, or 607 feet.

- 10Base5 can extend 500 meters, or 1,640 feet.

- 10BaseT, 100BaseT, 100Base VGAnyLAN, and 100BaseTX can all extend 100 meters, or 328 feet.

Know the speed limitations of each cable type.

- 10BaseN cables, where N is the type of cable, are rated for 10Mbps.

- 100BaseN cables, where N is the type of cable, are rated for 100Mbps.

Know the advantages and disadvantages of different cable features. 10Base2 is the cheapest cabling medium, but it is also the easiest to cause an entire segment of computers to lose connectivity. 10BaseT and 100BaseTX have moderate costs, but they suffer from attenuation and crosstalk—just like coaxial cabling. Fiber optical cabling has traditionally been the fastest medium. It is also free from interference, crosstalk, and wiretapping. Fiber is the most expensive medium.

Key Terms and Concepts

Attenuation An electrical signal dies after the specified maximum cable length is reached. (To extend a cable beyond the limit, use a repeater and another cable.)

Category 3 Twisted pair cabling that is rated for data communications up to 10Mbps.

Category 5 Twisted pair cabling that is rated for data communications up to 100Mbps.

Coaxial A single copper cable is enclosed in an outer sheath. 10Base2 cables are stranded cables; 10Base5 has a solid core.

Crosstalk Interference caused when two electrical cables are run beside each other. The magnetic field given off by each cable affects the other, which is is why UTP and STP wires are twisted inside the outer sheath.

EMI (electromagnetic interference) Corrupts electrical network communications. (For example, mechanical interference can occur when a cable is run down an elevator shaft.)

RFI (radio frequency interference) Corrupts electrical network communications.

Sample Questions

1. What is the maximum number of repeaters you can install on a single segment of a 10Base2 network?

A. 1

B. 2

C. 3

D. 4

Answer: D—Remember the 3-4-5 rule-a TenBase2 network can have three populated segments, four repeaters, and five total segments.

2. Which UTP Ethernet standard uses all four pairs of a Category 5 UTP cable?

A. 10Base2

B. 10BaseT

C. 10BaseF

D. 100BaseT4

E. 100BaseTX

Answer: D—100BaseT4. (10Base2 is coax, not UTP. 10BaseT and 100BaseTX both use only two pairs of Cat 5 UTP. 10BaseF uses fiber optic cable.)

3. Which connector is used with a 100BaseTX Ethernet cabling scheme?

A. BNC

B. SMA

C. RJ-45

D. RJ-11

E. FDDI

Answer: C—RJ-45. (BNC is used on 10Base2 Ethernet. SMA and FDDI connectors are used on fiber optic cable. RJ-11 connectors are used on telephone jacks.)

Identify the basic attributes, purpose, and function of the following network elements:

- Full- and half-duplexing
- WAN and LAN
- Server, workstation, and host
- Server-based networking and peer-to-peer networking
- Cable, NIC, and router
- Broadband and baseband
- Gateway, as both a default IP router and as a method to connect dissimilar systems or protocols

Multiple components are obviously needed to establish and maintain computer connection to a network. CompTIA will use the Network+ exam to evaluate your understanding of these components, including servers, workstations, and cable communications. You will also need to know that half duplexing allows for one-way communication while full duplexing allows for simultaneous two-way communication. And be careful when gateways are mentioned; gateways can connect you to the Internet or a dissimilar network depending on the context of the question.

Critical Information

As noted above, the exam looks for specific knowledge of duplexing, servers, workstations, hosts, and network devices. You will not have to configure a server, set up a router, or negotiate communications between two dissimilar networks using a gateway. However, certain gateway knowledge is necessary for the exam, and, as a network administrator, you will be required to identify and utilize all of these components. Beginning with duplexing, each item is discussed on the following pages.

Full Duplex and Half Duplex Communications

Once you have decided what protocol—IPX, IP, or NetBEUI—will be used, you will need to determine who will transmit on the wire, and when. If one person transmits at one time, then it is known as half duplex; if more than one person can transmit at the same time, then you have full duplex communication.

Half Duplex Communication

Half duplex communication allows only a single node to transmit at a time. There is always a dedicated sender and receiver, and when the sender is done the receiver can switch roles in order to transmit. Both entities cannot transmit at the same time.

Half duplex communication is distinguished by the fact that communication happens in both directions, but only in one direction at a time. A signal at the end of a single-direction communication indicates that the transmission is complete. Data travels in only one direction at a time, and it uses the same transmission frequency. Figure 1.18 shows half duplex communication.

F I G U R E 1.18: Graphical example of half duplex

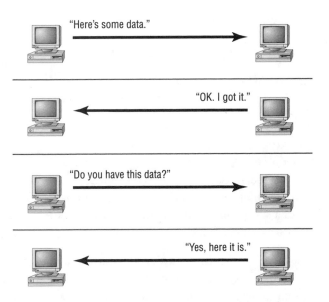

Full Duplex Communication

On the other hand, full duplex communication is more like a telephone conversation. Communication happens in both directions simultaneously. When using the telephone, it is possible for you to speak to a caller while they are talking to you. Similarly, with this type of networking, a system can send data in one direction while confirmation of previously sent data may be returned to that same system at the same time. This can greatly cut the time needed to send, confirm, and control given transmissions. One drawback is that full duplexing requires more complex hardware and software, which can raise costs and is why full duplexing is not used in all cases. Figure 1.19 shows full duplex communication.

F I G U R E 1.19: Graphical example of full duplex

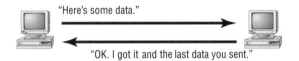

"Here's some data."

"OK. I got it and the last data you sent."

*Note: This exchange can occur simultaneously.

Network Types

Work on wide area networks and local area networks makes up the majority of a network administrator's job. The specific number of computers in a given LAN will vary. Remember that LANs are networks within individual buildings, whereas WANs can span cities, nations, and continents.

Local Area Network

The acronym LAN stands for local area network. The operative word in LAN is local. A LAN is a network limited to a specific area, usually the size of an office. By definition, a LAN cannot go outside the boundaries of a single building. If the network spans more than a single location, it becomes a WAN.

While technology today allows you to have a larger LAN than in previous years, practical administration limitations mean dividing a LAN into smaller, logical areas, called workgroups. A workgroup is a specific grouping, such as a single cubicle farm within a single building of a larger company. Figure 1.20 shows an example of a small LAN.

FIGURE 1.20: A small LAN

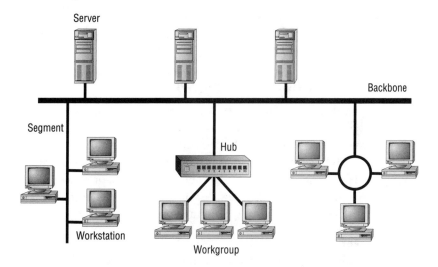

Wide Area Network

A wide area network is a computer network that can span several cities, nations, or continents, or, in other words, is any network that crosses metropolitan, regional, or national boundaries. Most networking professionals would define a WAN as any network that uses routers and public network links. The biggest WAN in the world is the Internet, which can be defined by both of these definitions.

To sum up, there are a few points that differentiate WANs from other types of networks:

- Greater distances involved than a LAN or a MAN

- Speeds are slower than a LAN or MAN

- Possible to connect on demand or have a permanent connection

- Several choices as to how data is transported

The Internet is actually a specific type of WAN. Since the Internet is a collection of networks that are interconnected, *internetwork* is the technical term used to describe it. That's actually where the name Internet came from; it is just an abbreviated form of the word internetwork.

It is also important to understand that a WAN can be either centralized or distributed. A centralized WAN uses a server to connect other computers (or brainless keyboards and monitors) to a central site. Distributed WANs, generally speaking, connect LANs together into one large WAN. The Internet is a great example.

Computer Roles on a Network

A typical network will consist of many servers, workstations, and hosts. As has been discussed earlier in this chapter, a server is a software or hardware device (either a PC or a dedicated server) that provides a service. A workstation is primarily a computer that enables a user to do local processing in their office or cubicle. And a host provides processing power and specialized services. Beginning with servers, each of these will be detailed in the following paragraphs.

Server

The word server is a generic term. In the truest sense, a server does exactly what the name implies and provides resources (*serves* them, in other words) to the various clients on a network. Servers are typically very powerful computers that run the software that controls and maintains the network. This software is known as the network operating system and is covered in more detail in Chapter 3.

Servers are often dedicated to a single purpose. That's not to say that an individual server can't perform many jobs, but, more often than not, you'll get better performance if you dedicate a server to a single task. Figure 1.21 shows a sample network that includes both workstations and servers; note that there are more workstations than servers.

Workstation

With several possible interpretations, workstation is a rather murky term. The classic definition refers to very powerful computers, such as those that are used for drafting or other math-intensive applications. This definition can also refer to computers with multiple central processing units (CPUs). The current definition of workstation refers to any computer that is connected to a network and is used to do work.

FIGURE 1.21: A sample network including servers and workstations

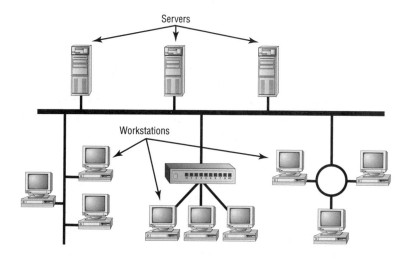

Workstations are computers that request resources. A client can be software or hardware that requests a service from the network. Workstations can be clients, but it is important to note that not all clients are workstations. You can have entities like printers that can request resources from the network, but they would be clients, not workstations.

Host

A host was originally a mainframe or minicomputer that provided processing to terminals. Currently, in the PC environment, the host provides a service, such as access to the Internet. A host is more like a server than a workstation.

Common Connection Devices

A network cannot exist without a cable and a network interface card (NIC). The NIC is the expansion card you install in the computer or other device to connect the device to the network cabling. Without these devices, you have no network because they are the two major physical components that comprise a network. There are microwave and infrared networks, but these are rare. Most of the commercial and educational networks are comprised of cabling. Routers are used to segment a large network or to connect one network to another.

Cable

Cabling makes up the major portion of the physical medium of a network. Computers are connected to hubs, hubs are connected to other devices (switches, routers, and other hubs), and all of these connections are made with wires, or network cabling. Types of cabling include Category 3, and Category 5 for twisted pair wires. Coaxial cabling has either a stranded or a solid copper core.

Network Interface Card

NIC stands for network interface card. To better understand the purpose of this component, you can take a look at each individual word in its name. First, you have already seen that a network is comprised of a minimum of two devices, which usually includes computers connected by a cable. This configuration allows valuable resources such as printers, Internet connections, data, or a combination of these, to be shared between users. Second, an *interface* couples two dissimilar points, translating a flow between them into something each side can understand. (For an NIC, that flow would be data.) And third, a card is the device used to join computers to a network. So, in short, the NIC is a type of expansion card.

NOTE   NICs have gotten small enough to be built into the motherboard. Built-in interfaces have the same functionality and are still called NICs.

Router

A router directs communications from one network to another based on the destination of a packet. Routers operate at the Network layer of the OSI model and commonly direct IP and IPX packets. NetBEUI is not routable and will not normally make it through a router. Figure 1.22 shows a router.

FIGURE 1.22: Router between two sections of a network

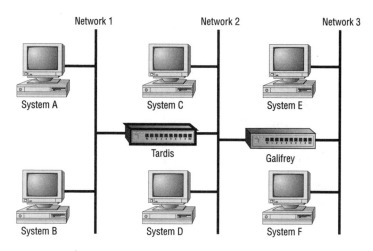

Bandwidth Usage

A computer cable can be used to send one signal or many signals simultaneously. Varying the frequency or phase of an electrical signal can encode multiple signals. This is known as broadband. Baseband technology uses all of the bandwidth to send or receive a single message.

Broadband

A broadband signal shares the cable with other signals on the same cable. There are two methods to accomplish this goal. One is time division multiple access (TDMA), which grants a time slot to send or receive data and is usually used in digital communications. The other method is frequency division multiplexing (FDM), which is generally used in analog transmissions and, as the name implies, uses frequency modulation (FM) to get the job done.

Baseband

Baseband is a digital signal that uses the entire cable. In other words, no other signals can be on the same cable during a baseband transmission. This is the opposite of broadband, where multiple signals can be on a single cable at the same time.

Gateways

The term gateway is generic. There are two definitions of the term gateway. The first definition is seen only on a TCP/IP network. For clients in a TCP/IP network, you must configure a default gateway. In this respect, the term gateway refers to a router that connects two networks. A default gateway is your primary router that gets you to another network or to the Internet. The other type of gateway is one that translates between protocols at all layers of the OSI model. In this respect, a gateway is a device that translates between dissimilar networks and protocols.

Default IP Router

As stated above, the default gateway is actually a router. This router is the first device checked when a message is sent out of your network to another. In small networks with only one router, the Internet router is sometimes called the default gateway.

Dissimilar Networks

Gateways can also connect dissimilar networks. Windows 9.*x* and NT networks connect to IBM mainframes and AppleTalk networks via different types of gateways. Common gateways are SNA and SAA gateways, which connect to IBM mainframe networks.

Exam Essentials

The exam will give you scenarios and definitions that need to be matched to terms. This objective covers duplexing, LANs, WANs, servers, workstations, hosts, cable, NICs, routers, and gateways. Server-based and peer-to-peer networking are also covered.

Know how to identify half duplexing and full duplexing. Full duplexing allows simultaneous two-way communication over a medium. Half duplexing restricts communication to one direction—from a sender to a receiver.

Know how to notice the difference between a LAN and a WAN. A LAN operates on one site. A WAN can span cities, nations, or continents.

Know how to identify a server, workstation, or host. A server is a network device that provides (or *serves*) resources to the rest of the network. A workstation is a computer on a network that a user uses to access network resources. A host is a general term for any device on a TCP/IP network that has an IP address.

Know how to differentiate between broadband and baseband. Broadband communications use different frequencies to allow multiple conversations to occur simultaneously on a wire. Baseband communications allow only one communication session to happen at any one instant.

Know how to identify the different types of gateways. A default gateway provides access to the Internet. A dissimilar network gateway connects a PC-based network to a completely different type of network. Other types of networks are SNA and AppleTalk networks.

Key Terms and Concepts

Baseband   Communication that takes up the entire bandwidth of a cable.

Broadband   Several different communications can transmit over the same cable simultaneously, using different frequencies and phases.

Full duplex   Simultaneous two-way communications, such as is possible on a telephone line.

Gateway   Can connect two dissimilar networks operating on all seven layers of the OSI model. A default gateway is the router that all IP packets are sent to when IP packets are destined for remote networks.

Half duplex   One-way communication where one side talks and the other side listens.

LAN (local area network)   A small collection of internetworked computers that do not communicate beyond one site.

MAN (metropolitan area network)   A medium-size collection of internetworked computers that are spread out over several sites within a single city and its suburbs.

Router   Directs packets on the Network layer of the OSI model and, typically, connects different companies or different network divisions in large companies.

SAA (systems application architecture)   Networks that are used to have IBM programs talk to each other.

SNA (systems network architecture)   Networks that are used to have IBM hosts and nodes talk to each other.

WAN (wide area network)   Comprised of internetworked computers where the network spans several cities, nations, or continents.

Sample Questions

1. What type of computer network is restricted to a minimal number of computers and may take up only one floor or building?

   A. LAN

   B. MAN

   C. WAN

   D. SAN

   Answer: A—Local area networks are restricted to a single site. (A metropolitan area network spans several sites within a city and its surrounding suburbs. A wide area network spans several cities, nations, or continents. A storage area network is used to manage disk farms and other storage media between several servers.)

2. What type of computer network encompasses several sites all within the same city or county?

   A. LAN

   B. MAN

   C. WAN

   D. SAN

Answer: B—A metropolitan area network spans several sites within a city and its surrounding suburbs. (Local area networks are restricted to one site. A wide area network spans several nations or continents. A storage area network is used to manage disk farms and other storage media between several servers.)

3. What communication technology allows the simultaneous, two-way sending and receiving of messages on the same medium between two devices?

    A. Baseband

    B. Gateway

    C. Half duplex

    D. Full duplex

    E. SAA

    Answer: D—Full duplex communication allows simultaneous, two-way communications. (Baseband communications use the entire cable to send a one-way signal. At the Application layer, gateways convert information from one type of network to another. Half duplex is one-way communication, with one device sending and the other listening. IBM programs to talk to each other using systems application architecture.)

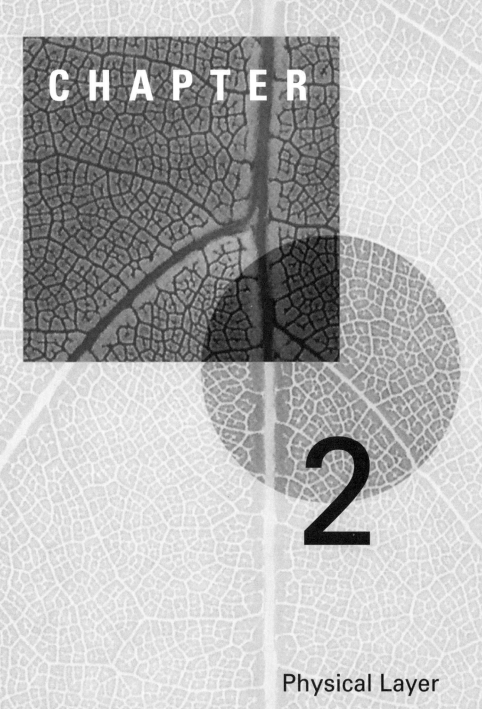

CHAPTER

2

Physical Layer

Network+ Exam Objectives Covered in This Chapter:

▶ **Given an installation, configuration, or troubleshooting scenario, select an appropriate course of action if a client workstation does not connect to the network after installing or replacing a network interface card. Explain why a given action is warranted. The following issues may be covered:** *(pages 87 – 96)*

- Knowledge of how the network card is usually configured, including EEPROM, jumpers, and plug-and-play software
- Use of network card diagnostics, including the loopback test and vendor-supplied diagnostics
- The ability to resolve hardware resource conflicts, including IRQ, DMA, and I/O Base Address

▶ **Identify the use of the following network components and the differences between them:** *(pages 96 – 105)*

- Hubs
- MAUs
- Switching hubs
- Repeaters
- Transceivers

Layer one of the OSI layer is the Physical layer, which is the bottom layer of the OSI model and manages electricity. Electrical signals are transmitted from the wire to the network interface card (NIC). Equipment such as hubs, repeaters, and transceivers are used to regenerate the signal and get it from one medium to another. Without an NIC, computers would not be able to talk to each other. NICs are now integrated right onto the motherboard of computers, as well as being on expansion cards.

As a network administrator, you will need to be able to configure NICs; EEPROMs, jumpers, and plug-and-play software are all used to manage the settings on NICs. Concerning these related objectives, the Network+ exam covers the different types of network equipment and network cards on the Physical and Data Link layers. You will need to be able to visually identify each component and define them in writing. The exam also checks that you know how to troubleshoot misconfigurations. Diagnostics include software and a hardware loop-back test.

Given an installation, configuration, or troubleshooting scenario, select an appropriate course of action if a client workstation does not connect to the network after installing or replacing a network interface card. Explain why a given action is warranted. The following issues may be covered:

- Knowledge of how the network card is usually configured, including EEPROM, jumpers, and plug-and-play software
- Use of network card diagnostics, including the loopback test and vendor-supplied diagnostics.
- The ability to resolve hardware resource conflicts, including IRQ, DMA, and I/O Base Address

Computers are connected to networks with network interface cards. The Network+ exam tests your ability to both recognize different types of cards and properly configure them. You should be familiar with how jumpers, EEPROMs, and plug-and-play software are used to configure communication settings on a card. You are also required to know what tool to select when troubleshooting network connectivity for NICs.

Critical Information

A network card is an expansion card that fits into a slot in a computer. NICs can be very small and integrated into a computer's motherboard, and they enable stand-alone PCs to connect to networks via an attached cable. The configuration of these cards has gotten much easier in the past few years. Originally, small jumpers that were less than a quarter-inch long had to be slipped over pins. Configuration is now as simple as powering down, inserting the card, powering up, and then letting plug-and-play configure the card. Although the NIC itself may be installed correctly, the computer often still won't connect properly to the network, so you must know how to troubleshoot network connectivity issues. Network cards are tested using vendor supplied diagnostic utilities and a hardware loopback device.

Network Card Configuration

There are several methods of configuring network expansion cards, including small plastic and metal jumpers, DIP switches, Electronically Erasable Programmable Read-Only Memory (EEPROM), and plug-and-play technology. Jumpers and DIP switches are hardware solutions that require you to manipulate tiny pins or switches, whereas EEPROMs and plug-and-play technology are configured via software, which makes them preferable.

Jumpers

Setting jumpers was the first method invented to configure an expansion card—and it's also the most difficult. Jumpers are small connectors that are used to connect pins, indicating a setting to the device. The connectors' sizes differ according to their manufacturer.

WARNING   These small jumpers are easily dropped and lost on the floor or in the computer case.

Placing a jumper over two prongs makes an electrical connection. This connection sets how the NIC will communicate with the computer. Note the small jumpers that fit over metal prongs in Figure 2.1.

F I G U R E 2.1: A jumper and how it is used

A jumper (above left) can be used to make a connection between various pairs of pins in an array of pins. On some devices you may need to jumper multiple pairs, using several jumpers. This arrangement of six pins offers eight different jumper settings.

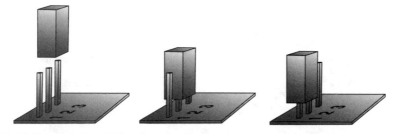

You'll often see devices with just three pins. These are common for devices that require only two settings, like on and off, or enabled and disabled.

DIP Switch

The dual in-line package (DIP) switch is a small block with a built-in lever. This lever changes the state of an electrical connection. Pushing the lever from one state to the other causes the same effect as putting a jumper over two prongs to make a connection. DIP switches offer one clear advantage over jumpers: Compared to jumpers, it is impossible to lose a DIP switch. Figure 2.2 shows how a DIP switch is preferable to a jumper.

Unfortunately, due to the increased cost of parts compared to prongs and jumpers, DIP switches are not always used. Today's cost-sensitive environment requires a manufacturer to reduce costs wherever possible.

The communication channel an NIC uses to communicate with the CPU is known as an interrupt request line (IRQ). IRQs, when set by hand, are easiest to set by using DIP switches. Some network cards

FIGURE 2.2: The DIP switch makes lost jumpers a non-issue.

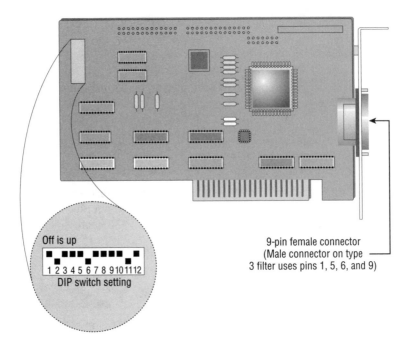

Off is up

1 2 3 4 5 6 7 8 9 10 11 12
DIP switch setting

9-pin female connector
(Male connector on type
3 filter uses pins 1, 5, 6, and 9)

are very clearly labeled on the circuit board with a nomenclature, such as "IRQ 3 4 5 7 9 10 11 12 13 14 15." An IRQ is the interrupt request that the NIC uses to open a communications channel with the CPU on the motherboard. Slide the appropriate switches from Off to On, and the network card will communicate on that IRQ. Other cards may have the same concept, with nomenclature such as JP8 A B C D E F G H I J K.

Plug-and-Play Software

Plug-and-play is basically a smart basic input/output system (BIOS). A BIOS is a set of services on a read-only chip that handles communications between hardware and the operating system. Rather than requiring that the network administrator manually configure the communication settings in a BIOS configuration utility, a plug-and-play BIOS on an expansion card talks to the BIOS on your motherboard to automatically configure the communications settings. This process is known as plug-and-play. If the BIOS is well-written, a card will work without any user intervention. The computer will automatically configure the device, and all you will have to do is install the network client.

To use a plug-and-play BIOS, activate it on the motherboard and the network card. (You may still need to configure some cards by hand even with plug-and-play turned on.) Each time the computer is powered up, the BIOS on the main board applies power to the communications bus on the motherboard, which allows the BIOS on the NIC and other devices to be read. Each device broadcasts its preferred settings. Barring a conflict, each device gets approval, and the boot cycle continues. If there is a conflict, a little arbitration occurs, and then the boot cycle continues. (Note that the BIOS on a plug-and-play board can usually be disabled, which makes a plug-and-play NIC behave like the EEPROM-based NIC.)

TIP   Plug-and-play is a function of design, not a bus type. Success of plug-and-play devices depends on whether the motherboard BIOS, NIC BIOS, and operating system are aware of plug-and-play.

Resource Conflicts   Plug-and-play still uses IRQ and memory addresses, though in most cases you won't need to alter them. Be aware that an NIC almost always needs a unique IRQ, and it always requires a unique memory address.

Network Card Diagnostics

When network connectivity fails, the problem can stem from many different issues. To diagnose the problem, you need to take a systematic approach, using several network interface card diagnostic methods. You will need to determine whether the network card is properly talking to the motherboard or if there are any resource conflicts. Then, using software diagnostics, you will need to ascertain whether the network card has internal problems. Lastly, using a hardware loopback test, you will look to see if signals are actually being transmitted and received.

Vendor-Supplied Diagnostics

Most NICs today come with some sort of software utility to verify that the NIC is functioning correctly and to test every aspect of NIC operation. This software is known as NIC diagnostics. Vendor-supplied diagnostics also test to make sure the computer motherboard, network card, and network cable can all send signals back and forth.

Software diagnostic programs typically consist of a sender portion and a receiver portion. Each portion is run on one of a pair of computers connected to the network. The sender sends a test packet out to the receiver. When the receiver receives the packet, it immediately sends a response indicating that it received the packet.

Hardware Loopback Test

A hardware loopback is a special connector for Ethernet 10BaseT NICs that receives signals from the NIC and responds with a return signal. An NIC cannot be completely tested without a hardware loopback test. Software diagnostics do not actually test transmission and reception through the port on the NIC. But the NIC's software diagnostics does use the hardware loopback test to assess transmission and reception capabilities. Figure 2.3 shows how a hardware loopback device connects to the back of an NIC.

F I G U R E 2.3: A hardware loopback and its connections

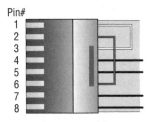

Pin#
1
2
3
4
5
6
7
8

In a loopback, pins 1 & 3 and
pins 2 & 6 are connected

The hardware loopback is usually no bigger than a single RJ-45 connector, with a few small wires on the back. If an NIC has hardware diagnostics that can use the loopback, the hardware loopback plug will be included with the NIC. To use them, simply plug the loopback into the RJ-45 connector on the back of the NIC and start the diagnostic software. Select the option in your NIC's diagnostic software that requires the loopback, and start the diagnostic routine. You will be able to tell if the NIC can send and receive data through the use of these diagnostics.

Exam Essentials

When you sit for the Network+ exam, you will need to be able to recall the following important facts.

Know how to identify EPROMs, jumpers, and DIP switches.   An EPROM is a block-shaped chip without any manually configurable parts on an NIC. A jumper is a small plastic and metal connector that slides over two metal pins on an NIC. DIP switches are small blocks on an NIC that can be slid back and forth to effect a manual hardware configuration.

Know how to use software to configure NICs.   The network administrator uses a vendor-supplied software utility to configure EPROMs. Plug-and-play software enables the NIC BIOS to automatically configure itself by talking to the motherboard BIOS. (Remember that an operating system that is aware of plug-and-play is required in order to take advantage of plug-and-play NICs.)

Know how to identify the correct tool for testing an NIC.   If you want to check the electrical output of a card, connect a hardware loopback device to the cable port. If you want to test internal components on the card, use vendor-supplied software diagnostics.

Key Terms and Concepts

BIOS (basic input/output system)   A collection of instructions on a read-only chip that allows hardware and software to talk to each other. On an NIC, it allows communication with a computer motherboard. On a motherboard, BIOS allows recognition and control of hardware devices such as hard disks, video, CPU, memory, and expansion cards.

DIP (dual in-line package) switch   Allows a setting to be changed on a card by flipping a tiny switch; preferable to jumpers.

EPROM (Erasable Programmable Read-Only Memory)   Uses ultraviolet light to erase settings on expansion cards. Software is then used to configure the new settings.

EEPROM (Electronically Erasable Programmable Read-Only Memory)   Allows a software utility to erase settings and configure an expansion card.

Jumper   A small plastic and metal component that slips over two pins. Pins and jumpers were the first means by which network and other expansion cards were configured.

NIC (network interface card)   Communication hardware that computers use to connect to a network.

Plug-and-play   Technology that automatically configures IRQs, base memory, and I/O memory. Plug-and-play software resides in the BIOS chip on an expansion card as well as on the motherboard's BIOS chip. Without proper negotiation between each BIOS, plug-and-play will not work.

Sample Questions

1. What component of a network card can have its settings programmed by a network administrator using a software program?

    A. EEPROM

    B. Jumper

    C. DIP switch

    D. Plug-and-play

    E. Testing diagnostics

Answer: A—An EEPROM is a read-only memory chip that contains NIC settings that can be modified by a special software utility. (A jumper is a hardware solution where two or more pins are linked by small connectors. A DIP switch is a miniature switch that is manipulated by hand. Plug-and-play is an automatic configuration method and does not have user intervention. Testing diagnostics are used to troubleshoot connections, not configure them.)

2. What network testing component can truly check the electrical output on the port of a network interface card?

   A. Software loopback

   B. Hardware loopback

   C. Vendor-supplied diagnostics

   D. Plug-and-play

   E. EEPROM

   Answer: B—A hardware loopback connects to the back of the network card where a cable would normally be attached. (A software loopback checks only the internal components of an NIC. Vendor-supplied diagnostics test only internal components and communication with the operating system. Plug-and-play is automatic configuration and cannot test electrical output.)

3. What two components talk to each other to auto-configure settings through plug-and-play technology?

   A. DIP switches

   B. Hardware loopback

   C. NIC BIOS

   D. EEPROM

   E. Motherboard BIOS

   Answers: C, E—The plug-and-play BIOS on the motherboard and the network interface card talk to each other to determine communication settings. (DIP switches are manually set. A hardware loopback is a test device. An EEPROM is used to store settings on an NIC, not determine what the settings should be.)

4. What is the difference between an EPROM and an EEPROM?

A. An EPROM uses UV light to erase communication settings on an NIC, whereas an EEPROM does not.

B. An EEPROM uses UV light to erase communication settings on an NIC, whereas an EPROM does not.

C. An EPROM uses UV light to set communication settings on an NIC, whereas an EEPROM does not.

D. An EEPROM uses UV light to set communication settings on an NIC, whereas an EPROM does not.

E. An EEPROM stores communication settings that are sent to it from an EPROM via UV light.

Answer: A—An EPROM uses UV light to erase communication settings on an NIC, whereas an EEPROM does not.

Identify the use of the following network components and the differences between them:

- Hubs
- MAUs
- Switching hubs
- Repeaters
- Transceivers

The Network+ exam will ask you to identify the devices commonly used to propagate electrical signals to multiple computers. Scenario-based questions will ask you to differentiate devices by text as well. To prepare for this aspect of the exam, pay close attention to the detailed information and figures about these devices in this section.

Critical Information

Two computers can be connected to each other using a single network cable. Technically, this makes a network. The networks of large companies, however, may consist of tens of thousands of computers. There are many different types of network components, each with different functions. Among these components, Hubs, switching hubs, and MAUs allow multiple computers to be connected to a single network. But when multiple floors or buildings need to be connected, hubs are not enough. Repeaters are then used to extend the length of a network by regenerating the electrical signal onto a new cable. A transceiver, still another network component, is used if a computer network card does not have the appropriate connector for the media type in use. Transceivers allow computers to attach to cabling that is not easily directly attached to a network interface card.

Hubs

A hub, or concentrator, serves as a central connection point for several network devices. A hub repeats what it receives on one port to all other ports. Notice the hub's multiple connection ports for computer cables in Figure 2.4.

FIGURE 2.4: A standard hub

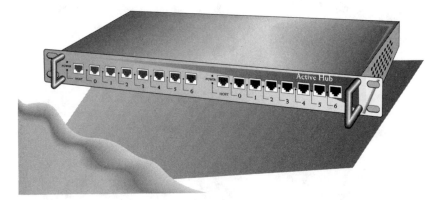

There are many different classifications of hubs, but the two most important are active and passive. An active hub actually amplifies and cleans up the signal it receives, thus doubling the effective segment distance limitation for the specific topology (e.g., extending an Ethernet segment another 100 meters). On the other hand, a passive hub is typically unpowered and only makes physical, electrical connections. A passive hub will typically shorten the maximum segment distance of a particular topology because the hub will borrow power from the signal in order to perform its job.

Multistation Access Unit

A Multistation Access Unit (MAU) is a Physical layer device unique to Token Ring networks that is designed to regenerate electrical signals to multiple ports and connected computers. The central device on an Ethernet star topology network is called a hub, but on a Token Ring network, the central device is known as a MAU (sometimes called an MSAU). Its functionality is similar to a hub, but the MAU provides the data path that creates the logical ring in a Token Ring network. Data can travel in an endless loop between stations and MAUs, as shown in Figure 2.5.

FIGURE 2.5: MAUs in a Token Ring network

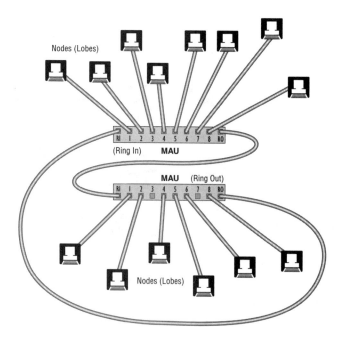

Switching Hubs

Switching hubs are actually switches. Switches are devices that direct network packets on the Data Link layer (OSI layer two) according to their MAC addresses. Switching hubs understand some of the traffic that passes through them. MAC addresses are used to direct information from one computer node to another. Layer two switches build a table of the MAC addresses of each connected station. Notice the switched communication in Figure 2.6. When two stations attached to the switch want to communicate, the sending station sends its data. The switching hub, or switch, then directs the packets to the port that leads to the recipient.

This part of the process is similar to the way a hub functions. However, when the switch receives data, rather than broadcasting it out all of its other ports like a hub would, the switch examines the Data Link header for the MAC address of the receiving station and then forwards it to the correct port. This opens a virtual "pipe" between ports, which can use the full bandwidth of the topology. If a server and several workstations were connected to the same 100Mbps Ethernet switch, for example, each workstation would be using a dedicated 100Mbps channel to the server and there would never be any collisions.

F I G U R E 2.6: A switch builds a table of all MAC addresses of all connected stations.

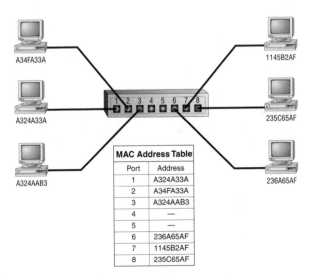

Repeaters

The physical device with the simplest design of all Physical layer devices is the repeater. A network repeater simply amplifies the signals it receives on one port and then resends (or repeats) them on another. Repeaters are used to extend the maximum length of a network segment. They are often found in locations where a few network stations are located far away from the rest of the network. Notice how the repeater in Figure 2.7 connects two sections of a network.

FIGURE 2.7: A repeater in action

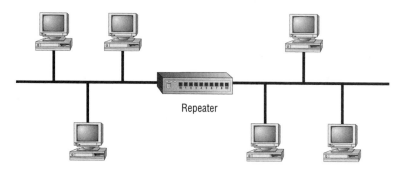

Repeater

The main downfall of a repeater is that it repeats everything it receives on one port—including noise—to all of its other ports. As a result, there is a limit to the number of repeaters that can be practically used on a network. The rule that dictates the maximum number of coaxial repeaters that can be used on a network and where they can be placed is the 5-4-3 rule. As you might remember from Chapter 1, this rule states that a single network can have up to five network segments connected by four repeaters; a total of three of the segments may be populated. If this rule is violated, one station may not be able to see the rest of the network because the signal becomes too distorted after being repeated this many times. Figure 2.8 illustrates the 5-4-3 rule and the maximum number of repeaters allowed.

FIGURE 2.8: The 5-4-3 rule for network repeaters

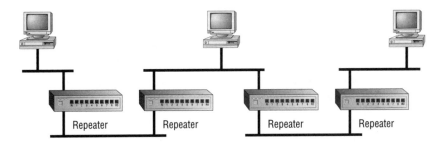

Transceivers

According to the strictest definition, a transceiver is the part of any network interface that transmits and receives network signals. Every network interface has a transceiver. The appearance and function of the transceiver varies with the type of network cable and topology in use.

Some network interface cards have an Attachment Unit Interface (AUI) port (typically a 15-pin DIN connector). The AUI port uses a different, external transceiver type and thus changes the media types to which the NIC can connect. For example, if you were using an Ethernet 10Base2 network interface card with an AUI port, you could connect to an Ethernet 10BaseT network by using an external transceiver attached to the AUI port.

TIP   Digital, Intel, and Xerox (collectively, DIX) invented Ethernet. They named a certain type of connection a DIX port, which, on an NIC, is the same thing as an AUI port.

Exam Essentials

The exam will require you to differentiate between devices and their function on the Physical layer.

Know how to identify the use of a hub.   A hub is essentially a multi-port repeater. Active hubs regenerate signals to allow each cable coming out from them to be the full length of their specification. Since passive hubs do not regenerate signals, they do not allow the total cable distance to be extended.

Know how to identify the use of a switching hub. A switching hub directs communications to the port that services the specific recipient of the message. This switch operates on the Data Link layer and greatly reduces network traffic.

Know how to identify the use of a MAU. Standard hubs do not work in Token Ring networks. A MAU is required to properly handle tokens.

Know how to identify the use of a repeater. A repeater regenerates the electrical signal coming from one port and sends it out of another port. The repeater enables the cable length to be extended. For example, with a repeater in a 100BaseT network, you can connect a second 100BaseT cable and extend the total allowable distance to 200 meters.

Know how to identify the use of a transceiver. A transceiver is used to connect a network card with a coaxial cable network. If you have a 10Base2 or 10Base5 cable, for instance, old network cards cannot directly connect to the cable. A transceiver is essentially a converter box that connects to the DIX port on an NIC and the coaxial cable on the other end.

Key Terms and Concepts

Active An active device is electrically powered to regenerate the network signal. The signal can be regenerated to a single connection, as in a repeater, or to many connections, as in a hub. An active device allows additional cables to be added without the initial cable being part of the maximum cable length.

AUI (Attachment Unit Interface) port See DIX port.

DIX port Digital, Intel, and Xerox (collectively, DIX) invented Ethernet. As such, they named the multi-pinned connection on the back of an NIC the DIX port. Transceivers connect to the DIX port, which is also known as an AUI port.

Hub   Operates on the Physical layer to distribute an inbound network signal to many outbound connections. The hub can be active or passive.

Passive   A passive device does not have an electrical power supply. The only electricity that is used comes from the network cables. Punch-down blocks and non-powered hubs are passive. The total distance a signal can travel stays the same even with the addition of a passive device.

MAU (Multistation Access Unit)   Used to attach multiple computers to a Token Ring network. A MAU is basically a special-purpose hub for token ring networks only.

Repeater   Powered device that regenerates an electrical signal. This device allows you to connect two sections of a network by using multiple cables.

Switch   Operates on the Data Link layer and directs packets using MAC addresses.

Transceiver   The component of an NIC (either built-in or added) that is responsible for transmission and reception.

Sample Questions

1. What type of network uses a MAU?

   A. UNIX

   B. Ethernet

   C. IP

   D. IPX

   E. Token Ring

   Answer: E—Token Ring networks use MAUs, which operate on the Physical layer. (UNIX is a network operating system that works in the upper layers of the OSI model. Ethernet is a different type of network than Token Ring. IP and IPX are protocols, which operate on the Network layer.).

2. Which type of hub doesn't require power?

   A. Active

   B. Passive

   C. Intelligent

   D. Switched

   E. Unswitched

   Answer: B—A passive hub does not use electricity. (An active hub uses electricity. An intelligent hub is a managed hub that can be remotely monitored. Switched hubs are actually switches, which operate on the Data Link layer. Unswitched hubs comprise the majority of hubs and, therefore, are not a specific enough type.)

3. Two lengths of cable need to be connected to connect two different buildings. Each cable is at its maximum length. What device is best suited to regenerate the signal from the first cable to the second?

   A. Transceiver

   B. Repeater

   C. Hub

   D. Switching hub

   E. MAU

   Answer: B—A repeater regenerates electrical signals to extend the distance network cables can reach. (A transceiver is used to connect a network card to a network cable. A hub sends electrical signals from many computers to each other. A switching hub is actually a switch and operates on the Data Link layer to direct packets. A MAU is used to regenerate electrical signals in a Token Ring network.)

4. What device is used to connect a DIX port on a network card to a thicknet cable?

   A. Transceiver

   B. Router

   C. Hub

   D. MAU

   E. Switch

Answer: A—Transceivers are used to directly connect an NIC without the proper port to the network cable. One side of the transceiver is a DIX port; the other side consists of the proper port, or Vampire Tap prongs. The Vampire Tap cuts through the outer casing of the network cable and establishes a connection with the core. (A router operates on the Network layer of the OSI model to direct packets. A hub connects many cables and computers through multiple ports. A MAU is a special device similar to a hub, but it is used in Token Ring networks. A switch is a network device that directs packets by operating on the Data Link layer of the OSI model.)

CHAPTER

3

Data Link Layer

▶ **Describe the following data link layer concepts:** *(pages 108 – 118)*
- Bridges, what they are and why they are used
- The 802 specs, including the topics covered in 802.2, 802.3, and 802.5
- The function and characteristics of MAC addresses

T he second layer of the OSI model is known as the Data Link layer. As was discussed in Chapter 1, this layer is responsible for creating, transmitting, and receiving packets. Layer two also sends information via the layer below it, the Physical layer. The Data Link layer is comprised of two components, or sub-layers: the Logical Link Control (LLC) sub-layer and the Media Access Control (MAC) sub-layer. The LLC allows data communications to jump to higher OSI model layers. The MAC is the lower of the two sub-layers and provides shared access to the NIC.

The Institute of Electrical and Electronics Engineers (IEEE) has outlined many Data Link layer protocols with their 802-series of specifications. Each specification outlines a different Data Link layer protocol with a different number after the 802 decimal point. 802.2 is the logical link control. 802.3 is Carrier Sense Multiple Access/Collision Detection (CSMA/CD). And 802.5 is Token Ring. Each specification dictates how signals are sent on a computer network cable. The types of communication, devices, and addresses specific to this layer are covered in this chapter.

▶ Describe the following data link layer concepts:

- Bridges, what they are and why they are used
- The 802 specs, including the topics covered in 802.2, 802.3, and 802.5
- The function and characteristics of MAC addresses

The Network+ exam covers devices and protocols on the Data Link layer. You will need to understand bridges, which function in this layer. Among the protocols that operate on this layer, you will need to know the 802 specifications in particular, as outlined by the Institute of Electrical and Electronic Engineers. Finally, you will need to know what a MAC address is and how it is used.

Critical Information

As you know, this exam objective deals with the Data Link layer. To pass the corresponding section on the exam, you will have to understand how communication occurs on the second OSI layer, where the IEEE 802 subcommittees define communications. These communications are directed to the MAC address of the destination computer. Lastly, a bridge is used to combine two networks into one logical net. Understanding of communications, addresses, and devices is required for Network+ certification.

Bridges

A bridge is a device that operates at the Data Link layer and is used to extend the maximum reach of a network. A bridge makes two physical segments appear as one network to the upper layers of the OSI model. Bridges permit communication that would otherwise be stopped by a router. In other words, if two sites on the same network use a protocol that is stopped by a router, then the use of a bridge is warranted instead.

In addition to forwarding packets that would normally be stopped by a router, a bridge is also used to keep traffic meant for stations on one side of a bridge on that side of the bridge. For example, if you have one group of workstations that constantly exchanges data over the same network segment and another group that doesn't often use the network, the busy group will diminish network performance for the other users. If you install a bridge to separate the two groups, only traffic destined for workstations on the other side of the bridge will pass through it; all other traffic stays within the local segment. Notice how two networks are combined into one in Figure 3.1.

FIGURE 3.1: A sample network before and after bridging

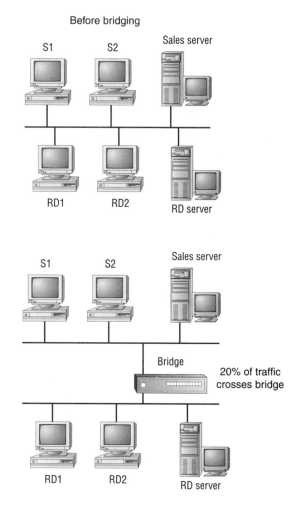

Bridges can connect dissimilar network types (Token Ring and Ethernet, e.g.) as long as the bridge operates on the LLC sub-layer of the Data Link layer. If the bridge operates at the lower, or MAC, sub-layer, the bridge can only connect similar network types (Token Ring to Token Ring and Ethernet to Ethernet, e.g.).

The IEEE 802 Specifications

The Institute of Electrical and Electronic Engineers 802 subcommittees define different network communication protocols. The 802 subcommittees that defined networks and their traffic are the most well-known. There are twelve 802 standards, but you only need to be familiar with three for the exam. 802.2 is the logical link control; 802.3 uses carrier sense, multiple access, and collision detection (CSMA/CD) with the packets; and 802.5 is Token Ring. Using these protocols, and depending on their MAC addresses, packets are directed to their destinations. Table 3.1 lists all of the IEEE 802 standards while Figure 3.2 shows how the 802 specifications line up in the OSI model.

FIGURE 3.2: The IEEE 802 subcommittees and working groups

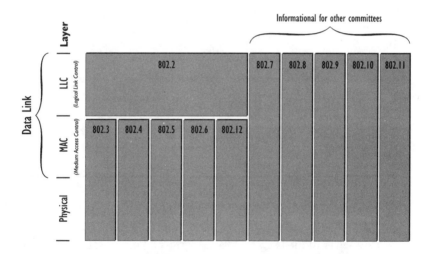

TIP You should generally know the other specifications and their numbers. The exam will only go into further depth on 802.2, 802.3, and 802.5.

T A B L E 3.1: IEEE 802 Networking Standards

802 Standard	Topic
802.1	Internetworking
802.2	Logical Link Control (LLC)
802.3	Carrier Sense Multiple Access/Collision Detection (CSMA/CD)
802.4	Token bus
802.5	Token Ring
802.6	Metropolitan area network
802.7	Broadband Technical Advisory Group
802.8	Fiber-Optic Technical Advisory Group
802.9	Integrated voice/data networks
802.10	Network security
802.11	Wireless networks
802.12	Demand Priority Access LAN

802.2 Standard

This IEEE standard specifies the operation of the Logical Link Control sub-layer of the Data Link layer of the OSI model. The LLC sub-layer provides an interface between the Data Link layer's MAC sub-layer and the OSI Network layer. Communication between different devices is managed by the LLC. Inside the computer, the LLC can utilize its service access points (SAP), which allow communications to jump to the upper layers of the OSI model without going through each layer.

802.3 Standard

Carrier Sense Multiple Access/Collision Detection is defined in IEEE standard 802.3. This standard specifies how multiple computers can send messages when they sense a live wire. If the messages hit each other, collision detection occurs, and each node realizes that the messages have been turned into gibberish. A random amount of time is then allowed to pass before each node attempts a retransmission. This standard is commonly known as Ethernet.

This is probably the most popular of the IEEE standards. It is the most widely implemented of all of the 802.*x* standards because of its simplicity and low cost. The 802.3 standard specifies a network that uses a bus topology, baseband signaling, and a CSMA/CD network access method. This standard was developed to match the Digital, Intel, and Xerox Ethernet networking technology. So many people implemented the 802.3 standard, which resembles the DIX Ethernet, that people just started calling it Ethernet.

802.5 Standard

The IEEE 802.5 standard is the Token Ring standard—one example of a common product becoming a documented standard. Typically, a standard is developed, and then products are written to conform to it. In the case of 802.5, however, IBM developed Token Ring in 1984, and the 802.5 standard soon followed.

Like Ethernet, Token Ring can use several cable types. It is most often installed using twisted pair cabling. The flexibility IBM offers in its cabling is to use either shielded or unshielded cable. Shielded cable adds to the cable investment because it is more expensive than unshielded cable and offers the advantage of resistance to unwanted electrical signals, which can impair network signals.

As its name suggests, Token Ring uses a logical ring, physical star topology with a token-passing media access. Like ARCNET, transmission rates for Token Ring increased over time. The 16Mbps Token Ring came along after the 4Mbps Token Ring. If you mix the 4Mbps ring with the 16Mbps ring, your entire ring will be 4Mbps. Unlike Ethernet, a computer cannot talk unless it has a token, which can cause some grief if a token gets "stuck."

Unlike ARCNET, Token Ring is still seen in a number of locations. There are two reasons for this. First, IBM made sure that Token Ring did a fine job of talking to IBM mainframes, and, secondly, Token Ring networks degrade with grace. This means that as network traffic increases the network slowly gets slower, and the single token, which can only travel in one direction, gets busy carrying all of that traffic. Ethernet can become so flooded that the entire network fails. Token ring networks provide for equal bandwidth access to all nodes. During high network usage, access for each node becomes slower, preventing one machine from hogging all of the bandwidth.

In a Token Ring network, just as in all ARCNET and most Ethernet schemes, there is a hub. Unlike the others, however, it isn't called a hub; IBM calls it a *MAU*, or Multistation Access Unit. The classification system for Token Ring cabling is also different. Telephone and computer networks rate twisted cable by category, but IBM rates Token Ring cable by type. One final difference between Token Ring and the others is the regeneration process. To reduce degradation, data signals get read, amplified, and repeated by every device on the network. This includes the MAUs and NICs and is one of the reasons Token Rings are fairly expensive. (An average Token Ring NIC is in the $200 range, whereas a similar Ethernet card can be less than $100.)

MAC Addresses

Every network interface card has an address, which is usually assigned at the factory. This address is protocol-independent and is often called the hardware address. But its technically accurate name is the MAC address because it exists at the MAC sub-layer of the OSI model. The MAC address is used on the Data Link layer where it identifies network devices or computers.

The MAC address itself is actually a 12-digit hexadecimal number burned into the network card. You might remember that the hexadecimal system uses all digits from zero through nine and A through F. Colons separate each pair of digits, like so:

07:57:AC:1F:B2:76

Normally, the MAC address of a network interface card is set at the factory and cannot be changed. For this reason, all NIC manufacturers keep track of their MAC addresses, and addresses are not duplicated between vendors. However, some manufacturers have begun reusing their blocks of MAC addresses. This makes it necessary for administrators to be able to change the MAC addresses of cards they receive from certain manufacturers, so, when duplicate MAC addresses are discovered, conflicts can be resolved with the use of factory-supplied programs.

Exam Essentials

Before taking the test, refer back to Table 3.1 and the definitions of the 802 layers. The IEEE subcommittees and OSI model are covered extensively in the exam. This section looks specifically at the second layer and its devices.

Know how to define the functions of a bridge. To upper layers of the OSI model, a bridge makes two separate segments look like one large extended network. It also stops messages meant for the original network and forwards messages meant for the second, or extended, segment. Different types of networks, such as Ethernet and Token Ring, can be connected using a bridge.

Know how to identify the characteristics of the 802.2 standard. The logical link control is defined in 802.2. The LLC is the upper sub-layer of the OSI Data Link layer, and it negotiates traffic between the MAC sub-layer and the Network main layer.

Know how to identify the characteristics of the 802.3 standard. Carrier Sense Multiple Access/Collision Detection is defined in 802.3. This specifies how multiple computers can send messages when they sense a live wire. If the messages hit each other, collision detection occurs and each node realizes the messages have been turned into gibberish. A random amount of time is allowed to pass before each node attempts a retransmission.

Know how to identify the characteristics of the 802.5 standard. 802.5 defines the characteristics of Token Ring networks. Token Ring nets use a token to restrict who can talk. If no one wants to talk, the token travels along the ring until someone picks it up in order to send a message. Only a machine with the token can use the network.

Know how to define and identify a MAC address. A Media Access Control address consists of twelve hexadecimal numbers in two-number pairs. A colon separates each pair. NICs have MAC addresses burned into them so computers can be uniquely identified on the Data Link layer of a network.

Key Terms and Concepts

Bridge   Operates on the Data Link layer of the OSI model and extends a network to make two separate segments appear as if they are one. Different media communications, such as Ethernet and Token Ring, can be connected using a bridge.

IEEE (Institute of Electrical and Electronics Engineers)   Determines specifications on many types of electrical systems. The most commonly known specifications are the 802 subcommittees, which define how electricity is sent and received in computer networks.

LLC (Logical Link Control)   Upper sub-layer of the Data Link layer of the OSI model. The LLC manages links between network devices. The LLC has service access points that allow communications to jump to the upper layers of the OSI model without going through each layer.

MAC (Media Access Control) address   A twelve-digit hexadecimal number that defines a network node on the Data Link layer of the OSI model. A unique MAC address is burned into each NIC at the factory. This is the lower sub-layer of the Data Link layer and allows shared access to the NIC.

Sample Questions

1. What OSI second layer network device can connect dissimilar networks, such as Ethernet and Token Ring?

   A. Router

   B. Gateway

   C. Bridge

   D. Switch

   E. Hub

Answer: C—A bridge operates on the Data Link layer and can connect dissimilar networks. (A router directs packets from one network to another. A gateway is either a special router or operates on multiple layers of the OSI model. A switch, generally speaking, connects only similar media types. A hub can only regenerate the same signal to multiple ports of the same network type.)

2. Which IEEE subcommittee defines Token Rings?

   A. 802.1

   B. 802.2

   C. 802.3

   D. 802.4

   E. 802.5

   Answer: E—802.5 defines Token Rings. (802.1 specifies internetworking. 802.2 specifies logical link control. 802.3 defines Carrier Sense Multiple Access/Collision Detection. 802.4 defines token bus.)

3. What is the upper sub-layer of layer two of the OSI model?

   A. Media Access Control

   B. Logical Link Control

   C. Physical layer

   D. Network layer

   E. Transport layer

   Answer: B—The Logical Link Control layer is the upper sub-layer of the OSI Data Link layer. (The Media Access Control sub-layer is the lower layer of the OSI Data Link layer. The Physical, Network, and Transport layers are all main sections of the OSI model and are not sub-layers.)

4. Which of the following is a correct example of a MAC address?

   A. 256.2.150.4

   B. 155.210.17.9

   C. 255.255.255.0

   D. 5G:43:B2:41:34:E2

   E. 2F:94:5B:2C:34:2E

Answer: E—This is a MAC address because it contains twelve properly formatted hexadecimal numbers. (**A** is an invalid IP address. **B** is an IP address. **C** is a subnet mask. **D** is an invalid MAC address because G is not a hexadecimal number.)

CHAPTER

4

Network Layer

Network+ Exam Objective Covered in This Chapter:

Explain the following routing and network layer concepts, including: *(pages 121 – 130)*

- The fact that routing occurs at the network layer
- The difference between a router and a brouter
- The difference between routable and nonroutable protocols
- The concept of default gateways and subnetworks
- The reason for employing unique network IDs
- The difference between static and dynamic routing

As you probably know from previous chapters, the third layer of the OSI model is the Network layer. Packets are routed, networks are connected, and communication paths are all determined on OSI layer three. Because the Network layer concepts are the foundation for other technologies (e.g. routing, logical network addressing), they are included on the exam.

Routers, which have also been discussed in previous chapters, operate on the Network layer, connect subnetworks, and work with protocols (such as IPX and IP). These two protocols use addresses that correspond to each network card in a node. Routers then direct packets between machines, which makes both IPX and IP routable protocols. The router also stops nonroutable protocols, such as NetBEUI, that can only be used for small networks. Nonroutable protocols don't have provisions for logical network address information within the packet; routers, therefore, can't forward them.

A brouter is actually a combination device. A bridge is combined with a router to create a brouter. This new device has the extension characteristics of a bridge and the direction features of a router.

A default gateway is the primary router used to get from one subnetwork to another. Do not confuse a default gateway with an application gateway, which converts between different protocols. Both types of gateways will be discussed later in this chapter.

Another networking concept that exists at the Network layer of the OSI model is network addresses (network IDs). Every network entity must have a network address to uniquely identify it and differentiate it from all other devices on the network. If two devices have the same network ID, neither one will be able to communicate with the rest of the network.

Static and dynamic routing is used to direct packets from one subnetwork to another. A static route is recorded in the routing tables of the router and does not change. Dynamic routing allows routing devices to automatically change the path used. Two dynamic routers talk to each other and automatically update paths, whereas static routers need human intervention.

Explain the following routing and network layer concepts, including:

- The fact that routing occurs at the network layer
- The difference between a router and a brouter
- The difference between routable and nonroutable protocols
- The concept of default gateways and subnetworks
- The reason for employing unique network IDs
- The difference between static and dynamic routing

This objective for the Network+ exam is probably the most complex because discusses the various concepts involved in setting up network addressing and routing. The majority of the routing and network addressing questions on the Network+ exam come from this objective.

Critical Information

To pass this objective, you will need to understand what routing is, including the different types of routing and the devices used to accomplish it. Routing takes place on the Network layer. The exam takes a close look at all devices on this layer. All devices, from routers and brouters to computer nodes, have network addresses, which allow packets to be routed to their intended destinations.

Routing on the Network Layer

Routing is the direction of packets using layer three of the OSI reference model. Packets are directed to different networks and nodes based on the destination's IP or IPX address. The sending node checks to see if the destination address is on the same network. If the destination node is on another network, the packets are forwarded to a router. The router then looks at the destination address and selects the appropriate path. Paths are stored in routing tables inside the router.

Network Address Formats

A brief discussion of TCP/IP and IPX addressing format specifics is essential to understanding the general concept of logical network addressing. Every network address in either TCP/IP or IPX has both a network portion and a node portion. The network portion of a network address assigns a number to every segment on that network. The node portion is the unique number that identifies a specific station on the segment. Together, the network portion and the node portion of an address ensure that a network address will be unique across an entire network.

The network portion of IPX addresses are eight-digit hexadecimal numbers. Network administrators assign IPX network addresses for different network segments, whereas manufacturers assign the 12-digit hexadecimal MAC addresses as the node portion. Figure 4.1 shows a sample IPX address.

FIGURE 4.1: A sample IPX address

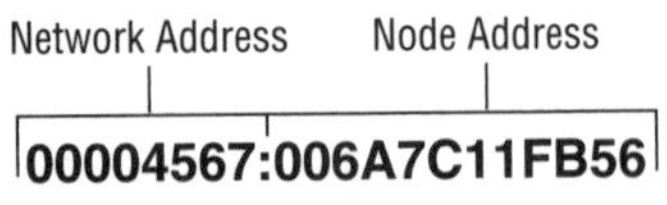

Network Address   Node Address

00004567:006A7C11FB56

TCP/IP addresses, on the other hand, use dotted decimal notations (in the xxx.xxx.xxx.xxx format, as shown in Figure 4.2). A TCP/IP address consists of four groups of eight-digit binary numbers (or up to three decimal digits), called octets, which are separated by periods. Each decimal number is typically a number from one to 254. The total range is actually zero to 255, where zero is used to denote a network and 255 is designated as a broadcast address. Computers are not assigned these special numbers.

The class of the TCP/IP address determines which is the network portion and which is the node portion. The network subnet mask, combined with the TCP/IP address of the workstation, lets you know where the destination is. The subnet mask is a dotted decimal number. If a subnet mask contains 255 (corresponding to a binary number of all 1s), the corresponding part of the IP address is part of the network address. For example, if you have the mask 255.255.255.0, then the first three octets are the network portion and the last portion is the node. Figure 4.2 shows a sample IP address and associated subnet mask.

F I G U R E 4.2: A sample IP address and subnet mask

199.217.67.34 IP Address

255.255.255.0 Subnet Mask

Routing Functions

Routing is the process of moving data through a network, where it sometimes passes through numerous network segments and routers can select the paths it takes. Connecting several smaller networks with routers creates an entity known as an internetwork. Routers get information about which paths to take from files on the routers themselves that are called routing tables. These tables contain network routing information that identifies which router network interface (or port) is to be placed on the data being routed, in order to send it to a particular network segment. Figure 4.3 illustrates these components and their participation in the routing process.

FIGURE 4.3: Routing components

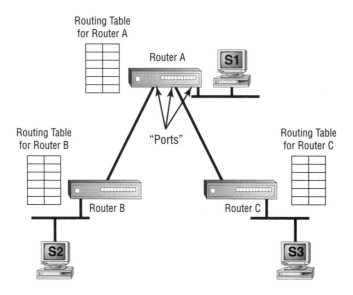

OSI layer three is responsible for the logical addressing and translation of logical names into physical addresses, but a little-known function of the Network layer is data prioritization. Not all data has equal importance. For example, it wouldn't hurt anyone if an e-mail message is delayed a fraction of a second, but delaying audio or video data by just a fraction of a second could be disastrous to the message. As mentioned in Chapter 1, this prioritization is known as quality of service, or QoS.

Another function of the Network layer is controlling congestion when routing data from source to destination, and building and tearing down packets. Most routing protocols function at this layer.

Routers and Brouters

As has already been shown, routers direct Network layer packets. Brouters, however, are unique devices that combine the functionality of both bridges and routers. Brouters are mainly used to connect different network topologies and bridge between them when the protocol being used cannot be routed. For example, if a brouter receives a packet that does not contain routing information, it will forward the packet to a local segment, like a bridge would. Unfortunately, if you try to use a brouter as just a bridge or a router, it will fall short in the functionality of either.

Routable and Nonroutable Protocols

You should note that there are several protocol stacks that can be routed. It is important to know which protocols are routable and which ones aren't, so when it comes time to design an internetwork you can choose the appropriate protocol. Table 4.1 shows a few of the most common routable and nonroutable protocol stacks and the routing protocols, if any, that they use.

T A B L E 4.1:   Routable and Nonroutable Protocols

Protocol Stack	Route Discovery Protocol	Routable?
IPX/SPX	RIP	Yes
IPX/SPX	NLSP	Yes
NetBEUI	None	No
TCP/IP	RIP	Yes
TCP/IP	OSPF	Yes
XNS	RIP	Yes

Default Gateways and Subnetworks

When configuring network routing, you may have to configure a default gateway. A default gateway is the router that all packets are sent to when a workstation does not know where the remote station is located on the local segment. TCP/IP networks sometimes have multiple routers as well and must use this parameter to specify which router is the default. Other protocols don't have very good routing functions at the workstation, so they must use this feature to find the router.

Subnetworks are subdivisions of larger networks; routers separate the divisions. Whenever a single network segment becomes saturated with network traffic, a network manager or administrator may decide to place routers in strategic locations to divide the network into subnetworks.

NOTE It is important to know that some people incorrectly call a subnetwork a subnet. In fact, a subnet is a construct used with TCP/IP; the full name is subnet mask, but it is frequently shortened to subnet.

Unique Network IDs

Every device on your network needs to have a unique ID. If two machines have the same ID, packets will get mixed up and problems will occur. Consider, for instance, what would happen if you had two printers on different floors with the same ID; users would be chasing after their printouts all over the building and letting you know of their dissatisfaction.

Each logical network address is protocol dependent. For example, a TCP/IP address is not the same as an IPX address. Additionally, the two different protocols can coexist on the same computer without conflict. However, two different stations cannot have the same protocol address on the same network. If that happens, neither station will be able to be seen on the network (as shown in Figure 4.4).

FIGURE 4.4: Address conflicts on a network

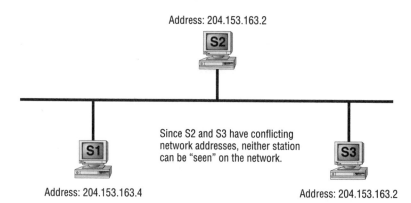

Address conflicts can be common with TCP/IP because IP addresses are assigned by administrators. Since IPX addresses use the MAC address as part of the IPX address, they have a part that is unique and can't be changed, which means they don't suffer from conflicts nearly as often.

Static and Dynamic Routing

There are two ways of getting information into the routing tables: static entries or dynamic entries. Static routing happens when the router's routing table is updated manually by the network administrator. The administrator enters every network address into the routing table and selects the port that the router should place data on when the router intercepts data destined for that network. Unfortunately, updating routing tables with every network change on networks with more than a few segments becomes prohibitively time-consuming.

TIP   When using a Windows NT server as a router, use the ROUTE command to add, change, or remove static routes.

Dynamic routing, on the other hand, uses route discovery protocols (or routing protocols) to talk to other routers and find out what networks they are attached to. Routers that use dynamic routing send out special packets to request updates about the other routers on the network and to transmit their own updates. Dynamic routing is the most popular routing technology.

With dynamic routing, there are two categories of route discovery protocols: distance vector and link state. Older route discovery protocols, like Routing Information Protocol (RIP) for TCP/IP and for IPX, use the distance vector method. In distance vector routing, a router sends out its routing table when it is brought online. When one router receives another router's routing table, it adds one hop to the hop count of each route in the list of routes, and then it rebroadcasts the list. (A hop is one pass through a router.) This process typically takes place every 60 seconds.

The main downside to distance vector route discovery is the overhead required to broadcast the entire routing table every 60 seconds. Link state route discovery is more efficient. Link state routers send out routing tables too, but they do it a lot less often (typically, every five minutes or so). If there is an update, just the update is sent. NetWare Link State Protocol (NLSP) for IPX and Open Shortest Path First (OSPF) for TCP/IP are two link state route discovery protocols.

Exam Essentials

This objective is based on the Network layer and routing, so you should possess a good understanding of the different routing protocols, methods, and devices.

Know how to identify a router and the layer on which routing occurs. A device that directs packets on the third layer of the OSI model is a router.

Know how to differentiate between a router and a brouter. A router operates only on the Network layer of the OSI model, whereas a brouter is the combination of a bridge and a router that works on both the Data Link and Network layers.

Know how to identify both routable and nonroutable protocols. Refer back to Table 4.1. IPX/SPX, TCP/IP, and XNS-based protocols are routable. NetBEUI is not a routable protocol.

Know how to define gateways and subnetworks. Subnetworks are segments of a larger network that has been divided by routers. A gateway is the router that transmits data from one subnetwork to another.

Know how to differentiate between static and dynamic routing. Static routing is something network administrators want to avoid when dealing with thousands of routers because they must manually enter static routes into router tables. Dynamic routing occurs when routers automatically send each other route tables and any updates.

Key Terms and Concepts

You should know the acronyms and terms that relate to routing. Different acronyms and common terms are listed below.

Brouter A brouter is a device that has the characteristics of both a router and a bridge. It operates on both the Data Link and Network layers.

Dynamic routing   Route paths, tables, and updates are automatically sent from one router to another.

NLSP (NetWare Link Services Protocol)   A dynamic link state route discovery protocol (for IPX).

OSPF (Open Shortest Path First)   A dynamic link state route discovery protocol (for TCP/IP).

RIP (Routing Information Protocol)   A dynamic routing communication method. Routers automatically update their routing tables using RIP. Both IPX and TCP/IP have an implementation of RIP.

Router   Directs packets from one network to another based on the destination ID. (The Network layer destination ID is typically an IP or IPX address.)

Static routing   Route paths and tables are manually updated by a network administrator.

XNS (Xerox Network System)   The protocol that is the basis for Novell's IPX/SPX protocols.

Sample Questions

1. Routing occurs on what layer of the OSI model? (Layers are listed from bottom to top.)

   A. One

   B. Two

   C. Three

   D. Four

   E. Five

   Answer: C—Routing occurs on the Network layer, or layer three of the OSI model.

2. What protocols are routable?

   A. IPX

   B. SPX

   C. TCP

   D. IP

   E. NetBEUI

   Answers: A–D—(Only NetBEUI is not routable.)

3. What device operates on the Data Link layer and the Network layer?

   A. Hub

   B. Brouter

   C. Bridge

   D. Router

   E. Switch

   Answer: B—A brouter operates on both the Data Link and Network layers. (A hub operates on the Physical layer. A bridge operates on the Data Link layer. A router operates on the Network layer. A switch operates on the Data Link layer.)

4. What type of routing is bandwidth intensive because the entire routing table is sent every 60 seconds?

   A. Brouter

   B. XNS

   C. OSPF

   D. NLSP

   E. RIP

   Answer: E—RIP sends the entire table every minute. (A brouter is a network device, not a type of routing. XNS is a network communications protocol. OSPF and NLSP are dynamic routing protocols that only send updates.)

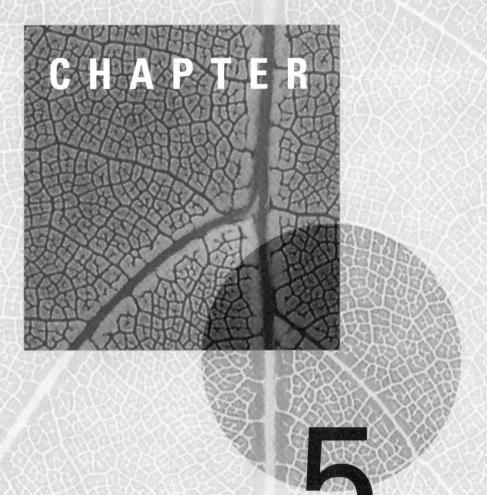

CHAPTER

5

Transport Layer

Network+ Exam Objective Covered in This Chapter:

▶ **Explain the following transport layer concepts:** *(pages 133 – 138)*
- The distinction between connectionless and connection transport
- The purpose of name resolution, either to an IP/IPX address or a network protocol

Y ou probably remember that the fourth layer of the OSI reference model is the Transport layer. This layer handles flow control, error correction, and the sequencing of packets. This chapter will cover these topics as well as the resolution of names from different layers and from friendly names.

A connection-oriented transport means that the sender and receiver maintain an active channel. Packets are sent in this active channel, and each end of the connection ensures that packets get through. If information is lost or received in the wrong order, the destination computer requests a resend. Basically, a connection-oriented transport guarantees delivery of messages.

A connectionless transport means there is no active communication between the sender and receiver about the quality of a transmission. Packets are sent out and may or may not reach their destination. With a connectionless transport protocol, if the packets don't reach their destination, the sender simply resends the packets. This method of transport is used for messages that are not important or that require a low overhead (thus achieving greater performance).

Whether the transmission of packets is guaranteed with connection-oriented communications or not, addresses need to be resolved. Address resolution is the conversion of a device name to a network address. Computers are commonly referred to by their NetBIOS name, such as *\\servername,* or their domain name, *servername.com.* These names need to be resolved down to their respective IPX or IP address. Once you have an IP or IPX address, it is then resolved to a MAC address.

Explain the following transport layer concepts:

- The distinction between connectionless and connection transport
- The purpose of name resolution, either to an IP/IPX address or a network protocol

The Network+ exam will test your knowledge of connection-oriented and connectionless transports. TCP and SPX are connection oriented; they maintain an active communication link between the sender and the receiver. UDP and IPX are connectionless protocols. When messages are sent, whether connection oriented or connectionless, the specific destination addresses must be determined.

Application layer programs and users select domain names and Net-BIOS names, which need to be converted or resolved. The computer names are converted to Network layer addresses, such as IP addresses. Resolution from Network layer addresses to MAC addresses then occurs. Be sure to understand that computers talk to each other using MAC addresses, and resolution is used to get there. The exam will test your knowledge of transport types as well as name resolution.

CRITICAL INFORMATION

As you have seen, this objective covers connection types and name resolution during packet transmission. Names are resolved to addresses in neighboring layers, such as the Network and the Data Link layers, and from separated layers, such as the Application and the Network layers. Connection types refer to whether parties during a communication maintain active links.

Connection Type

Protocols that operate at the Transport layer use connection services to provide error and flow control. There are two types of connection services: connection oriented and connectionless.

Connection-Oriented Transport

Connection-oriented connection services use acknowledgments and responses to establish connections between sending and receiving stations. When a receiving station successfully receives a packet sent by the sending station, the receiving station sends an acknowledgment back to the original sender to indicate to the sender that the packet was successfully received at the receiving station. The acknowledgments are also used to ensure that the connection is maintained for the duration of the communication. (TCP and SPX are examples of connection-oriented protocols.) Figure 5.1 shows communication beginning between two computers using connection-oriented services.

F I G U R E 5.1: Initiating communication using a connection-oriented connection

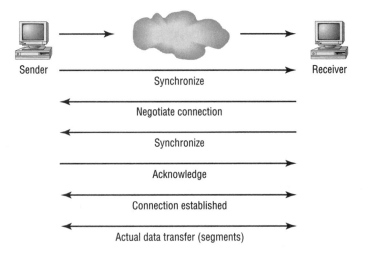

Connectionless Transport

Connectionless communications are hit or miss. The sender transmits packets, but there is no acknowledgment of receipt from destination computers. This type of communication does not have the error and flow control that connection-oriented services do, but it does have one advantage: speed. Connectionless connection services don't have the overhead of maintaining the connection, so the sacrifice in error control is more than made up for in speed. (UDP and IPX are examples of connectionless protocols.)

Name Resolution

Name resolution is the conversion of a name from one OSI layer to another. When you convert a station name to an IP or IPX address, names are resolved down from the Application layer to the Network layer. When the router talks to a switch, the IP address is resolved from the Network layer to the Data Link layer

A node IP address like 185.45.2.23 is not the easiest way to reference a host. Some protocol stacks (like TCP/IP and IPX, for example) can use Transport layer logical (or friendly) names for hosts in addition to their Network layer logical addresses. These logical names make it easier for hosts to be found on the network by human beings. For example, you can enter http://www.sybex.com in your Web browser's Location bar and quickly locate Sybex's home page; this is an example of a friendly name.

Computers on the Internet need an IP address. Converting www.sybex .com to 206.100.29.83 is an example of name resolution.

At the Transport layer, various protocol stacks implement a name resolution protocol to translate Network layer addresses into Transport layer logical names. These name resolution protocols (DNS for example) are used so the upper-layer processes can use logical names for network entities and so the lower–layer protocols can use the network addresses that they require.

Exam Essentials

This small objective tests your ability to understand connection types and name resolution. Study the quick listing below before moving on.

Know how to define connectionless and connection-oriented communications. For connection-oriented communication, receivers acknowledge that packets are received, and both senders and receivers maintain active communication connections. Connectionless transport methods don't maintain an active communication connection.

Know how to identify connectionless and connection-oriented protocols. IPX and UDP are connectionless. SPX and TCP are connection oriented.

Know how to define name resolution and give an example of it. Name resolution occurs when devices convert names from one OSI layer to another layer. For example, www.sybex.com resolves to 206.100.29.83. The IP address 206.100.29.83 can also be resolved to its MAC address.

Key Terms and Concepts

For the exam, you should know the acronyms that relate to the protocols mentioned and understand the concepts of connection type and name resolution.

Connection oriented   Communication type that maintains active links between senders and receivers. Receivers automatically acknowledge when packets are received from senders.

Connectionless oriented   Communication type that does not maintain active links between senders and receivers. Messages are transmitted without acknowledgment about the receiver being online.

Name resolution Process that converts OSI upper-layer addresse. to lower-layer addresses. Station names are converted to Transport layer addresses (i.e., IP or IPX addresses), and Transport layer addresses are converted to Network layer addresses.

SPX (Sequenced Packet Exchange) Part of Novell's IPX/SPX protocol suite, which operates on the Transport layer and is a connection-oriented protocol.

TCP (Transmission Control Protocol) Part of the DOD specifications for the TCP/IP protocol suite, which communicates between different operating systems and operates in a connection-oriented fashion on the Transport layer.

Sample Questions

1. What protocols are connection oriented?

A. IPX

B. SPX

C. TCP

D. UDP

E. All of the above

Answers: B, C—SPX and TCP are connection oriented. (IPX and UDP are connectionless and are connectionless oriented.)

2. What layer of the OSI model processes flow control, error correction, and packet sequencing?

A. Physical

B. Data Link

C. Network

D. Transport

E. Session

Answer: D—The Transport layer processes flow control, error correction, and packet sequencing.

...ing the IP address, or NetBIOS address, of a Web server is ...wn as what?

. Name resolution

B. Connection oriented

C. Connectionless oriented

D. Transmission

E. Transport

Answer: A—Name resolution is the process of resolving a logical host name to a network address for a resource. (Connection-oriented and connectionless-oriented communications relate to whether links are actively maintained between senders and receivers. Transmission is the sending of information. Transport is the fourth layer of the OSI model.)

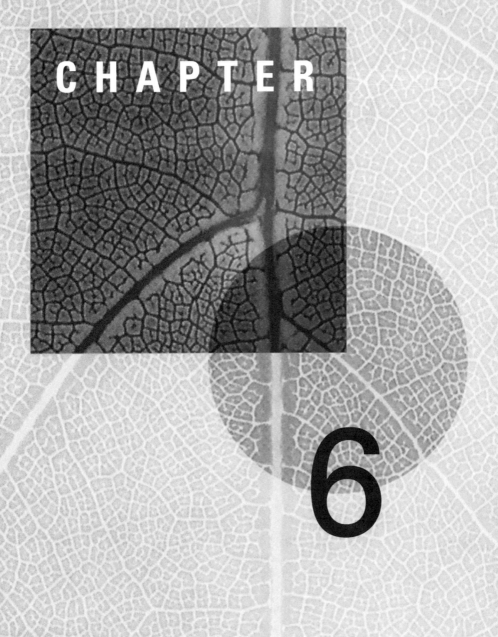

CHAPTER

6

TCP/IP Fundamentals

Network+ Exam Objectives Covered in This Chapter:

▶ **Demonstrate knowledge of the following TCP/IP fundamentals:** *(pages 141 – 154)*

- The concept of IP default gateways
- The purpose and use of DHCP, DNS, WINS, and host files
- The identity of the main protocols that make up the TCP/IP suite, including TCP, UDP, POP3, SMTP, SNMP, FTP, HTTP, and IP
- The idea that TCP/IP is supported by every operating system and millions of hosts worldwide
- The purpose and function of Internet domain name server hierarchies (how e-mail arrives in another country)

▶ **Demonstrate knowledge of the fundamental concepts of TCP/IP addressing, including:** *(pages 155 – 160)*

- The A, B, and C classes of IP addresses and their default subnet mask numbers
- The use of port number (HTTP, FTP, SMTP) and port numbers commonly assigned to a given service

▶ **Demonstrate knowledge of TCP/IP configuration concepts, including:** *(pages 160 – 166)*

- The definition of IP proxy and why it is used
- The identity of the normal configuration parameters for a workstation, including IP address, DNS, default gateway, IP proxy configuration, WINS, DHCP, host name, and Internet domain name

The Transmission Control Protocol/Internet Protocol (TCP/IP) stack of protocols has become very popular in the world of networking. TCP/IP was designed specifically for use on the Internet, and, with the explosion of Internet use worldwide, more and more companies are connecting to the Internet. To make their networks easier to manage, companies choose to standardize on TCP/IP because they can use it on both their networks and the Internet. All network operating systems now support TCP/IP utilities and protocols. Companies all over the world are now standardizing on TCP/IP protocols (including SMTP, FTP, and HTTP) so they have only one suite of protocols to manage.

The TCP/IP suite is compatible with all common desktop operating systems, including the following:

- Microsoft Windows 95/98

- Microsoft Windows NT

- IBM OS/2

- Apple Macintosh

- Unix (including Linux, SCO, Unix, and UnixWare)

The Network+ exam tests you on the concepts involved in configuring TCP/IP on your network, including those specified in the following objective.

Demonstrate knowledge of the following TCP/IP fundamentals:

- The concept of IP default gateways

- The purpose and use of DHCP, DNS, WINS, and host files

- The identity of the main protocols that make up the TCP/IP suite, including TCP, UDP, POP3, SMTP, SNMP, FTP, HTTP, and IP

- The idea that TCP/IP is supported by every operating system and millions of hosts worldwide

- The purpose and function of Internet domain name server hierarchies (how e-mail arrives in another country)

The chapter's first objective covers the fundamentals of TCP/IP. All networks that have a presence on the Internet today use TCP/IP. It is important that you understand the fundamentals of the TCP/IP protocol stack. The Network+ exam will test you on these concepts to ensure that you have a solid foundation in TCP/IP concepts.

Critical Information

Internet Protocol addresses are used to identify all computers on both the Internet and on the networks of most companies. These addresses are assigned either manually or through a DHCP (Dynamic Host Configuration Protocol) server. Once a computer has an IP address, packets are sent using TCP or UDP (User Datagram Protocol). If the packets are destined for another network, a router is used. A default gateway is the primary router used by a computer to send information to other networks.

Many services are available to a computer once it has an IP address and a default gateway. E-mail services are provided by POP3 (Post Office Protocol version 3) and SMTP (Simple Mail Transfer Protocol). Files are downloaded with FTP (File Transfer Protocol), and Web pages are viewed using HTTP (Hypertext Transfer Protocol). Lastly, network devices are monitored using SNMP (Simple Network Management Protocol).

The U.S. Department of Defense (DOD) specifies that the TCP/IP protocol suite provides communications between dissimilar operating systems. With this mandate and universal numbering scheme, TCP/IP is the most widely used protocol suite worldwide.

IP Default Gateways

An IP default gateway is the primary router for a computer. As you know, routers direct packets from one network to another network on layer three of the OSI Model. Subnetworks and networks are connected via routers, and they are also divided into smaller networks. Large companies can have several smaller networks and routers while small companies may only have one or two routers. Multiple routers can service a single computer. When there are several possible paths over the network, several routers are used, but each PC has a default gateway assignment. This default assignment is the router used when the operating system cannot determine which router is the best choice.

DHCP

The Dynamic Host Configuration Protocol is the communication method used to automatically assign IP addresses to computers. Automatic assignments allow network administrators to easily manage thousands of computer addresses. A DHCP server leases addresses so a computer can communicate on your network. When a lease expires, the DHCP client asks for a renewal.

When setting up DHCP services, you assign a block of IP numbers that you are willing to lease to a computer for a set duration. In effect, the computer borrows an IP address and returns it to the pool of addresses when it is done using the address. Once an address is loaned out, another computer cannot use that particular IP address. A contiguous pool of addresses is known as a *scope*.

Setting a lease duration for too long uses up valuable IP address that cannot be used during that lease. Conversely, too short a time creates extra network traffic while all stations try to renew their addresses. The actual duration, or value, depends on the needs of your company. In a desktop environment where computers don't move around much, a lease of several weeks is practical. For dialing in to a company server or connecting to the Internet, a lease period that is measured in minutes is more reasonable.

DHCP servers set how computers talk on the TCP/IP protocol suite. IP addresses, subnet masks, DNS servers, WINS servers, and IP default gateways can all be set for the DHCP client. The following sections include descriptions of each of these features.

DNS

The Domain Name System (DNS) resolves Internet domain names to IP addresses and back again. For example, www.sybex.com is resolved to 204.70.161.70 via a DNS server. Users and computer programs routinely access servers and their shared folders via domain names. When you download a file from a company, you might access companyname .com\download. This is easy to remember because names do not change often. However, IP addresses can change with regular administrative updates. Users would then have to locate the new IP address for the server they want to access, but DNS servers handle all of the updates and make accessing these servers much more efficient.

Network administrators change computer IP addresses in the listings on DNS servers. Users never realize that changes have occurred. The next time a user attempts to access www.sybex.com, their DNS server is queried and, if all goes as intended, the new IP address is accessed without any errors.

All computers that use domain names for communications need a way to resolve the names. This means that either DNS servers are manually set or DHCP servers are used to assign computers a DNS server. Without a server, machines will need a local list of addresses called a host file.

NOTE Fully Qualified Domain Name (FQDN) is the complete Internet name of your computer. For example, www is not an FQDN, but www .mycompany.com is an FQDN.

WINS

The Windows Internet Naming Service (WINS) is an implementation of a NetBIOS Name Server (NBNS). WINS does for NetBIOS names what DNS does for host names. NetBIOS names are resolved to IP addresses through WINS servers. As the NetBIOS name of a station changes, WINS makes changes to the WINS database to reflect the new name. Additionally, WINS servers can speak with and update each other, pushing and/or pulling the data to another WINS server, which stores the data in the form of an MS Access database.

HOSTS File

A HOSTS file is a text file that contains Internet domain names and their corresponding IP addresses. The file gets its name from the list of network hosts that it contains. Each computer has a HOSTS file when no DNS server is available, and the TCP/IP protocol suite looks to resolve the name locally via the file. A separate HOSTS file must be maintained manually on each workstation for lookups to be successful, whereas DNS uses a centralized database of names.

HOSTS files work well when only a few changes are made over a period of time, such as a week. Even today, within a private network, the HOSTS file may perfectly address a company's needs. Several things determine if a manually created HOSTS file fits your needs. For instance, how often do changes need to be made. If network additions rarely happen, you shouldn't have to make name database changes often. Thus, you could implement a HOSTS file on each workstation. A HOSTS file is shown below for your examination.

```
#
# 102.54.94.97 rhino.acme.com # source server
# 38.25.63.10 x.acme.com # x client host

127.0.0.1       localhost
204.153.162.78  www
204.153.162.79  ftp
```

While the sample provided here, taken from Windows NT, is rather self-explanatory, a few points need stressing. As the sample file says, if you want to leave comments in the HOSTS file, use the # symbol. The HOSTS file is being repeated here because of the importance of what it is saying. The # symbol is reserved to indicate that anything to its right should be ignored for the rest of the line. Comments are important so you can document any changes you make to HOSTS files. The line without a # symbol begins with 127.0.0.1 and has one or more blank spaces. Finally, the IP address has a host name to respond to. In this case, it is the local, or host, computer.

The HOSTS file is a flat file, which is a simple listing in plain text. There is no database design and no intelligence.

LMHOSTS File

An LMHOSTS file provides a local list of NetBIOS names to IP address resolutions. Computers resolve NetBIOS names in one of three ways: broadcast messages, local LMHOSTS files, and WINS servers. Broadcast messages are the worst solution because every computer on a network segment gets the resolution request and the destination NetBIOS computer then responds with its IP address. LMHOSTS files are faster and cleaner; a local file resides on each computer with the needed lists. Unfortunately, each file needs to be manually updated. WINS servers are the best solution because updates are automatic and centralized.

WARNING HOSTS and LMHOSTS files can be confused. Both resolve names to IP addresses. Remember that HOSTS files correspond to Internet domain names, or host names, while LMHOSTS files correspond to NetBIOS names.

TCP

As you may recall, the Transmission Control Protocol is used to transmit and receive packets on the Transport layer (OSI layer four). TCP tests packets for errors, requests resends if needed, and reports unsolvable errors to the upper OSI layers.

Along with error checking, TCP establishes and monitors connections. Both the sending and receiving computer nodes create a TCP connection. This is why TCP is considered to be connection oriented. This creation is a virtual circuit; a guaranteed and monitored connection frees programs further up the OSI model from being concerned with details of reliability. Large blocks of data are broken down into smaller units, and TCP numbers and sends each smaller block. This is done so that TCP on the receiving end knows how to reassemble the data back into the original order. Before too much data is sent, the TCP protocol on the sender's end waits for an acknowledgement (called an ACK) from the receiver. Should a segment fail to arrive in good condition, the data is re-sent.

All of this packet-counting, full-duplex communication carries a price: overhead. Quite a bit of network traffic occurs that is not actual data. This gives rise to an alternative that is quite popular in use, if not so well-known in name, and that is UDP.

UDP

The User Datagram Protocol operates on the Transport layer (OSI layer four)—as doesTCP—but UDP lacks the reliable delivery and error checking of TCP. Just like TCP, this transport breaks up larger pieces of data and even numbers them. But, unlike TCP, the station that receives a UDP packet doesn't need to acknowledge the receipt of every packet. Instead, it simply responds to any request made by the sending workstation. For example, if you were to send data across an internetwork, it doesn't matter in what order the pieces of your message arrive as long as it all arrives. Once received, the message is put into the correct order. Another characteristic of UDP is that it does not create a virtual circuit; therefore, UDP is referred to as a connectionless protocol.

POP3

The Post Office Protocol is used to download e-mail from a server to an e-mail client. Version 3, or POP3, is currently in use. Eudora and Microsoft Outlook Express use the POP3 protocol to download e-mail to your local PC. A personal home account from your Internet Service Provider (ISP) most likely also uses POP3. This is because the ISP would prefer to have tens of thousands of users' e-mail messages downloaded instead of remaining on the ISP's servers.

NOTE   Some POP3 servers allow you to keep copies of e-mail messages on the mail servers. Remember that the default is to download the messages to local PCs and their e-mail clients.

SMTP

The Simple Mail Transfer Protocol sends e-mail. Server-to-server transmissions use SMTP. When you send a note from your client to your server, SMTP is also used. Dissimilar operating systems work well with the SMTP e-mail protocol, which originates from the TCP/IP suite. A Windows 9.*x* e-mail client, for example, can send a note to your NT Exchange server; the NT server can then send the message through the Internet to a Unix sendmail server or a Novell GroupWise e-mail server. The SMTP protocol allows e-mail to be sent without having the same vendor's operating system or e-mail package.

SNMP

The Simple Network Management Protocol is the management protocol created for sending information about the health of the network to network management consoles. Network devices have SNMP agents, or traps, loaded on them. These traps send a message to the SNMP management console when an event occurs. Traps can monitor the health of a hard drive, heat in a server, the status of a router, and other vital statistics. The devices are organized according to communities. An SNMP-enabled device has a community string, which stores information in a database called a Management Information Base (MIB).

FTP

The File Transfer Protocol is both a protocol and a program. It transfers files, which is a good cause for care in security. It wouldn't do to simply let someone transfer a program that also transmits a virus. Therefore, FTP is usually set up to allow users to take files but not transmit them. For example, anyone is free to download fixes to allow a new printer to be installed for an operating system. The administrator sets up a folder, installs the new printer driver, marks it as a read-only, and allows anyone who logs in using the name "anonymous" to download the update. *Anonymous* is used because some sort of user name must be supplied, and this has become the name of choice.

FTP has a cousin known as TFTP, or Trivial File Transfer Protocol. TFTP is a simpler version of FTP and lacks functions for folder (directory) browsing. If you were using TFTP in the preceding example, you would need to know exactly what the name of the new printer driver is. Due to this and other limitations, its use is rare.

HTTP

The Hypertext Transfer Protocol is used to transmit Web pages to a Web browser from a Web server. The current pages sent are based on the HyperText Markup Language (HTML). A very close relative of HTTP is HTTPS; the *S* represents the word Secure. This protocol is slower than HTTP due to the overhead of security encryption. Many consider this format a requirement for conducting online financial transactions.

IP

Internet Protocol addresses are decimal numbers that designate the network ID and node ID of a computer. IP is used on the Network layer (OSI layer three). There are two parts to an IP address. The first few digits correspond to what network the device is on, while the last few digits designate a particular workstation or node on that network. The class of an IP address dictates which part of an address is the network portion and which part is the node portion. IP also receives segments of data from TCP on the Transport layer and breaks them into packets known as *datagrams*. These datagrams are not sequenced, connection oriented, or guaranteed. Basically, IP packets are created and then directed through various networks via routers.

TCP/IP Support

As has already been discussed, TCP/IP is the most prevalent protocol. This protocol suite works with Windows 9.*x*, Windows NT, Net-Ware, and Unix, among others, because the U.S. Department of Defense has specified that all operating systems sold to them must be able to communicate with each other. Specifically, TCP/IP has to be available. The DOD desires to ensure communication regardless of the operating system used. Notice how the TCP/IP DOD network model is matched up to the OSI reference model in Figure 6.1 on the following page.

FIGURE 6.1: OSI and DOD network models

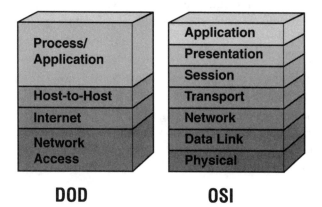

Internet Domain Name Server Hierarchies

The most common type of host name is www.companyname.com. But that does not tell the whole story. A company domain or organization can also be divided into smaller domains, such as server4.research .companyname.com. Starting from the left, the first item (*server4*) is the service or machine host name. The next item (*research*) and all other names before the last period are sub-domains (all those before *companyname*). The second-to-last item (*companyname*) denotes the organization or corporation. And the item (*com*) after the last period tells what type of network the machine is in. The original Internet domains include those listed in Table 6.1.

TABLE 6.1: Original Internet Domains

Suffix	Usage
.com	Commercial
.mil	Military
.edu	Education
.org	Organization
.net	Network

NOTE These Internet suffixes were originally designed in the United States. Today, many other suffixes exist around the world.

It is important to understand how e-mail travels from one server to another—or from my server to your server, for example. If I were to send e-mail from my `server4.research.companyname.com` to your `server8.yourcompany.net`, my e-mail server looks to resolve your address by going to the DNS server for *research*. *Research* does not know you, so it forwards the message up to *companyname*. *Companyname* does not know you, so the request for name resolution goes outside of my business. The *com* name server does not know the IP address of your *server8* because it is on the *net* network. *Com* transfers the request over to the *net* name server; because the *net* name server knows about *yourcompany*, it sends me your IP address for *yourcompany.net*. I then query *yourcompany.net* for the *server8* IP address. Once we both know each other's IP address, the e-mail can be sent.

NOTE Many routers along the way will have more than the minimum amount of information necessary to do name resolution. This eliminates the need to go to the top of each hierarchy and reduces the time involved.

Exam Essentials

This objective examines the use of TCP/IP. You will need to be able to identify the correct service for the desired action.

Know how to identify IP assignment and management services.
DHCP servers assign computers with an IP address, its related subnet mask, router, and other TCP/IP settings. DNS servers resolve Internet host names to IP addresses. WINS servers resolve NetBIOS names to IP addresses. HOSTS files are local text files that do the same thing as a DNS server, but through a file for a single local computer.

Know how to identify the main protocols in the TCP/IP suite.
TCP is a connection-oriented protocol. UDP is a connectionless-oriented protocol. POP3 downloads e-mail from a server by using an e-mail client. SMTP sends e-mail messages. SNMP is a network management protocol. FTP transfers files. HTTP serves Web pages. IP is a connectionless-oriented Network layer protocol.

Know how to describe the process of sending IP packets worldwide. IP packets require destination name resolution. This is accomplished by traversing up the domain hierarchy, over, and down until a name server is reached that has the needed listing. See the preceding Critical Information section for details.

Key Terms and Concepts

Know the acronyms that relate to TCP/IP services. Different acronyms and common terms are listed below.

DHCP (Dynamic Host Configuration Protocol) The communication method used to automatically send IP address assignments from server to client.

DNS (Domain Name Service) DNS servers resolve domain names to IP addresses, such as resolving `www.sybex.com` to 204.70.161.70.

NOTE 204.70.161.70 is *not* the actual IP address of `www.sybex.com`; it is just an example.

FTP (File Transfer Protocol) Used to send and receive files from dissimilar operating systems.

HTML (HyperText Markup Language) Defines how Web pages are written.

HTTP (Hypertext Transfer Protocol)   Sends Web pages from Web server to Web clients. HTML documents are normally transmitted.

IP (Internet Protocol)   A connectionless-oriented protocol that sends and receives packets on the Network layer.

POP3 (Post Office Protocol version 3)   Downloads e-mail from servers to local e-mail clients.

SMTP (Simple Mail Transfer Protocol)   A TCP-based protocol that allows dissimilar e-mail servers to send e-mail to each other. E-mail clients can also use SMTP to send e-mail up to their servers.

SNMP (Simple Network Management Protocol)   Monitors and manages agents called SNMP traps on network devices.

TCP (Transmission Control Protocol)   A connection-oriented protocol specified by the U.S Department of Defense and originated before the OSI model that matches up with the OSI Transport layer.

UDP (User Datagram Protocol)   Similar to TCP except that it is a connectionless-oriented protocol.

WINS (Windows Internet Naming Service)   WINS servers resolve NetBIOS names to IP addresses, such as resolving \\myserver to 204.70.161.70.

Sample Questions

1. What type of server primarily manages NetBIOS name resolutions for Microsoft networks?

   A. WINS

   B. DNS

   C. DHCP

   D. UDP

   E. TCP

Answer: A—WINS servers are used to resolve NetBIOS names to IP addresses. (DNS servers are used to resolve domain names to IP addresses. DHCP servers are used to assign IP addresses and subnet information to clients. UDP is a connectionless-oriented protocol. TCP is a connection-oriented protocol.)

2. Which of the following is not one of the original Internet domains?

   A. .com

   B. .mil

   C. .us

   D. .edu

   E. .net

   Answer: C—.us does not stem from the inception of the Internet; it was added when the Internet spread in popularity worldwide. (.com is for commercial use. .mil is for the U.S. military. edu is for educational institutions. .net is for ISPs.)

3. What static file is used to hold Internet host names and their corresponding IP addresses on a PC?

   A. HOSTS

   B. LMHOST

   C. RIP

   D. CONFIG.SYS

   E. AUTOEXEC.BAT

   Answer: A—The HOSTS file is used for local resolution of host names to IP addresses. (The LMHOST file is used for NetBIOS names and IP addresses. RIP is used in routing tables. CONFIG.SYS and AUTOEXEC.BAT manage the drivers, programs, and settings that are loaded when a Windows 9.x PC is booted.)

Demonstrate knowledge of the fundamental concepts of TCP/IP addressing, including:

- The A, B, and C classes of IP addresses and their default subnet mask numbers
- The use of port number (HTTP, FTP, SMTP) and port numbers commonly assigned to a given service

Critical Information

IP networks are assigned by InterNIC, and InterNIC does not hand out more addresses than are required, so there are a limited number of IP addresses available. IP networks are categorized by classes, and subnetworks are used to further classify IP networks. Additionally, multiple services can reside on a single computer and be addressed through assigned ports.

Network Classes

IP networks are divided into classes. These classes determine what subnetworks are and what computer nodes are. Consider this concept in binary and decimal terms. You have four numbers separated by decimal points, and each number consists of eight binary numbers:

00000000.00000000.00000000.00000000 to

11111111.11111111.11111111.11111111

and in decimal numbers:

0.0.0.0 to

255.255.255.255

To decide how large your network is, determine the maximum number of nodes needed. If 254 or less are needed, then you only need the last decimal number assigned to you, or x.x.x.0255. To figure out the maximum number of computer nodes, convert the ones above from binary to decimal. You then supply each computer with an ID and the subnet mask 255.255.255.0. This mask says that the ID with the first three numbers x.x.x is local to your network. The same is true if you have the last two decimal numbers assigned to you, or x.x.0255.0255. 255.255.0.0 indicates that any ID that has a different first or second decimal is outside of your network. Any ID with the same first two numbers is inside your net.

The largest network, a Class A network, only has one set number—the first decimal, or x.0255.0255.0255. Companies with Class A networks generally are very large and have been around since the inception of TCP/IP. There are two easy ways to define your network. The first method is by class type, A through E. The second method is to look at the first decimal number of the IP address; the decimal range in which the first number in the IP address falls denotes the type of network. Table 6.2 summarizes class types and their default subnet masks.

TIP This exam objective only requires that you understand Class A through Class C networks and their default subnet masks.

T A B L E 6.2: Network Classes

Class	Decimal Range	Default Subnet Mask	Maximum Nodes
A	1–127	255.0.0.0	16,777,214
B	128–191	255.255.0.0	65,534
C	192–223	255.255.255.0	254
D	224–239	Multicast net	
E	240–255	Reserved net	

NOTE The IP address 127.0.0.1 is reserved for the local host. The local host is an address given to the local computer that you are currently working on. When you use the ping utility on 127.0.0.1, you are actually pinging your own computer.

WARNING Class D and E networks should be avoided unless you have a compelling specific requirement.

Port Numbers

The Internet Assigned Number Authority (IANA) assigns communication ports 0 through 1023. These values are used to distinguish between several applications that try to communicate with the same host. Distinct communication channels are created on the Transport layer to correspond to each upper-level service. Table 6.3 shows the common services and their corresponding ports.

TABLE 6.3: Common Services and Their Ports

Service	Port
FTP	21
Telnet	23
SMTP	25
Gopher	70
HTTP	80
POP3	110
IRC	194

There are three ports of which you should be especially aware: HTTP FTP, and SMTP. FTP operates on port 21. Web pages are transmitted on HTTP port 80. And e-mail is sent using SMTP on port 25.

WARNING If you are sending e-mail, then use SMTP and port 25. If you are downloading e-mail from a server, use POP3 on port 110.

Exam Essentials

This objective is based on network classes and ports for common services. The Network+ exam will test your knowledge on classes of networks, subnet masks, and communication ports.

Know how to identify the class of network you have. Look at the first number in the IP address. Class A falls between one and 127. Class B is between 128 and 191. Class C networks are between 192 and 223. Class D and Class E networks are not covered on the exam.

Know how to identify the correct default subnet mask for each type of network. 255.0.0.0 is used for a Class A networks. 255.255.0.0 is used for Class B networks. 255.255.255.0 is used for Class C networks. Realize that these are all default subnet masks; other values can also be used.

Know how to identify common communication ports. FTP uses port 21. Telnet uses port 23. SMTP uses port 25. And HTTP uses port 80. See Table 6.2 for additional port numbers.

Key Terms and Concepts

You need to know the different classes of networks for the exam, as well as other terms.

Class A network Can handle up to 16,777,214 nodes. The default subnet mask is 255.0.0.0. The first digit of a Class A IP ranges from one to 127.

NOTE The 127 designation has special uses; 127.0.0.1 is the local host computer.

Class B network   Can handle up to 65,534 nodes. The default subnet mask is 255.255.0.0. The first digit of a Class B IP ranges from 128 to 191.

Class C network   Can handle up to 2,254 nodes. The default subnet mask is 255.255.255.0. The first digit of a Class C IP ranges from 192 to 223.

Default subnet   An IP network is subdivided by covering some of the leftmost numbers by using 255 and viewing some rightmost IPs by using a 0.

Gopher   Gopher sites are public and private access sites that can be browsed by using gopher browsers. Gopher sites use port 70 and are the precursor of HTTP Web sites.

IANA (Internet Assigned Number Authority)   Assigns communication ports 0 through 1023. These ports are used for popular services.

IRC (Internet Relay Chat)   Operates on port 194. It is used to carry on text-based conversations in near real time over IP networks.

Subnet Mask: A special IP address used to indicate the class of an IP address.

Sample Questions

1. IP address 13.1.12.34.9 is an example of what class of address?

   A. Class A

   B. Class B

   C. Class C

   D. Class D

   E. Class E

Answer: A—The first number in the IP address is 13; 13 is less than 127, so the address falls into Class A's network range of 1127. (128191 is a Class B network. 192223 is a Class C network. Class D and Class E networks are reserved for special purposes.)

2. What port is used to download e-mail from a server via an e-mail client?

   A. 21

   B. 23

   C. 25

   D. 80

   E. 110 *(POP3)*

   Answer: E—E-mail is downloaded from a server using POP3 on port 110. (Port 21 is used for FTP. Port 23 is used for telnet. SMTP utilizes port 25. And Web pages are transmitted using port 80.)

3. Port 25 is used to provide what service?

   A. SNMP to monitor e-mail

   B. SMTP to send e-mail

   C. SMTP to receive e-mail

   D. POP3 to send e-mail

   E. POP3 to receive e-mail

   Answer: B—SMTP sends e-mail using port 25. (SNMP monitors via another port. POP3 receives e-mail from a server via an e-mail client on port 110.)

Demonstrate knowledge of TCP/IP configuration concepts, including:

- The definition of IP proxy and why it is used
- The identity of the normal configuration parameters for a workstation, including IP address, DNS, default gateway, IP proxy configuration, WINS, DHCP, host name, and Internet domain name

Critical Information

To have use of the TCP/IP stack for an Internet connection, a workstation must have the TCP/IP protocol and the correct network adapter driver installed. After these items are installed, they must be configured. You must understand the following two major concepts to configure TCP/IP correctly:

- IP proxy

- Workstation configuration parameters

IP Proxy

A TCP/IP proxy, or just IP proxy, is a network service that makes Internet requests on behalf of workstations on your network. (This technology is also known as *network address translation.*) IP proxies act as translators between LANs and the Internet, intercepting all requests going out to the Internet and replacing each sender's IP address with that of the IP proxy. When the response comes from the Internet, the response is addressed to the IP proxy instead of to a particular workstation. The proxy replaces its own address in the response with the address of the station for which the response is destined and then sends the packet on the internal network. This technology is useful when you want to use a single TCP/IP address over the Internet (or have only one TCP/IP address available) regardless of what workstations are sending it. An IP proxy also allows an administrator to manage Web connection on a port-per-port basis.

Workstation TCP/IP Configuration Parameters

Generally speaking, TCP/IP is fairly simple to configure for most computers; you have to configure only a few parameters. Quite a few optional parameters add extra TCP/IP functionality to a workstation when they are implemented. The following configuration parameters are available:

- Host IP address and subnet mask

- DNS information

- Default gateway

- IP proxy configuration (optional)

- WINS (optional)

- DHCP (optional)

- Host name

- Internet domain name

IP Address and Subnet Mask

When you are configuring a workstation for TCP/IP, you must configure an IP address and a subnet mask on the TCP/IP stack of the workstation. The workstation cannot communicate on a TCP/IP network unless you configure at least those two parameters. The IP address must be unique on that network to uniquely identify that station on the network. The subnet mask indicates what kind of IP address is being used on that workstation. If your network is connected to the Internet, your Internet Service Provider assigns a block of TCP/IP addresses (usually a range of dotted-decimal numbers) and a subnet mask for you to use. If you aren't connected to the Internet (or aren't going to be connected in the future), you can pick any IP addressing scheme that you want to use, as long as the class of address and subnet mask match.

You must input the IP address and the subnet mask in the TCP/IP protocol configuration for your particular operating system. The location where you enter this information varies between operating systems. In Windows 9.*x*, you open the Network Control Panel (choose Start ➤ Settings ➤ Control Panel) and double-click Network); click the TCP/IP protocol and then click Properties. You can then enter the TCP/IP address and subnet mask in this window in the fields designated for them. Reboot your system, and the system will have basic TCP/IP communications capabilities.

DNS

When you configure a workstation to use DNS, you must set three parameters: the DNS server's IP address, the local host name, and the Internet domain name of the host that you are configuring. Where you configure these parameters depends on the operating. Windows 9.*x*, you add this information to the DNS tab of the ⎯ Protocol Properties dialog box, which you access from the Network control panel as described in the preceding section.

Default Gateway

The default gateway is a parameter that indicates to the TCP/IP stack where the workstation should send all packets that are destined for other networks. You must specify the default gateway on the workstation if you want it to be able to send packets to hosts on other networks. The address that you type for this parameter is the IP address of the router interface (connection) that connects your workstation's network segment to the Internet. By default, this parameter is blank; you must fill it in to be able to send IP packets to other networks.

As is true of the other parameters, where you configure this parameter depends on the OS. To configure the default gateway in Windows 9.*x*, you still use the properties of the TCP/IP protocol, but you enter the information in the Gateway tab of the TCP/IP Properties dialog box.

IP Proxy Configuration

Many IP proxy servers are available, including Microsoft's and Novell's, and each IP proxy has a different method of configuration. Most IP proxies, however, don't require any workstation configuration. The server is configured with two IP addresses: one on the NIC that connects to the Internet and the other on the NIC that connects to the internal network. All IP addresses on the internal network (LAN and proxy server) can use any IP addressing scheme (as long as it fits within a certain class). The IP proxy is configured to translate a browser request between these two addresses. Access to the proxy server is configured through the browser. In Windows 95, on the desktop, right-click the browser's icon and choose Properties; then choose the Connection folder. The second radio button allows you to choose a proxy server. Choose a radio button and then enter either the proxy server's name or its IP address.

NOTE   This parameter is optional; it is required only if your network uses an IP proxy to access the Internet.

WINS

You must configure the WINS parameter on TCP/IP workstations that run any version of Microsoft Windows (including 9.*x* and NT). This parameter indicates to the Windows machine what method it should use to resolve NetBIOS computer names over TCP/IP. To configure WINS on a workstation, you must enable WINS and specify a primary WINS server. To configure WINS on a Microsoft Windows 95/98 workstation, for example, choose Start ➤ Settings ➤ Control Panel ➤ Network ➤ TCP/IP ➤ Properties ➤ WINS Configuration.

DHCP

No specific parameter tells a workstation which DHCP server to use (unlike the other TCP/IP parameters). To use DHCP to assign a TCP/IP address, you must direct a workstation to use the DHCP server. This setting is usually the default in most Windows TCP/IP stacks. This setting usually is a check box that asks a variant of "Obtain an IP address automatically?" If you change this setting, you must configure the workstation with a static IP address and subnet mask. If you accept the default setting, the DHCP server automatically assigns an IP address and a subnet mask, as well as any other parameters configured on the DHCP server (such as the default gateway).

Host Name

The host name is the DNS name of a particular workstation. You must configure the host name so other workstations on the network can identify a workstation by DNS name rather than just by IP address. You can assign host names in many ways, depending on the OS that you are using. On Windows 9.*x* workstations, you use the DNS tab of the TCP/IP Properties dialog box to configure the host name of that workstation. By default, this parameter is blank. This parameter tells the workstation what host name to use in all TCP/IP communications.

Internet Domain Name

The final parameter that you should configure on a workstation is the Internet domain name of the network on which this workstation resides. You obtain this information from the Internet Service Provider to which

you are connecting—if you do not have your own domain na..
parameter is optional. If you fill in this parameter, the workstation
knows what Internet domain it is part of and can use that information
in future TCP/IP communications. You configure this parameter in different places in different operating systems, but in Windows 9.*x* you
use the DNS tab of the TCP/IP Properties dialog box.

Exam Essentials

This objective is based on workstation TCP/IP configuration concepts. The Network+ exam will test your knowledge of IP proxies and
the normal configuration parameters for a workstation.

Know how to define IP Proxy and discuss its use.   IP proxies act
on behalf of a workstation to allow secure communications over the
Internet. They prevent an individual workstation's IP address from
being sent to the Internet.

**Know the normal TCP/IP configuration parameters for a
workstation.**   These parameters include IP address, DNS, default
gateway, IP proxy configuration, WINS, DHCP, host name, and Internet
domain name.

Key Terms and Concepts

In addition to the terms discussed in previous sections, the following
terms are also covered in this section.

IP proxy   Act on behalf of workstations to allow secure communications over the Internet. They prevent individual workstation IP
addresses from being sent to the Internet.

Default gateway   The configuration parameter on workstations
that indicates which router to send packets to when the packet destination addresses aren't on the local workstations.

Sample Questions

1. Which TCP/IP parameters can you configure on a workstation?

   A. IP address

   B. DHCP server address

   C. DNS server

   D. WINS server

   Answers: A, C, D—All listed parameters other than DHCP can be configured on a workstation. (DHCP server addresses are found using broadcasts. The workstation broadcasts a request for an IP address, and the DHCP server responds.)

2. What local file can you alter on a Windows 95/98/NT machine to resolve the NetBIOS name \\ntfsone to its TCP/IP network address?

   A. hosts

   B. lmhosts

   C. iphosts

   D. nthosts

   Answer: B—The LMHOSTS file is used to resolve NetBIOS names to IP addresses. (A is incorrect because it is used to resolve DNS host names to IP addresses, *not* NetBIOS names. C and D are bogus answers.)

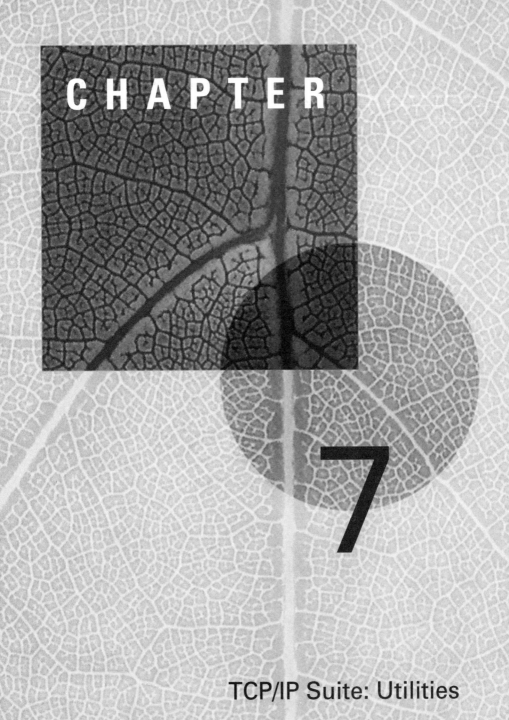

CHAPTER

7

TCP/IP Suite: Utilities

Network+ Exam Objective Covered in This Chapter:

Explain how and when to use the following TCP/IP utilities to test, validate, and troubleshoot connectivity: *(pages 169 – 184)*

- ARP
- Telnet
- NBTSTAT
- Tracert
- NETSTAT
- ipconfig/winipcfg
- FTP
- Ping

This chapter covers the main workstation-based tools that are used to diagnose and report the status of TCP/IP on a network. With these tools, you can check configurations, troubleshoot connections, and transfer files. Each utility has a different use. You must know each utility's proper use and various options. Address Resolution Protocol (ARP) commands allow you to view or modify the ARP address resolution table. The Telnet utility is used to establish a virtual terminal session with a remote host over a TCP/IP network. NBTSTAT allows you to view a station's NetBIOS over TCP/IP (NBT) statistics. Tracert allow you to view the route a packet takes from your workstation to a specified destination. NETSTAT is a useful troubleshooting utility used to gather TCP/IP and other protocol statistics. The ipconfig/winipcfg utilities (for Windows 9.*x* and Windows NT, respectively) allow you to view the TCP/IP configuration for that workstation. FTP is both a protocol and a utility used to transfer files between TCP/IP hosts. Finally, the ping utility is used to test whether or not a station's TCP/IP address has been configured correctly.

Explain how and when to use the following TCP/IP utilities to test, validate, and troubleshoot connectivity:

- ARP
- Telnet
- NBTSTAT
- Tracert
- NETSTAT
- ipconfig/winipcfg
- FTP
- Ping

This objective covers some of the various utilities used to troubleshoot a workstation's TCP/IP communications with the rest of the network. With the large amount of networks running TCP/IP, it is important for you to know the functions of these utilities as well as how to use them.

Critical Information

A good understanding of the following TCP/IP diagnostic commands and terms will help you to test and validate IP connectivity as well as to troubleshoot and administer your network.

ARP

The Address Resolution Protocol is within the TCP/IP protocol stack that uses broadcasts to translate TCP/IP addresses to MAC addresses.

In addition to being a protocol, ARP is also a Windows 9.*x*/NT utility that is used to manipulate and view the local workstation's ARP address resolution table.

The Windows ARP Table

The ARP table in Windows 9.*x* and Windows NT comprises a list of TCP/IP addresses and their associated physical (MAC) addresses. This table is cached in memory so that Windows doesn't have to perform ARP lookups for frequently accessed TCP/IP addresses (e.g., servers and default gateways). Each entry contains not only an IP address and a MAC address but also a value for *time to live*, which indicates how long each entry should stay in the ARP table.

There are two kinds of entries: static and dynamic. First, dynamic entries are made whenever an ARP request is made by the Windows TCP/IP stack and the MAC address is not found in the ARP table. The ARP request is then broadcasted on the local network segment. When the MAC address of the requested IP address is found, that information is added to the ARP table on the local computer. Static entries serve the same function as dynamic entries, except they are made manually through the use of the ARP utility.

The ARP Utility

The ARP utility runs from the command line in both Windows 9.*x* and Windows NT 4.*x*. To start the command prompt in both operating systems, simply click on the Start menu and choose Programs. Then, in Windows 9.*x*, choose MS-DOS Prompt, or choose Command Prompt in Windows NT 4.*x*. Once there, you can run the ARP utility simply by typing ARP at the command prompt (along with any switches you need to use). By itself, the ARP command only gives you the switches you must use in order to use the ARP utility correctly.

The ARP utility is useful mainly for duplicate IP address resolution problems. Say, for example, that a workstation receives its IP address from a DHCP server, and it accidentally receives the same address as another workstation. When you try to ping it, you get no response. This is because your workstation is trying to determine the MAC address and it can't because two machines are reporting the same IP address. To help solve this problem, you can use the ARP utility to view your local ARP table and see which TCP/IP address is resolved to which MAC address. This is accomplished by using the ARP command, with the "–a" switch, like so:

```
ARP -a
```

This will display the entire current ARP table, which will produce an output that looks similar to the following:

```
Interface: 204.153.163.3 on Interface 2
Internet AddressPhysical AddressType
204.153.163.200-a0-c9-d4-bc-dcdynamic
204.153.163.400-a0-c0-aa-b1-45dynamic
```

TIP The "–g" switch will accomplish the same result.

In addition to displaying the ARP table, the ARP utility can also be used to manipulate it. If you use the ARP command with the "–s" switch, you can add static entries to the table. (These entries stay in the ARP table until the machine is rebooted.) A static entry hardwires a specific IP address to a specific MAC address so that when a packet is sent to the IP address it is also automatically sent to the MAC address. The format for doing that is:

```
ARP -s [IP Address] [MAC Address]
```

Simply replace the [IP Address] and [MAC Address] fields with the appropriate data, like so:

```
ARP -s 204.153.163.5 00-a0-c0-ab-c3-11
```

After doing this, using "arp –a", you can view the new ARP table, which should look something like this:

```
Interface: 204.153.163.3 on Interface 2
Internet AddressPhysical AddressType
204.153.163.200-a0-c9-d4-bc-dcdynamic
204.153.163.400-a0-c0-aa-b1-45dynamic
204.153.163.500-a0-c0-ab-c3-11 static
```

Finally, if you want to delete entries from the ARP table, you can either wait until the dynamic entries time out or you can use the

"–d" switch with the IP address of the static entry that you'd like to delete, like so:

```
ARP -d 204.153.163.5
```

This will delete the respective entry from the ARP table.

NOTE When either adding or deleting entries, the ARP utility won't give you a confirmation that the process has happened successfully.

Telnet

Telnet allows users to access other machines through a network as if he or she were at the remote terminal's keyboard. It was originally used for opening terminal sessions from remote Unix workstations to Unix servers. (The name Telnet is a shortening of terminal emulation for networks.) This protocol has evolved into an invaluable trouble-shooting tool. Today, the Telnet utility on both Windows 9.*x* and Windows NT is used as a basic GUI tool for testing TCP connections. You can Telnet to any TCP port to test if it is responding. This is especially good for checking SMTP and HTTP (Web) ports. You probably remember from the last chapter that each upper-layer service in a TCP stack has a number for its address. Each network service that uses a TCP port will respond to a TCP request on that port (if the defaults are used).

To test whether a TCP service is responding, start either the Windows 9.*x* or Windows NT Telnet utilities (see Figure 7.1) by going to Start ➤ Run ➤ telnet. Once the Telnet utility is running, choose Remote System from the Connect menu; this will bring up the screen shown in Figure 7.2. In the Host Name box, type the IP address or DNS host name of the host running the TCP service to which you want to connect. For example, if you want to check whether a Web server is responding to TCP port 80 (its default port), you would enter the IP address or DNS host name of the Web server (204.153.163.2 in this case) and then, in the Port box, type the number that corresponds to the service that you want to check. In the case of HTTP (Web servers), the port would be 80, so you would type in the number 80. Once you've done that, click Connect.

F I G U R E 7.1: The Windows 9.*x* and Windows NT Telnet utility

F I G U R E 7.2: Entering host and port in the Telnet utility

NBTSTAT

The NBTSTAT command-line utility is used to track NetBIOS over TCP/IP statistics. (Remember that NetBIOS names are used to identify computers in Windows 9.*x* and Windows NT.) NBTSTAT is used to show the details of NetBIOS name resolution and incoming and outgoing NetBIOS over TCP/IP connections. Because NetBIOS name resolution is primarily a Windows 9.*x* or Windows NT network issue, the NBTSTAT command can only be found on Windows 9.*x* or NT networked computers.

The NBTSTAT utility is a command-line utility. If you type NBTSTAT by itself on the command line, it will only show a basic description of NBTSTAT and the options that can be used with it. The options for NBTSTAT allow you to configure the way NBTSTAT displays information about NetBIOS over TCP/IP hosts. Some of the switches that can be used are listed in Table 7.1. Also, in Figure 7.3, notice the name table that is listed when an "–s" is used.

T A B L E 7.1: NBTSTAT—Its Switches and What They Do

Switch	Effect
–a	Lists a remote machine's NetBIOS name table
–A	Resembles –a, but IP address of host used instead of NetBIOS
–c	Displays remote NetBIOS name cache on the workstation
–n	Displays NetBIOS names for the machine you are running on
–r	Compiles statistics of NetBIOS names resolved to TCP/IP
–R	Purges NetBIOS cache; reloads LMHOSTS file
–S	Lists all NetBIOS sessions, incoming and outgoing
–s	Resolves remote host IP addresses into host names

F I G U R E 7.3: Sample output of the "NBTSTAT –S" command

```
C:\NBTSTAT -S

              NetBIOS Connection Table
Local Name         State     In/Out  Remote Host            Input   Output
------------------------------------------------------------------------
S1         <00>  Connected   Out    204.153.163.4          256B    432B
S1         <03>  Listening
```

TIP Dashes, followed by the appropriate letter, are always used for NBTSTAT utility switches. Switches are also case sensitive. Generally speaking, lowercase switches deal with NetBIOS host names and uppercase switches deal with TCP/IP host addresses.

The "–s" switch for the NBTSTAT utility is useful to determine how a workstation is resolving NetBIOS names and whether WINS is configured correctly. If WINS is not configured correctly, the numbers under Resolved by Name Server or Registered by Name Server will always be zero.

Tracert

The TCP/IP tracert (traceroute) command shows you every router interface hop that a packet goes through in a TCP/IP network. To use this utility, go to the command prompt and type tracert <IP Address> | <DNS name>, filling in the fields that you want to find the route for. You will then get a list of DNS names and/or IP addresses of which router interfaces the packet transverses; tracert will tell you how long it takes for each hop. Figure 7.4 shows a sample tracert output that was performed from a workstation connected to an ISP (Corporate Communications in Fargo, ND, in this case) to the search engine *Yahoo!*

F I G U R E 7.4: Sample tracert output

```
C:\>tracert www.yahoo.com
Tracing route to www10.yahoo.com [204.71.200.75]
over a maximum of 30 hops:

  1    110 ms     96 ms    107 ms  fgo1.corpcomm.net [209.74.93.10]
  2     96 ms    126 ms     95 ms  someone.corpcomm.net [209.74.93.1]
  3    113 ms    119 ms    112 ms  Serial5-1-1.GW2.MSP1.alter.net [157.130.100.185]
  4    133 ms    123 ms    126 ms  152.ATM3-0.XR2.CHI6.ALTER.NET [146.188.209.126]
  5    176 ms    133 ms    129 ms  290.ATM2-0.TR2.CHI4.ALTER.NET [146.188.209.10]
  6    196 ms    184 ms    218 ms  106.ATM7-0.TR2.SCL1.ALTER.NET [146.188.136.162]
  7    182 ms    187 ms    187 ms  298.ATM7-0.XR2.SJC1.ALTER.NET [146.188.146.61]
  8    204 ms    176 ms    186 ms  192.ATM3-0-0.SAN-JOSE9-GW.ALTER.NET [146.188.144.133]
  9    202 ms    198 ms    212 ms  atm3-0-622M.cr1.sjc.globalcenter.net [206.57.16.17]
 10    209 ms    202 ms    195 ms  pos3-1-155M.br4.SJC.globalcenter.net [206.132.150.98]
 11    190 ms      *        191 ms  pos0-0-0-155M.hr3.SNV.globalcenter.net [206.251.5.93]
 12    195 ms    188 ms    188 ms  pos4-1-0-155M.hr2.SNV.globalcenter.net [206.132.150.206]
 13    198 ms    202 ms    197 ms  www10.yahoo.com [204.71.200.75]

Trace complete.
```

NETSTAT

NETSTAT is used to determine what TCP/IP connections (both inbound and outbound) your machine has. It will also let you view packet statistics (similar to the MONITOR.NLM utility on a NetWare server console), such as how many packets have been sent and received, the number of errors, and so on. The utility, when used without any switches, may produce an output that shows all of the outbound TCP/IP connections, similar to the Web connection shown in Figure 7.5. This utility, used without any switches, is very useful in determining the status of outbound Web connections.

FIGURE 7.5: Output of the NETSTAT command without any switches

```
C:\NETSTAT
Active Connections
```

Proto	Local Address	Foreign Address	State
TCP	default:1026	204.153.163.2:80	ESTABLISHED
TCP	default:1027	204.153.163.2:80	ESTABLISHED
TCP	default:1028	204.153.163.2:80	ESTABLISHED
TCP	default:1029	204.153.163.2:80	ESTABLISHED

The Proto column in the output shows the protocol being used; since this is a Web connection, the protocol is TCP. In the Local Address column, you will see the source address as well as source port. In this case, default means that the local IP address and the source ports are four separate TCP ports being used to open four separate TCP connections. Notice that the Foreign Address for all four connections is the same (204.153.163.2:80), meaning that the address of the destination machine is 204.153.163.2 and the destination port is TCP port 80 (in other words, HTTP for the Web). The State column indicates the status of each connection and shows only statistics for TCP connections. Most commonly, this column will indicate "ESTABLISHED" once a connection between your computer and the destination computer has been established.

NOTE   If the address of your computer or the destination computer can be found in the HOSTS file on your computer, the destination computer's name will show up in either of the address columns (rather than the IP address).

The NETSTAT utility functions differently depending on which switch is used. A NETSTAT command uses its switches to control the display of the statistics it collects. To use a switch with the NETSTAT command, simply type NETSTAT, followed by a space, and then the switch name. There may be other options to type with each switch, but the syntax is basically the same. The switches you can use with the NET-STAT command are listed in Table 7.2. Also, in Figure 7.2, notice the output of the NETSTAT command.

T A B L E 7.2:   NETSTAT—Its Switches and What They Do

Switch	Effect
–a	Shows all TCP/IP connections (TCP and UDP)
–e	Summarizes the packets sent as of that instant
–r	Displays the current route table for the workstation
–s	Compiles statistics on TCP, UDP, IP, and ICMP protocols
–n	Displays network addresses instead of associated network names
–p	With "s," specifies protocols (IP, TCP, UDP, or ICMP)

ipconfig/winipcfg

The IP configuration utility that comes with Windows 9.*x* is called winipcfg, and the Windows NT utility is called ipconfig. They display TCP/IP current information on machines, like the current IP address, DNS configuration, WINS configuration, and default gateway.

For Windows 9.*x*, you use winipcfg to check the workstation's TCP/IP configuration, which can be run from the command prompt or at a DOS prompt command line by going to Start -> Run and then winipcfg. See Figure 7.3 for a sample winipcfg screen.

TIP   With DHCP, you can use the Release All and Renew All buttons to remove DHCP information and to request new TCP/IP configuration information from DHCP servers.

F I G U R E   7.6: Windows 9.*x* winipcfg utility

After clicking on the More Info button (see Figure 7.6), you will get information on the DNS name of the machine and the IP address of the DNS server that the workstation is using (see Figure 7.7). Plus there is information on NetBIOS over TCP/IP, addresses of DHCP and WINS servers (if any are present), and lease information about how old the DHCP addresses are.

In an attempt to get closer to Unix (which uses ifconfig), Microsoft named the Windows NT version ipconfig, which is NT's command-line based IP configuration utility. In Windows 98, winipcfg and ipconfig both work.

FIGURE 7.7: Windows 9.*x* IP Configuration utility More Info screen

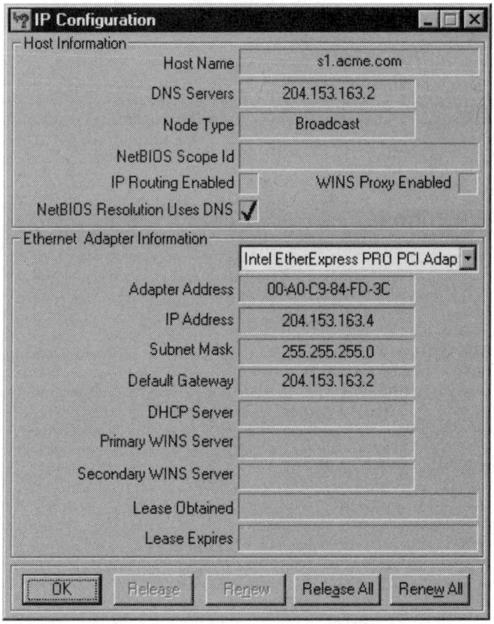

Because ipconfig is command-line based, output of the command is controlled through the use of switches. There are only four switches that can be used with this command; they are listed in Table 7.3. Notice what the /all switch displays in Figure 7.8.

TABLE 7.3: ipconfig Switches

Switch	Description
/?	Help: lists all switches and their uses
/all	Displays all TCP/IP configuration information
/release	Releases all TCP/IP configuration information from DHCP
/renew	Releases and then renews TCP/IP information from DHCP

F I G U R E 7.8: ipconfig with the /all switch

```
C:\>ipconfig /all

Windows NT IP Configuration

        Host Name . . . . . . . . . : s1.devarim.com
        DNS Servers . . . . . . . . :
        Node Type . . . . . . . . . : Broadcast
        NetBIOS Scope ID. . . . . . :
        IP Routing Enabled. . . . . : No
        WINS Proxy Enabled. . . . . : No
        NetBIOS Resolution Uses DNS : No

Ethernet adapter E100B1:

        Description . . . . . . . . : Intel EtherExpress PRO PCI Adapter
        Physical Address. . . . . . : 00-A0-C9-D4-BC-DC
        DHCP Enabled. . . . . . . . : No
        IP Address. . . . . . . . . : 204.153.163.2
        Subnet Mask . . . . . . . . : 255.255.255.0
        Default Gateway . . . . . . :
```

FTP

The File Transfer Protocol transfers files on computers running FTP server services (or daemons) to clients. Downloads of patches, manuals, and other software in binary code or ASCII are all easily performed through a variety of computer platforms that have only one thing in common—they all run the TCP/IP stack and have the FTP server or client running on them.

To begin a file transfer, type ftp <ip address> or <site name> at the command prompt. Or you can enter the command once you are in FTP:

> FTP> open ftp.sybex.com

If the FTP is available and running, you will receive a response from the FTP server welcoming you to the server and asking you for a username, like so:

> ftp> open ftp.sybex.com
> Connected to ftp.sybex.com
> 220 nemesis FTP server (Version wu-2.4.2-academ _
> [BETA-14](4) Tue Oct 14 17:57:04
> MDT 1997) ready.
> User (ftp.sybex.com:(none)):

You must enter a valid username in order to gain access. (Usernames are case sensitive.) To proceed, type in your username (or the anonymous username) and press Enter. Before you can gain access and become able to download or upload files, you must enter a password. If you enter the wrong username and/or password, the server will tell you so by displaying:

```
530 Login Incorrect
Login failed.
```

The server will also leave you at the FTP command prompt. Table 7.4 lists some FTP commands and what they do.

T A B L E 7.4: Command Summary

Switch	Effect
Help	Displays help for available FTP commands
CD	Changes directory on remote machines
LCD	Changes directory on local machines
DIR	Displays a long and descriptive list of files on remote machines
ASCII	Transfers an ASCII file mode
BINARY	Transfers a binary file mode
GET	Retrieves a single file from remote machines
PUT	Sends or transmits files to remote machines
Prompt	Toggles on or off interactive mode
Quit	Alternates the command used to exit FTP

When you're finished with the FTP utility, simply type *quit* or *bye* to quit and return to the command prompt.

Ping

Ping is used to see if a destination computer is talking on the TCP/IP stack; it is one of the most basic TCP/IP utilities. You use this command to test whether a host is reachable and is responding. The syntax is: `ping <Hostname>` or `<IP Address>`. If you ping any station with an IP address, the ICMP (Internet Control Message Protocol) that is part of that host's TCP/IP stack will respond to the request. This ICMP test and response might look something like this:

```
ping 204.153.163.2

Pinging 204.153.163.2 with 32 bytes of data:

Reply from 204.153.163.2: bytes=32 time<10ms TTL=128
Reply from 204.153.163.2: bytes=32 time=1ms TTL=128
Reply from 204.153.163.2: bytes=32 time<10ms TTL=128
Reply from 204.153.163.2: bytes=32 time<10ms TTL=128
```

When a reply is received from the destination station (204.153.163.2 in this case), you know that the host is reachable, and you can determine how quickly it is responding to IP requests (for this example, an average of 10ms per packet round-trip). Table 7.5 shows ping utility switches.

T A B L E 7.5: Windows Ping Utility Switches

Switch	Description
–?	Help: displays the switches available for ping
–a	Resolves addresses to host names while ping occurs
–n #	Pings target machine a specific number of times (specified by #, the pound symbol)
–t	Pings continuously until Ctrl C is pressed
–r #	Records the route taken during the ping hops

Exam Essentials

Be familiar with and understand how to use the troubleshooting commands available in the TCP/IP protocol suite, including ARP, NBTSTAT, NETSTAT, FTP, ping, ipconfig/winipcfg, tracert, and Telnet.

**Know how to describe and use the troubleshooting inf
and statistics that ARP, NBTSTAT, and NETSTAT proviae you.**
ARP shows whether an IP address is being resolved to your MAC
address (or someone else's in case of conflicts). NETSTAT produces
TCP/IP statistics, and NBTSTAT produces NetBIOS over TCP/IP
statistics.

**Know how to diagnose a network by using TCP/IP's trouble-
shooting commands.** Ping echoes back if a machine is alive and
active on a network. Tracert shows the path the ping packets take
from source to target. And Telnet enables a user to participate in a
remote text-based session.

Know how to use the FTP process. Files are transferred from a
server using the FTP program. This process begins initiating a connection to an FTP server by using the FTP utility and logging on. Then
you can use the ls and get commands to browse and download files,
respectively. You can end the FTP session by typing *quit*.

Key Terms and Concepts

Know the acronyms and definitions relating to the TCP/IP tools
presented.

ARP (Address Resolution Protocol) Resolves IP addresses to
MAC addresses.

ICMP (Internet Control Message Protocol) Used to send control
and troubleshooting packets over an IP-based network.

ipconfig/winipcfg Displays the TCP/IP settings for a computer.

NBTSTAT Displays NetBIOS statistics over TCP/IP.

NETSTAT Displays statistics about the interfaces of current
TCP/IP network connections.

PING (Packet Internet Groper) A TCP/IP diagnostic tool
command that verifies that a target computer is alive and responding
to packets from a sending machine through ICMP.

ICMP (Internet Control Message Protocol) ICMP communications are used to send control and troubleshooting packets over an IP based network.

ipconfig/winipcfg Displays the TCP/IP settings for your computer.

RARP (Reverse Address Resolution Protocol) Resolves MAC addresses to IP addresses (the opposite of ARP).

Tracert (traceroute) Similar to ping except tracert tracks the path packets take every step of the way to the target computer.

Sample Questions

1. On a Windows 98 machine, which of the following utilities do you use to see the local TCP/IP configurations?

   A. winipcfg

   B. NBTSTAT

   C. ipconfig

   D. None of the above

   Answers: A, C—NBTSTAT is a TCP/IP command that provides statistics, and winipcfg and ipconfig work in Windows 98 to display TCP/IP configurations.

2. What command is used to resolve MAC addresses to IP addresses?

   A. NETSTAT

   B. ARP

   C. Telnet

   D. RARP

   Answer: D—RARP is the protocol used to resolve IP addresses to MAC addresses (the opposite of ARP). (NETSTAT is a TCP/IP statistics reporting command. ARP resolves IP addresses to MAC addresses. Telnet is a program that enables a user to access another machine.)

CHAPTER

8

Remote Connectivity

Network+ Exam Objectives Covered in This Chapter:

Explain the following remote connectivity concepts:
(pages 187 – 198)

- The distinction between PPP and SLIP
- The purpose and function of PPTP and the conditions under which it is useful
- The attributes, advantages, and disadvantages of ISDN and PSTN (POTS)

Specify the following elements of dial-up networking:
(pages 199 – 205)

- The modem configuration parameters that must be set, including serial port, IRQ, I/O address, and maximum port speed
- The requirements for a remote connection

Whether you connect to your corporate network while out of the office or dial up a personal ISP, you are using remote connectivity. The days of not taking work home with you have long since passed. (Those days might never have existed in some companies.) Technology makes it possible to work at home as if you are sitting in your office. The same network resources are available even if you are halfway across the world.

The Network+ exam tests your knowledge of the technology that makes remote connections possible. You will not have to set up a remote session for the exam. This is an important distinction; there are no simulations on the Network+ exam. But as a prospective certified network administrator, you will have to describe different access methods. Also, you may be asked to find possible logic flaws in certain scenarios.

This chapter will discuss the types of physical connections and protocols used for remote connections. The most common form of remote connection is the Point-to-Point Protocol (PPP), which has surpassed the Plain Old Telephone Service (POTS) protocol. An even older protocol is the Serial Line Internet Protocol (SLIP). Lastly, Integrated Services Digital Network (ISDN) is a medium-speed connection that used to be considered high speed. In addition, this chapter will discuss the requirements for a remote connection and the parameters you must configure on a workstation for a successful remote connection. These parameters include modem IRQ, I/O address, and COM port address, as well as the various software settings.

Explain the following remote connectivity concepts:

- The distinction between PPP and SLIP
- The purpose and function of PPTP and the conditions under which it is useful
- The attributes, advantages, and disadvantages of ISDN and PSTN (POTS)

This exam objective outlines the various types of protocols used in remote connections and their respective details. Because each protocol has advantages that make it best suited for a particular application, each protocol is used primarily in a specific application. For this reason, the Network+ exam tests you on the details of each remote access protocol.

Critical Information

You will need to define the most common analog and digital dial-up devices for the Network+ exam, including analog modems and other digital communication devices. A modem is a remote communication device that converts a computer's digital signals into analog signals that can then travel over standard POTS phone lines. Modems are currently capable of 56Kbps data transfer under the V.90 standard.

An ISDN terminal adapter is a digital device that allows a network access to the ISDN transmission medium. This device is often mistakenly called an ISDN "modem," but since it doesn't translate between analog and digital, it can't technically be called a modem. However, because the device is similar in physical appearance to a standard, external modem, it is often called an ISDN modem.

The ISDN terminal adapter bonds two 64Kbps channels to give 128Kbps throughput. Once you have selected the modem type, you need to look at the communication protocol. The Data Link layer has PPP and SLIP, the two most common protocols, to send the packets over modems. You must understand the details of both modems and ISDN terminal adapters and their communication protocols for the exam.

PPP

The Point-to-Point Protocol is used to connect a remote workstation to a network. PPP is the most commonly used communication protocol for transporting TCP/IP over a dial-up connection. PPP uses the Link Control Protocol (LCP) for communication between the PPP client and the host. (LCP is the protocol that is used to test the link and specify PPP client configuration.)

Because it operates at the Data Link layer of the OSI model, PPP can support several upper-layer network protocols as well as run over many different types of physical media. With PPP, information can be encrypted, whereas SLIP, as you will see in the next section, does not have any built-in encryption capabilities. With error checking and the ability to run over many types of physical media, PPP has almost completely replaced SLIP.

Advantages

- Supports multiple network protocols
- Error correction
- Automatic configuration of TCP/IP and other protocol parameters
- Can use a number of physical media

Disadvantages

- Higher overhead than other protocols
- Not compatible with some older configurations

Workstation Configuration

The beauty of PPP from the technician's standpoint is the simplicity of configuration. Once the workstation makes a connection to a router using PPP, the router will assign the workstation all other TCP/IP parameters using DHCP, including the workstation's TCP/IP address and DNS server addresses. A technician only needs to enable the PPP protocol and specify the phone number of the router. To configure a Windows 9.*x* dial-up connection, select PPP from the Type of Dial-Up Server drop-down list in the Server Types tab (Figure 8.1). PPP will take care of the rest of the workstation configuration.

F I G U R E 8.1: PPP and other choices are available in Windows 9.*x* under Dial-Up Networking, at the Server Types tab

SLIP

The Serial Line Internet Protocol is designed to transport TCP/IP over serial connections (like modem dial-up links over POTS). Rick Adams developed SLIP in 1984 for the Berkeley flavor of Unix. Today, it is found in other NOS offerings, in addition to Unix. The use of SLIP has declined in recent years, but that has nothing to do with the fact that it operates in both the Physical and Data Link layers. SLIP is slipping in popularity due to a lack of features when compared to other choices, like PPP.

SLIP is used today primarily to connect workstations to the Internet or other networks using TCP/IP over a 1.2 to 19.2Kbps serial connection. The protocol does not support compression, encryption, or dynamic allocation of IP addresses.

Advantages

- Low overhead

- One method of getting TCP/IP over serial connections

Disadvantages

- No error checking

- No packet addressing

- Can only be used on serial connections

Workstation Configuration

When you set up SLIP for a remote connection, you must have a SLIP user account on the host machine and usually a batch file or script on the workstation to configure the session. When you use SLIP to log in to a remote machine, you must configure a terminal mode after login to the remote site so the script can enter each parameter for you. If you don't use a script, you will have to establish the connection and then open a terminal window to log in to the Remote Access Server (RAS) manually.

PPTP

Point-to-Point Tunneling Protocol (PPTP) is the Microsoft-created brother to PPP. PPTP is used to create virtual PPP connections across the Internet so two networks can use the Internet as their WAN link and still retain private network security. The beauty of PPTP is both its simplicity and its security.

Microsoft was proud enough of PPTP to submit it to the Internet Engineering Task Force (IETF) as an Internet standard. Cisco had also offered its opinion on the PPTP standard. Both firms' proposals were denied, and they are now attempting to combine efforts to get a common encrypted PPTP standard through the IETF, but there is currently no industry-wide standard.

To use PPTP, you set up a PPP session between the client and the server, typically over the Internet. Once the session is established, a second dial-up session is created. This second session tunnels through the existing PPP connection, creating a secure session. Using this method, the Internet can be used to create a secure session between the client side and the server. This type of connection is also called a Virtual Private Network, which is very affordable when compared to direct connections.

Advantages

- Lower-cost Internet WAN connection

- Secure connection

Disadvantages

- Not available on all types of servers

- Not a fully accepted standard

- More difficult to set up than PPP

- Tunneling can reduce throughput

F I G U R E 8.2: A PPTP implementation connecting two LANs together over the Internet

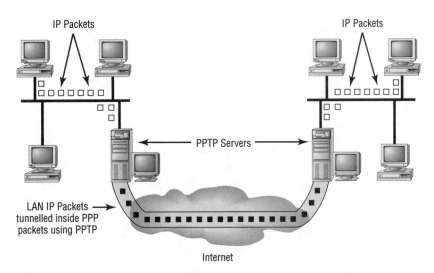

Workstation Configuration

There are two ways to implement PPTP. The first way is to set up a server to act as the gateway to the Internet and as the server that does all of the tunneling. The workstations will run normally, without any additional configuration. This method is normally used to connect whole networks together. Figure 8.2 (on the previous page) shows a network set up in this manner.

The second way to implement PPTP is to configure a single, remote workstation to connect to a corporate network over the Internet. The workstation is configured to connect to the Internet via an ISP, and the VPN client is configured with the address of the VPN Resource Access Server, as shown in Figure 8.3. PPTP is often used to connect remote workstations to corporate LANs when a Remote workstation must communicate with a corporate network over a dial-up PPP link through an ISP (and the link must be secure).

F I G U R E 8.3: Workstation connection to a corporate LAN over the Internet using PPTP

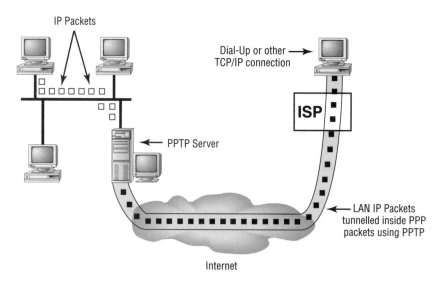

TIP Windows 98 and Windows NT 4 have this functionality included; Windows 95 must add it.

PSTN/POTS

Many phone company outsiders refer to the Public Switched Telephone Network (PSTN) as the Plain Old Telephone Service. This is the telephone wiring system that connects your home phone to phones in the rest of the world. Modems used over POTS are the most popular method of connecting remote users to local networks.

As its name indicates, PSTN is a public, switched phone system. This means that anyone can lease the use of the switch-governed network. While one or more wires are connected to your home and/or office, they are not always in use. In effect, your wiring and equipment is offline, or not part of the network. Yet you still have a reservation (your phone number) to join the network at almost any time.

The POTS system in your town is made up of a few standard components. The first is the wiring itself. Most POTS systems installed in your town use unshielded twisted pair (UTP) wire (discussed in detail in Chapter 1). The phone company runs a UTP cable (called the local loop) from your location (called the demarcation point, or demarc for short) to a phone company building called the central office. All of the pairs from all of the local loop cables that are distributed throughout a small regional area come together at a central point. This centralized point has a piece of equipment called a switch attached. On one side of the switch is the neighborhood wiring; on the other side of the switch are lines that may connect to another switch or to a local set of wiring. The number of lines on the other side of the switch depends on the amount of usage that particular exchange typically uses. Figure 8.4 illustrates a PSTN system that utilizes these components.

FIGURE 8.4: Simplified block diagram of a local PSTN (POTS) network

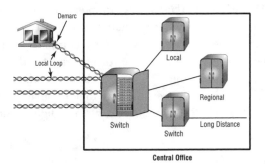

Advantages

- Inexpensive to set up
- Widely accessible
- No LAN cabling costs
- Worldwide connections available

Disadvantages

- Analog bandwidth limited by the FCC to 53K
- Aging infrastructure
- Only two wires used in some cases

ISDN

The Integrated Services Digital Network sends digital computer networking signals down UTP wiring, which is normally used for analog telephone communications. That is where the similarity with PSTN/POTS ends. Instead of carrying an analog (voice) signal like POTS, ISDN is set up for a digital (computer) signal. This is the source of several differences between ISDN and other remote connection methods, especially POTS.

A major difference between ISDN and POTS is how lines are powered. The phone company uses a battery to supply power to lines for POTS. This is referred to as a self-powered operation, but it isn't truly self-powered because the power comes from the phone system. However, the phone company customer does not need to supply any power to the line, and this differs greatly from the way ISDN works.

For ISDN communications, the phone company does not power the telephone lines; the customers' equipment must be powered separately. This is done with what is usually (and incorrectly) called an ISDN modem—the device that connects a computer or networking component to the ISDN line. The correct term for this device is actually ISDN terminal adapter. The reason the name ISDN modem is incorrect is that there is no conversion from digital signals to the analog signals that POTS uses (ISDN signals are already digital). Since the ISDN line

and the computer are both digital, there is no MODula
DEModulation (MODEM) involved. Terminal adapters are
ally referred to as ISDN modems because the term modem is so
easily recognizable.

The ISDN line has an interesting feature that is represented by the
word *integrated*—the first word of the acronym ISDN. The line is
integrated because a typical ISDN line is actually comprised of two
phone lines, which are one pair of copper wires. This makes it possible to use one section of the ISDN line for a voice call while the
second section can be used for data.

For a typical ISDN line, the bandwidth is divided into channels. The
data are carried on special bearer, or B, channels, each of which can
carry 64Kbps of data; a typical ISDN line has two B channels. A third
channel that is used for link management is known as the signal, or D,
channel. Also referred to as the data channel, the D channel only has
16K of bandwidth, which is less than today's typical modem.

In many cases, to maximize throughput, the two bearer channels, or
B lines, are combined into one data connection for a total bandwidth
of 128Kbps. This is known as *bonding*. This still leaves the data
channel, or D line, free for signaling purposes.

Advantages

- Moderately fast connection

- Higher bandwidth greatly increases remote access connection speed

- No conversion from digital to analog

- Higher bandwidth than POTS (bonding yields 128Kb bandwidth)

Disadvantages

- More expensive than POTS

- Specialized equipment required at phone company and at remote
  computer

- Distance limitations are greater than POTS

- Not all ISDN equipment can interconnect

NOTE Due to interfacing with phone company switches, not all ISDN equipment works together. This is because not all switches are from the same manufacturer. Therefore, terminal adapters (ISDN modems) must match the equipment at the phone company. Combine this necessity with a lack of ISDN-experienced personnel and ISDN installation horror stories become too commonly heard.

Exam Essentials

This objective is based on remote communication protocols. You will need to know about PPP, SLIP, ISDN, and POTS. The exam will specifically test for usage and definitions.

Know how to differentiate between PPP and SLIP. PPP is the more advanced remote access protocol of the two, with these features: multiple protocol support, compression, encryption, and dynamic IP management. SLIP has both Physical layer and Data Link layer specifications and requires much more setup and administration than PPP.

Know how to define PPTP and the conditions for which it would be useful. PPTP is a tunneling protocol that allows LANs to be extended to remote users or sites. The encrypted tunneling is performed over an unsecured larger network, such as the Internet.

Know how to differentiate between ISDN and POTS. ISDN is a digital remote access protocol that typically has a single D channel, two B channels, and 128K of bandwidth. POTS is the network of analog phone lines running to and in typical United States homes. The FCC currently limits analog data communications to 53K, and modems on the market can handle 56K in uncompressed transmissions.

Key Terms and Concepts

For the exam, you will need to understand the acronyms and terms—
and their definitions—that relate to remote access protocols and
modem types.

Bearer channel Two B channels typically make up an ISDN connection. The two 64K channels are typically bonded to provide
128K for data transfer.

Bonding Two or more separate communication channels are
linked together to make them logically appear as one higher bandwidth coonection.

Data channel The D channel is the communication control
channel for an ISDN connection.

ISDN (Integrated Services Digital Network) A digital method of
modems communicating remotely with networks and servers. A
single 16K D channel and two 64K B channels make up a typical
ISDN connection.

POTS (Plain Old Telephone Service) The telephone cabling that
is wired to most homes in the Unites States. Two or four wires may
be used in these pre-existing phone lines.

PPP (Point-to-Point Protocol) Used for remote access. Features
including multiple protocols, encryption, compression, and dynamic
IP assignment make this the most popular dial-up protocol.

PPTP (Point-to-Point Tunneling Protocol) Allows Microsoft
LANs to be extended to remote offices over the Internet through
encryption. The LAN communications are tunneled inside of the
encrypted packets, which are typically IP packets.

PSTN (Public Switched Telephone Network) Telecommunications
industry term for the Plain Old Telephone Service.

SLIP (Serial Line Internet Protocol) The oldest remote access protocol which, as such, does not support multiple mid-layer protocols,
encryption, compression, or dynamic IP assignment.

Sample Questions

1. What remote access protocol works over modems, allows for dynamic assignment of client IP addresses, and can transmit more than one protocol?

   A. IRQ

   B. PPP

   C. SLIP

   D. POTS

   E. I/O

   Answer: B—PPP allows multiple protocols and can dynamically assign IP addresses. (IRQs are communication links from hardware to computer CPUs. SLIP only allows one protocol (TCP/IP) and cannot dynamically assign IPs. POTS is a voice system for telephone service. I/O is the base memory address for programs in a computer.)

2. A typical ISDN line has two B channels and one D channel. How much bandwidth is there for data transfer?

   A. 16K

   B. 32K

   C. 64K

   D. 128K

   E. 256K

   Answer: D—By bonding two bearer channels, you get an effective bandwidth of 128K. (A single data channel is 16K but is used for signaling coordination. A single bearer channel yields 64K of bandwidth.)

Specify the following elements of dial-up networking:

- The modem configuration parameters that must be set, including serial port, IRQ, I/O address, and maximum port speed
- The requirements for a remote connection

When you configure a workstation for remote connections using dial-up networking methods, there are several items you must contend with. These items include the hardware configuration of the modem, and the software and hardware requirements of the connection itself. The Network+ exam will test your knowledge of these two elements of dial-up networking.

Critical Information

By now, you know about the software protocols used in remote communications, but you also need to understand the hardware and other settings for the modems used in dial-up networking connections. This objective requires knowledge of serial ports, IRQ addresses, I/O base memory addresses, and maximum port speeds.

Modem Configuration

Because most remote access situations involve dial-up connections, the Network+ exam will test you on the concepts you must know to configure a remote dial-up connection properly. Every remote asynchronous computer connection over analog telephone lines uses a modem of some sort because a computer's digital signals must be changed to analog signals in order to travel over telephone lines. Therefore, it is important that you understand modem configuration parameters—the requirements necessary to configure a remote workstation for remote access to a corporate network.

Serial Port

The two main issues with external modems concern the available serial ports and the types of Universal Asynchronous Receiver/Transmitter (UART) chip. With the large number of external serial expansion devices available, including modems, cameras, and printers, spare serial ports won't often be available, and you'll have to purchase an internal modem. The UART chip is responsible for managing serial communications. The type of chip determines the maximum port speed that that particular serial port can handle; there are two main types of chip: 85xx and 165xx. Serial ports that use the 165xx chip can communicate at a maximum speed 115,200Mbps. 85xx UARTS restrict communications to 9600bps.

IRQ

Interrupt Request Lines (IRQ) are special communication lines from a piece of hardware to a CPU. The hardware device uses these lines to signal the CPU that it needs attention from the processor. Every device needs to have its own IRQ line if it uses the ISA bus, regardless of whether or not a card takes up an actual expansion slot. The default assignments for an Intel-based PC are listed in Table 8.1

T A B L E 8.1: Default IRQ Assignments for the ISA Bus

IRQ	Default Assignment
0	System timer
1	Keyboard
2	Cascade to IRQ 9
3	COM 2 & 4
4	COM 1 & 3
5	LPT2
6	Floppy controller
7	LPT1

T A B L E 8.1: Default IRQ Assignments for the ISA Bus *(cont.)*

IRQ	Default Assignment
8	Real-time clock
9	Cascade to IRQ 2
10	Available
11	Available
12	Bus mouse port
13	Math coprocessor
14	Hard disk controller
15	Available

A few things need to be noted when you are connecting a modem to a PC. A modem uses a COM port, whether an internal modem is installed or an external modem is connected. The modem needs to be set to COM 1, 2, 3, or 4 to operate correctly. If two devices are set to the same COM port, neither one will function. Bear in mind that COM 1 and COM 3 share an IRQ, and COM 2 and COM 4 also share an IRQ. So you must be careful to configure a modem to use a COM port so that it doesn't share an IRQ with any other serial device that sends data to the processor in continuous streams (like a mouse or other serial input device). If your modem is set to COM 3 and your mouse is hooked to a serial port set to COM 1, neither device will function properly.

TIP To remember which IRQ goes with which port, notice that IRQ 3 is an odd number while COM 2 and COM 4 are even numbers. Odd goes with even. The same holds true for COM 1, COM 3, and IRQ 4— odd goes with even.

I/O Address

I/O addresses are base memory addresses that a processor uses to send data between itself and a device. Hardware devices interrupt a CPU via IRQs, and a CPU is basically a super number cruncher that utilizes memory. So if you assign a portion of memory to a device, the CPU can just access that memory section to send a message. Table 8.2 shows the common assignments for COM port to I/O addresses.

TABLE 8.2: COM Port to I/O Addresses

COM Port	IRQ Address	I/O Address
1	4	3F8-3FF
2	3	2F8-2FF
3	4	3E8-3EF
4	3	2E8-2EF

TIP You will be required to know COM ports and their associated IRQ ports and I/O addresses. If presented with a scenario, you should be able to notice conflicts between all three settings (COM ports, IRQ addresses, and I/O addresses).

Port Speed

The 85xx chips are UARTs that have 8-bit buffers that are limited to a maximum speed of 9600Bps and are typically found in PCs manufactured before 1986 (before IBM ATs). Since the IBM AT was released, computers have had the faster 164xx and 165xx UARTs. These chips use 16-bit buffers and transmit data at a maximum speed of 115,200Bps. Any modem faster than 9600Bps that is going to be connected to a PC for remote access requires that the PC use 165xx UARTs in order to get the maximum speed possible. Otherwise, the connection speed will be limited to the fastest output speed of the 85xx UART, or 9600Bps.

TIP Be sure to set the communication speed in the software configuration for both the modem and the operating system of your computer. They are in different places, and one is often overlooked.

Remote Configuration Requirements

Several software and hardware settings must be in place before you can connect via remote access. If any of the required settings is incorrect, the user will not be able to gain access. A remote user needs the following items:

- The ability to use a local workstation

- A properly configured modem that communicates with the OS

- An account on the Remote Access Server

- Client software on the local workstation to authenticate to the remote NOS

- Privileges to log in remotely to the RAS

- Privileges to navigate the remote network and to access resources

- Unrestricted login time

Exam Essentials

This objective is based on setting up a modem and configuring it for remote connectivity to a server or network.

Know how to configure the settings to get a modem to work on your computer. The I/O base memory address, IRQ address, COM port, serial port, and maximum port speed all need to be set. Be sure that the settings of the modem do not conflict with existing hardware in the computer. Study the text and tables in the Critical Information section for common configurations and other important information.

Know the requirements for a remote connection. A remote connection consists of many things. If you start at the top level of the OSI model on the workstation and work your way down, over, and back up to the server, you will not miss anything. For example, make sure that you have the proper communication software, such as PPP. Ensure that you have an account on the machine that you are dialing. Properly configure the modem. Match the modem type with the telephone connection type. Have a properly configured RAS server. And have a server account that has remote access privileges.

Key Terms and Concepts

You should know the acronyms and terms that relate to dial-up hardware.

I/O base memory address   A memory address below 1 megabyte that a device uses to exchange data with the processor.

IRQ (Interrupt Request Line)   Used by a hardware component to communicate with and request time from the CPU of a computer.

Modem   The MODulator DEModulator converts electrical signals from the computer into tones to be transmitted over telephone lines and converted back into electrical signals by another modem at the other end.

Port speed   The speed at which a computer can communicate over a serial or parallel connection.

RAS (Remote Access Server)   Hosts multiple remote connections from other workstations. The connections can be over the Internet or via dial-up modems.

Serial   A phyical connection port, or the means of computer communication where one bit is transferred after another. (This is the opposite of a parallel connection.)

UART(Universal Asynchronous Receiver/Transmitter)   Chips used to manage serial port communications on a computer.

Sample Questions

1. To what IRQ address should you set the internal modem if you have a bus mouse, two local printers, and an external image capture device on COM 3 of your Windows 9.*x* PC?

A. 1

B. 2

C. 3

D. 4

E. 5

Answer: C—IRQ 3, COM 2 and COM 4 are available for a modem.

2. What software configurations do you need to set for remote access?

A. A RAS-enabled account on the server

B. The I/O base memory address on the workstation

C. The IRQ settings on the workstation

D. The COM port settings on the workstation

E. An account that allows you to use the workstation

Answer: **All of the above**—remote connectivity is a complex setup with many steps.

TIP Do not forget that you need the correct accounts with remote access privileges as well as proper software configurations.

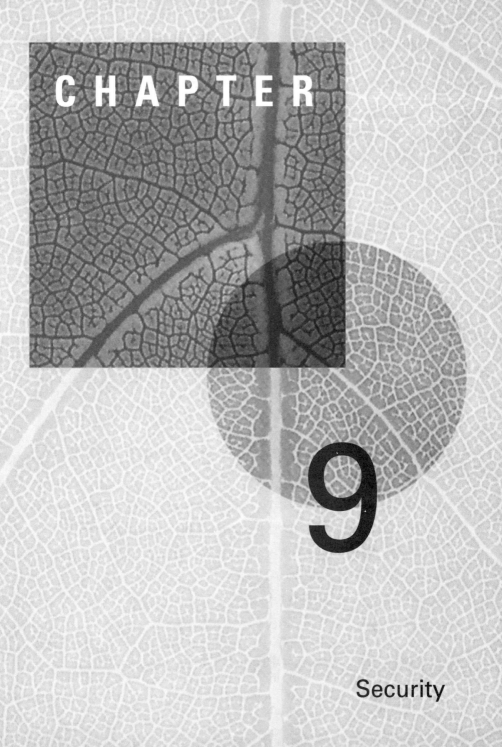

CHAPTER

9

Security

Network+ Exam Objective Covered in This Chapter:

▶ **Identify good practices to ensure network security, including:** *(pages 208 – 218)*

- Selection of a security model (user and share level)
- Standard password practices and procedures
- The need to employ data encryption to protect network data
- The use of a firewall

As you well know, your data is important, so leaving it unprotected is akin to leaving open the front door to your home when you go to work in the morning. Without a firewall to safeguard your data, you do not even have a proverbial front door to close. Inside your home, rooms can be locked as well; the same is true with user-level and share-level access. And as strong locks are important to your home, strong passwords are important to your network. Finally, encryption is used to encode data for a secure transmission. This chapter will take a look at these topics as they relate to the exam.

Identify good practices to ensure network security, including:

- Selection of a security model (user and share level)
- Standard password practices and procedures
- The need to employ data encryption to protect network data
- The use of a firewall

Network security is extremely important because your data could easily be taken or deleted. For this reason, the Network+ exam will test you on the various aspects of network security, including security model selection, standard password procedures, encryption, and the use of firewalls.

Critical Information

The Network+ exam requires you to be comfortable with the terms associated with sharing, encryption, firewalls, and passwords. You must understand the different types of each method and the issues associated with implementing them on your network.

Security Models

You can share files over a network by using one of two security models, either the user level or the share level. Each model differs in the locus of control for the security information. User-level protection provides a better degree of granularity, but share-level protection is a simpler method of setting security on network data.

User Level

User-level security has a centralized database of user accounts. All security information for a specific server (or possibly for an entire network) is stored in this centralized database. This security model implements access rights on individual files and directories. User accounts are allowed to read, write, change, and take ownership on these files. This is true whether the user is logged in to the machine at the console or is accessing the computer remotely over the network. User-level security is the preferred method of securing files. All users only know their own username and password and have no need to share them with others.

Share Level

With a share-level network, you will view data security from a broader standpoint. Access is controlled through a shared network folder, and a single password is used to access files and directories. The network support staff usually has a difficult time knowing who is accessing the files that share is providing. Share-level security is best used in combination with user-level security.

Password Management

Password management encompasses the processes and techniques used to ensure the security of passwords. Passwords, like any other portion of your network, will not take care of themselves. The best password ever thought of can still be cracked. Fortunately, most network operating systems include various tools to help administrators keep passwords secure. The following information should also assist in that process.

Lock-Outs

From time to time, and for whatever reason, passwords can be incorrectly entered. After several unsuccessful attempts to access an account with an incorrect password, the account will likely become locked. (The standard is to allow three login attempts before the account is locked.) The user is then prevented from logging in, even if the correct password is finally entered. At that point, the user usually needs to get their password reset by the network support staff. When the password is reset, the administrator or help desk member should require the user to change their password at the next login. Another option is to have the account automatically unlock after a certain period of time.

Password Expiration

Passwords, even the best ones, do not remain as secure over time. It is more likely that someone will eventually be able to crack a password if it never changes. Therefore, most companies abide by a standard where certain user passwords expire every 30 days. When that occurs, users will need to reset their passwords. Make sure that they must first log in to the network before they are allowed to change a password, and limit the number of times or days a user can skip changing their password at login. (When a password has expired, some systems give the user a few grace logins; the operating system allows the user to change their password at a more convenient time.)

Unique Passwords and Histories

A password that has never been used before is referred to as a unique password. Unique passwords reduce the chances of break-ins. Keeping a password history ensures that unique passwords are used. A history is a confidential electronic record of a user's past several passwords. When a user attempts to reuse any of the former passwords stored in their password history, the password change fails. The operating system then requests another password change, and a password that has never been used by the user must be entered.

Minimum Length

A short password may be more easily cracked. There are only so many combinations of three characters, for instance, and a much higher combination of eight or 10 characters. It is important for password security, therefore, that you set a specific number of characters as a minimum password length. A limit of at least eight characters is a good starting point for your users. (The upper limit is based on the capabilities of your particular operating system, as well as your users' ability to memorize them.) But remember that passwords that are too long are more likely to be forgotten.

Weak Passwords

Users should be discouraged from using weak, easily cracked passwords. Weak passwords include a user's proper name, pet's name, spouse's name, children's names, company's name, occupation, favorite color, license plate number, birth date, anniversary date, and username. Words from a dictionary, including the words *password* and *server* and any text from the face of a user's PC or monitor, should also be avoided. But it is acceptable to combine any of the preceding items with leading or trailing numbers, or any of the preceding terms may be typed backwards.

Strong Passwords

A strong password is one that is difficult to crack. Strong passwords should be used for all network user accounts to ensure network security. The password should be eight characters in length or longer, and a combination of numbers, letters, and special characters should be used. Additionally, a strong password should not include any word on the preceding list of weak passwords. And although they are often complex, strong passwords do not have to be difficult to remember; you can make them easily remembered by using a mnemonic name (2easy4u!, e.g.).

Locking Workstations

Passwords are pointless if they are not used in every situation. If a user goes to take a break, they should lock their workstation with a password. This usually means setting a password-protected screen saver or a security utility so the workstation is unusable until the correct password is entered. Network administrators should especially be sure to always lock their machines. (What you think will be just a quick trip to the water fountain can often end up being a half-hour discussion *at* the water fountain, leaving your machine vulnerable the entire time.)

Data Encryption

Encryption is the process of encoding data before transmission across an insecure medium. It is used in internal communication, external communication, and storage. Password files and data on servers are important data that must be safeguarded. The network operating system, in some cases, can automatically encrypt usernames and password databases. The authentication process for a program or user encodes transmissions with the server; this ensures that the password stays secure during transmission. Data is often encrypted on intranets, and on extranets for remote users.

Intranets

Computers within the same company can send encrypted data between themselves. E-mail servers can send encrypted messages between each other in the same site; this ensures data confidentiality. When a company connects to the Internet, it puts up a firewall for protection from outside entities.

Extranets and Remote Users

Virtual Private Networks (VPNs) are secure networks that are constructed over the Internet and enable separate office locations to appear as if they are in the same network. Separate locations outside of a secure internal network are tied in to the main network and called extranets. Servers, databases, and printers can all be shared on an extranet. The VPN connection is encrypted to keep prying eyes from looking at the data as it goes across the public wires of the Internet. Individual remote users also work away from a main network (from home or on the road) and desire to be able to access company resources; encryption of data for transmission across the Internet also make this possible.

Public and Private Keys

Public keys and private keys enable data encryption and decryption. Private keys are known as symmetrical keys. Both senders and receivers have the same key; a single key is used to encrypt and decrypt all messages going in both directions. Public key technology, or a Diffie-Hellman algorithm, uses two keys to facilitate communication—a public key and a private key. Public keys encrypt messages being sent, and private keys decrypt messages being received.

Firewalls

Firewalls are network devices, often combinations of hardware and software, that prevent unauthorized access to your LAN from the Internet; they may also prevent access to the Internet from your LAN. Network+ certification does not provide you with all of the resources and understanding needed to design, install, and manage a firewall. However, this section should help you to work more knowledgeably with existing firewalls. After the exam, you might also work as part of a team to install or upgrade your company's firewall solution. (Remember that firewalls can operate on all three major networking operating systems.)

Demilitarized Zones

Web servers, FTP servers, and mail relay servers receive the highest usage from people outside of your network. Hackers also go after those servers first. A standard setup has three network cards coming off of a firewall. The first goes to the outside world. The second goes to these servers; this area is called a demilitarized zone (DMZ) because it is not on either the public side of the firewall (the Internet) or the private side (directly on your LAN). The third network card connects your intranet. Notice the three separate connections to the firewall in Figure 9.1 on the next page.

Protocol Switching

TCP/IP is the protocol used on the Internet. Therefore, many external attacks will be based on this protocol stack. The Ping of Death and SYN floods both use IP packets. One way to protect your intranet is to switch protocols (to a non-TCP/IP protocol and back again) inside your firewall. The IP-based attack aimed at your development server will never be successful if you are using IPX inside. A second approach is to switch from IP to IPX in a dead zone, and then switch back to IP once inside your network.

FIGURE 9.1: Firewall with a DMZ

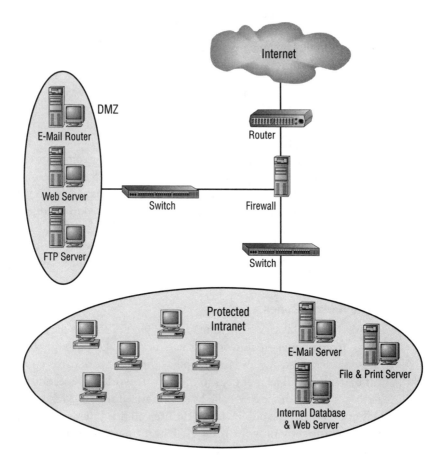

Access Control Lists

The first form of defense everyone should have against outside attacks is access control lists (ACLs). These lists reside on your routers, deciding what machines can use the router and in what direction. ACLs have been around for years and are implemented separate from a firewall. These lists prevent people from Network B from coming into Network A, as shown in Figure 9.2.

F I G U R E 9.2: Two networks with an ACL router

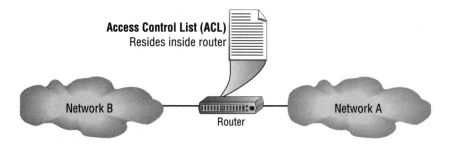

Note that people in Network A pass through the router into Network B. IP spoofing can still occur, and someone in Network B can pretend to be in Network A.

Dynamic State List Servers

A dynamic state list resides on a firewall. This list changes as communication sessions are added and deleted. A computer in Network A can request a Telnet session with a server in Network B, for example. The firewall between the two then keeps a log of the communication packets that are sent each way, and only the computers that are in a current communication session initiated by a station in Network A are allowed to send information into Network A through the firewall. Notice that the wily hacker in Figure 9.3 (on the next page) attempts to insert a packet into the communication stream but fails. This is because the packet doesn't have the right packet number. The firewall was waiting for a specific order of packets, but the hacker's packet is out of sequence.

Proxy Servers

Proxy servers act on behalf of network clients to completely separate packets from internal and external hosts. A message is sent from an internal client out to a server on the Internet, for example. When the packet arrives at the proxy server, it stops the packet and breaks it down and handles it by using an application on the proxy server. That application then creates a new packet requesting information from the external server. Figure 9.4 (also on the next page) illustrates this process.

FIGURE 9.3: Hacker denied by dynamic state list

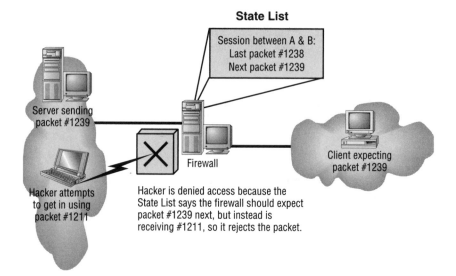

State List

Session between A & B:
Last packet #1238
Next packet #1239

Server sending
packet #1239

Firewall

Client expecting
packet #1239

Hacker attempts
to get in using
packet #1211

Hacker is denied access because the
State List says the firewall should expect
packet #1239 next, but instead is
receiving #1211, so it rejects the packet.

FIGURE 9.4: Packet going to a proxy

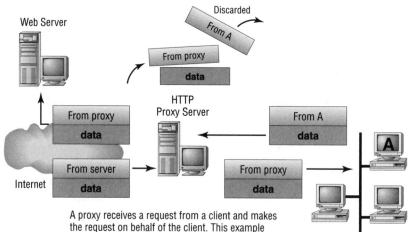

Web Server

Discarded
From A

From proxy
data

HTTP
Proxy Server

From proxy
data

From A
data

From server
data

From proxy
data

Internet

A

A proxy receives a request from a client and makes
the request on behalf of the client. This example
shows an HTTP proxy server.

Exam Essentials

The Network+ exam will test you on the terms and procedures for selecting proper technologies and passwords for optimum networking security.

Know how to select a security model.   User-level security allows you to set different access levels for each user. Share-level access assigns one password for the share.

Know how to select a strong password.   Strong passwords consist of alphanumeric and special characters, are at least eight characters long, and are changed at least every 30 days.

Know how to differentiate between types of firewalls.   Access is controlled in three main ways: access control lists, dynamic state inspection, and by proxy. ACLs are non-changing lists of authorized hosts. Dynamic state lists ensure that sessions are not hijacked. Proxies recreate the packet with a different Network (or higher) layer address.

Key Terms and Concepts

You will need to know the acronyms and terms that relate to network security. Different types and common terms are listed below.

ACL (access control list)   A flat text file on a router that lists which addresses can go where; precursor of the modern-day firewall.

Dynamic state list server   A type of firewall that manages packet sequence and origin to reduce the chance of hackers hijacking communication sessions.

Firewall   Protects internal networks from external networks, such as the Internet; manages access from one network to another.

Password   A secret combination of characters and letters that, in conjunction with a username, allows a specific user access to a network and its resources.

Proxy server   A firewall that recreates the packets and services of the communication that is trying to get through.

Share access   A shared network folder with only a single password.

User access   Usernames and passwords give different users different levels of access.

Sample Questions

1. If you have five users in a college dormitory sharing a printer with minimal security requirements, what access level would you assign?

   A. User level

   B. Share level

   C. Proxy

   D. Access control list

   E. Dynamic state list

   Answer: B—Share access has a single password for everyone to know and use to access resources. (User level has separate usernames and passwords and is more than a minimal security requirement. Proxies, ACLs, and dynamic state lists are types of firewalls for high security situations.)

2. Public key encryption is based on what technology?

   A. Single use codes

   B. Secret multiple use codes

   C. Prime number algorithms

   D. Transposition

   E. DES

   Answer: C—Prime number algorithms are used in public and private keys. (Single use codes were used in the military in the past. A secret code, or private key, requires that you somehow transmit the key to share. Transposition is the simplest encryption and is often used by children in decoder rings. DES encryption is a specific U.S. government implementation of a private key system.)

CHAPTER

10

Implementing the Installation
of the Network

Network+ Exam Objectives Covered in This Chapter:

▶ **Demonstrate awareness that administrative and test accounts, passwords, IP addresses, IP configurations, relevant SOPs, etc., must be obtained prior to network implementation.** *(pages 221 – 228)*

▶ **Explain the impact of environmental factors on computer networks. Given a network installation scenario, identify unexpected or atypical conditions that could either cause problems for the network or signify that a problem condition already exists, including:** *(pages 229 – 236)*
- Room conditions (e.g., humidity, heat, etc.)
- The placement of building contents and personal effects (e.g., space heaters, TVs, radios, etc.)
- Computer equipment
- Error messages

▶ **Recognize visually, or by description, common peripheral ports, external SCSI (especially DB-25 connectors), and common network componentry, including:** *(pages 236 – 245)*
- Print servers
- Peripherals
- Hubs
- Routers
- Brouters
- Bridges
- Patch panels

▶ **Given an installation scenario, demonstrate awareness of the following compatibility and cabling issues:** *(pages 246 – 250)*
- The consequences of trying to install an analog modem in a digital jack
- That the uses of RJ-45 connectors may differ greatly depending on the cabling
- That patch cables contribute to the overall length of the cabling segment

Anetwork installation has many parts and is quite complex. As you prepare for your installation, the best thing to do is to devote a few days to planning everything out. If you are merely adding additional workstations, then just implement your standard operating procedures (SOPs). If you need to implement an entire network, you may have to create a detailed layout of the network, come up with the SOPs and network documentation, create implementation time schedules, and just generally plan and research every aspect of the network implementation.

The Network+ exam will test your awareness of planning requirements, visual appearance of equipment, and computability issues. Therefore, this chapter will discuss all of these requirements, including documentation.

Demonstrate awareness that administrative and test accounts, passwords, IP addresses, IP configurations, relevant SOPs, etc., must be obtained prior to network implementation.

This chapter will first look at the administrative and test accounts and their passwords, IP addresses, and procedures needed to install a network. This is standard information that is needed for any operating system. Whenever you are implementing a new network (or upgrading an old one), you must have obtained all of the information you will need before beginning the installation. If you don't, you may run into problems during the installation and have to start over.

Critical Information

A standard operating procedure is a set of documentation that dictates exactly how the administration of the network is done. SOPs will save you time and headaches during a network installation. If everyone involved with the project is working out of the same playbook, then installations will go much more smoothly.

Administrative and Test Accounts

Because an account without limitations is a disaster waiting to happen, the wise person uses test accounts to confirm the basic functionality that conforms to the needs of local users. This also limits the possibility that the administrator's account is overlooking a security challenge that regular users are facing. Service accounts, on the other hand, are used to give outside network maintenance personnel the ability to perform administrator-level functions on your network. This may be necessary when you have a problem that you can't solve and must call in outside personnel. Or you may have these outside personnel install some new network software that you haven't got time to install. A naming conventions document (part of the SOPs) should be created that should also specify the names for these accounts and how limited their security rights should be.

Passwords

Along with the user accounts, you should have gotten the users passwords prior to implementing the network. This is almost self-explanatory because, without the correct password, you will not be able to log on to the system as that user. If you are the person giving out the password, you may want to change it after the installation or upgrade has been performed so network security is not compromised.

IP Addresses and Configurations

To reduce training and operational expenses, a great number of companies are standardizing on TCP/IP. All network addresses, including TCP/IP addresses, must be obtained before performing a network implementation. This factor introduces its own set of considerations. For instance, each IP address must be unique, and just guessing at one is bound to create havoc. Clearly, you need a well-documented IP address and associated parameters, such as where the IP address comes from. Your SOPs should tell you how network addresses should be formatted and how they are distributed.

In addition to understanding how to find an IP address for the workstation you are installing, you need to know other configurations. These additional configurations include the addresses of your DNS server, WINS server, DHCP server, default gateway, and subnet mask, and they all need to be at hand before you start working on the network.

Relevant SOPs

Almost every company has standard operating procedures. These procedures outline diverse company operations and explain how they are performed. Typically, these procedures are written down in the company's procedures manual.

There are many types of SOPs, covering everything from sick day policies to how long employees get for lunch. The SOPs that are pertinent to the exam are those that dictate how networks function and are used. When doing networking administration, you will need to research documentation that outlines company policies that include the following issues.

- Internet access

- Printing

- Storage allocation

- E-mail usage

- User administration

The above items comprise just a short list of networking considerations, each of which can affect how a network is installed and used.

These items, along with several others, make up the network SOPs. The following list represents some of the most common network SOPs.

- Naming conventions

- Protocol standards

- Workstation configuration

- Network device placement

Naming Conventions

Every network entity should be given a name that is unique on the entire network. A naming conventions document is one type of SOP that specifies details about how network entities are named, and it is governed by the guidelines of the directory service being used. The following list includes some topics commonly included in a naming conventions document, and they are each detailed after the list.

- Server naming

- Printer naming

- User accounts

NOTE Currently, you have three different directory services possibilities to contend with—NTDS, NDS, and DNS. Remember to use the formatting of these directory services when creating computer names. (Directory services are covered in Chapter 1.)

Server Naming

Users access various resources within a network with server names. Finding a naming convention for servers isn't as difficult as finding one for users, so getting a unique name isn't usually a problem. The issue that usually comes up is exactly how to name a server—based on location or function? The naming conventions document would specify which method to use or might call for a combination of the two.

Printer Naming

There are still more naming conventions to be considered when looking at company policies. Just as it is important to name servers and users, you must also give logical names to your printers so they can be referenced easily. A couple of examples of the logic behind naming printers will give you some ideas. At some sites, printer function, location, or both are what determine printer names. If, for example, a dot matrix printer is used to print multiple-part forms, it might be called Forms. With more than one forms printer, you may need to use two-word names, such as Forms-Ship and Forms-Finance. High-quality printers may be named Laser, or something like Laser-Legal can be used for a printer that is always loaded with legal-size paper.

User Accounts

Generally speaking, the simplest username may be the user's first name. This usually works well in a company with only a few users, and it fits the often-found informality of a small office. This is a fairly insecure method, however, and won't work well in a larger organization. It also won't work if the firm has two or more people with the same first name. Additionally, hackers can easily guess any user's username and use it to gain access.

The user naming convention generally should allow people to have their own unique user IDs. The convention should ensure that there are no duplicates. Larger firms typically use a first initial followed by part or the entire last name as a standard. Consider the treatment of someone named Jose L. Sanchez, for example. Jose's full name, Jose L. Sanchez, is rather long. It does fit within the naming parameters of NT4, but it's a lot to type when logging in. Therefore, when creating a username for Jose, an SOP may call for the first initial of the first name followed by some or all of the last name. In this example, JSanchez is a short yet unique login name.

TIP A common standard is to make a login name eight characters or less. This is mainly because older network operating systems are sometimes limited to eight character usernames.

Prior to Network Configuration

Determining the current condition of a network is an initial step in networking. Collecting information best begins this process; it's better to have the information beforehand than to have to go back and look for it later. Spending 15 minutes reading documentation before doing an install or upgrade can save you hours of labor later in the process.

Exam Essentials

This objective is based on preparing the network administrator for an installation.

Know how to gather administrative and test accounts and passwords. Before you begin work on a workstation or network, obtain the needed user test accounts and passwords. These can be obtained from the network administrator or the workstation's user, typically.

Know how to gather IP configuration information before network installs. The IP addresses of all workstations, servers, printers, routers, gateways, as well as their associated subnet masks, need to be recorded and accessible ahead of time. You also need to determine the IP addresses of your default router, DNS server, WINS server, and proxy server at that time.

Know how to check and implement SOPs. Every company has standard operating procedures, and you should be familiar with your SOPs before installing equipment or making any changes. Make sure you use proper naming conventions for equipment and accounts.

Key Terms and Concepts

You should know the acronyms and terms that relate to network planning and installation.

Administration account   Used to install equipment and software and have network or workstation management privileges.

Printer Hardware device that produces hard copy, usually paper, versions of electronic documents. Print jobs are sent from a user's workstation to a print server, which manages the job and sends the text file to the printer.

Server Software and hardware devices that provide services to a user's request. Proxy servers provide firewall services, and print servers provide print services, for example.

SOP (standard operating procedure) A company's specific methods for implementing network administration and other operations; usually in written form.

Test account A generic user account that is used to check installs.

User account Authenticates users and then provides them with access to a network.

Sample Questions

1. What account(s) do you need in order to install a network?

   A. Your manager's account

   B. Generic user account

   C. Administrator account

   D. Auditor account

   E. Your account

   Answers: B, C—A test account is needed to ensure user operation, and an administrator account is needed to install hardware and software. (Do not use your boss's account. An auditor's account is used for legal or security audits; no actual work should ever be done with an auditor's account. Your account should not have administrative capabilities, because you might inadvertently make a mistake in your daily operations while logged in as yourself.)

2. For which of the following do you need IP addresses in order to properly set up TCP/IP on a workstation?

   A. Another workstation

   B. DNS server

   C. All routers

   D. WINS server

   E. Workstation being worked on

   F. Web server

   G. Subnet mask

   H. Default gateway

   Answers: B, D, E, G, H—Your DNS server is required to resolve domain names to IP addresses. Your WINS server resolves netBIOS names to IP addresses. The IP address of your workstation is needed if a DHCP server is not used. The workstation subnet mask is needed to determine whether packets should be sent to the default router. And the default gateway routes packets to the appropriate networks and routers. (Another workstation's IP address is not needed. The IP addresses of all routers are not needed. Your Web server IP address is not needed when configuring IP on a workstation.)

3. What is the name of your list of rules, regulations, and methods for running your network?

   A. SOP

   B. DNS

   C. WINS

   D. DHCP

   Answer: A—Standard operating procedures are the rules and methods used to install and manage your network. (DNS servers resolve domain names to IP addresses. WINS servers resolve netBIOS names to IP addresses. DHCP servers automatically assign IP addresses to workstations.)

Explain the impact of environmental factors on computer networks. Given a network installation scenario, identify unexpected or atypical conditions that could either cause problems for the network or signify that a problem condition already exists, including:

- Room conditions (e.g., humidity, heat, etc.)
- The placement of building contents and personal effects (e.g., space heaters, TVs, radios, etc.)
- Computer equipment
- Error messages

An often-overlooked aspect of a network implementation is the environmental conditions in which the network equipment will be operating. The environment can be harsh and contribute to early equipment failure or strange problems. This objective covers the basic environmental conditions that can affect network equipment and errors that can result from an improper environment.

Critical Information

Network equipment is very susceptible to climate variations. Computers are a lot like human beings in that respect. They don't operate at their best unless they are operating in a climate that is "comfortable" for them. Too much humidity or heat can cause premature failure. For this reason, it is important to be mindful of the environment that your network hardware is operating in. The Network+

exam will test you on the various environmental conditions and their impact on your equipment.

Room Conditions

Network devices (including computers and servers) are very sensitive to temperature extremes; extreme hot and cold can cause computers to fail prematurely. The room temperature for network devices should be roughly the same as that for human beings. The temperature and humidity should be kept consistent at 60–65° and around 30% relative humidity. Keeping these values constant can prove to be a challenge because every computer constantly produces heat.

NOTE Computer rooms are much cooler (60-65°F) than the equipment stored in them. This is because the computer equipment generates a lot of heat that needs to be counteracted by a cool room.

Larger companies have special rooms for network equipment. Raised flooring protects the equipment from flooding and provides room for cabling, and special air conditioners and humidifiers help keep the room's climate consistent. The equipment also needs to be set up to automatically page the building maintenance and network management staff when the temperature or humidity fluctuates outside of an acceptable norm. If no one works in the server room, a physical walk-through is required at least four times a day.

Placement of Building Contents and Personal Effects

Never prioritize personal convenience over computer stability. For instance, space heaters should not be placed near computer terminals under desks. Personal televisions should not be situated near monitors, and radios should be kept away from computer equipment. This is because excessive heat, electromagnetic interference (EMI), radio frequency interference (RFI), and electrostatic discharge (ESD) may ruin or corrupt your computer equipment.

Electromagnetic Interference Problems

Electromagnetic interference is caused by electrical devices that create magnetic waves. These magnetic waves can disrupt nearby electronic devices that they reach and are a challenge to find because they are unseen. Sources of this type of pollution are typically motors and transformers. Motors are found in many places, including air conditioners, heaters, other common appliances, and even elevators. As has been noted in previous chapters, a familiar EMI scenario arises when network cable is run though an elevator shaft, causing EMI to travel in the cable across the floors of the building in conjunction with the movement of the elevator.

Transformers are found inside every fluorescent light. Running cable through ceilings containing a whole bank of these transformers can flood network cabling with EMI. This can be very challenging to discover because the EMI only shows up when the lights are on.

To locate EMI, follow a cable with an inexpensive compass and look for strong, odd needle movement. Move around to find the direction of the erratic behavior. This way, you can track an EMI source that is hiding behind a physical barrier, such as a wall.

Radio Frequency Interference Problems

Radio frequency interference occurs when a device sends out radio waves that interfere with other devices. Unlike its cousin, EMI, RFI operates at a higher frequency that is too fast for a simple compass to respond to. Therefore, without very specialized and expensive test equipment, logic is the best tool to use against RFI.

A battle against RFI begins by looking for its sources, including television and radio transmitters, cellular phones, and two-way radios. Each of these devices transmits a specific radio frequency. Once you have located these RFI sources, you can win the battle against RFI by moving either the source or the affected equipment.

The only way to protect against both EMI and RFI is to use shielded network cables. Shielded cable, as is used in shielded twisted pair (STP) and coaxial cable, can reduce the effects of both EMI and RFI.

You can also use fiber optic cable, which is immune to EMI and RFI, throughout your entire network.

Electrostatic Discharge Problems

Another problem that can wreak havoc with a network (and any electronic component, for that matter) is electrostatic discharge. Everyone has experienced ESD. ESD happens when two or more items with dissimilar static electrical charges are brought together. Nature doesn't like things to be unequal, so static electrical charges will jump from an item with more electrons to another that has fewer electrons in order to equalize electron-distribution. This jump can be seen as an electrical spark and is called an electrostatic discharge. The high number of electrons from an ESD moving through delicate circuit junctions of silicon chips can destroy these connections and render the chips useless.

Computer Equipment Placement

Beware of placing dissimilar computer equipment next to each other. Normally, you will not have problems placing a Unix box next to a NetWare box or a Windows NT box. However, the issue is not with software but with hardware. Additional computers generate a large increase in temperature, and this can cause serious problems if your air conditioner cannot handle the increased load.

Error Messages

In addition to SOPs and environmental issues, you should check for error messages on servers before installing or upgrading your network. Errors on servers can indicate the general well-being of a network.

Errors can be found by studying log files, which are records of a station's every action. Servers create logs such as those seen in the Windows NT Event Viewer or the NetWare ABEND.LOG to record when problems occur. What does a log file contain? That depends on how the engineer has set up the server. It is possible to create logs with varying degrees of detail. For example, it is possible to log multiple details of print jobs—printed by whom, how many pages, on what printer, and at what time. Is that too much detail? That depends on the needs and policies of the company.

The location of log files varies depending on the network operating system in use and what tools are available. Sometimes you can use standard data manipulation tools to organize the information the log file is giving you. For example, it is possible to export log files in a comma-delimited format for import into a database or spreadsheet. Instant access to logs is also available with any modern NOS. For example, in NT4, the Event Viewer can be found under Start ➤ Programs ➤ Administrative Tools on the Windows NT server console. Figure 10.1 displays a sample log file from the Windows NT Event Viewer.

F I G U R E 10.1: A sample log file

Date	Time	Source	Category	Event	User	Computer
1/7/99	12:53:09 PM	BROWSER	None	8015	N/A	S1
1/7/99	11:39:17 AM	BROWSER	None	8033	N/A	S1
1/7/99	11:39:17 AM	BROWSER	None	8033	N/A	S1
1/7/99	11:39:17 AM	BROWSER	None	8033	N/A	S1
1/7/99	11:37:14 AM	symc810	None	9	N/A	S1
1/7/99	11:36:50 AM	symc810	None	9	N/A	S1
1/7/99	11:36:05 AM	symc810	None	9	N/A	S1
1/7/99	11:35:21 AM	symc810	None	9	N/A	S1
1/7/99	11:33:15 AM	Disk	None	7	N/A	S1
1/7/99	11:33:11 AM	Disk	None	7	N/A	S1
1/7/99	11:33:07 AM	Disk	None	7	N/A	S1
1/7/99	11:33:04 AM	Disk	None	7	N/A	S1
1/7/99	11:33:00 AM	Disk	None	7	N/A	S1
1/7/99	11:32:56 AM	Disk	None	7	N/A	S1
1/7/99	11:32:52 AM	Disk	None	7	N/A	S1
1/7/99	11:32:48 AM	Disk	None	7	N/A	S1
1/7/99	11:32:44 AM	Disk	None	7	N/A	S1
1/7/99	11:32:40 AM	Disk	None	7	N/A	S1
1/6/99	7:04:41 PM	BROWSER	None	8015	N/A	S1
1/6/99	7:04:41 PM	BROWSER	None	8015	N/A	S1
1/6/99	7:02:59 PM	EventLog	None	6005	N/A	S1
1/6/99	7:04:41 PM	BROWSER	None	8015	N/A	S1
1/6/99	6:57:00 PM	Service Control M	None	7000	N/A	S1
1/6/99	6:56:54 PM	EventLog	None	6005	N/A	S1
1/6/99	6:57:00 PM	E100B	None	5007	N/A	S1
1/6/99	6:00:37 PM	Service Control M	None	7000	N/A	S1
1/6/99	6:00:32 PM	EventLog	None	6005	N/A	S1
1/6/99	6:00:37 PM	E100B	None	5007	N/A	S1

Event Viewer - System Log on \\S1

Log View Options Help

Exam Essentials

This objective requires knowledge of environmental issues that can cause networking problems or be indicators of those problems.

Know how to select and configure a room for network equipment. All rooms need to be locked, restricted, and monitored. Equipment rooms need to be on a separate air conditioning and heating system that is monitored by both machine and personnel. Plan for the fact that additional equipment will increase the load on the cooling system.

Know how to position personal comfort devices. Keep radios, TVs, space heaters, message magnets, and similar devices away from computer equipment. These devices may produce EMI and RFI, which are invisible killers of network equipment.

Know how to track problems through messages the computer gives you. Read error messages that appear on the screen, and note any errors that appear. Also look in log files for records of errors and the details of past problems.

Key Terms and Concepts

You need to be familiar with the acronyms and terms that relate to network installation and environmental influences.

Computer room Servers are secured in a locked, monitored, dedicated, specially cooled room.

EMI (electromagnetic interference) Occurs when electrical equipment generates a magnetic field that disrupts the electrical operations or communications of another device.

ESD (electrostatic discharge) Static electrical charges build up and are released, potentially damaging the computer equipment in the vicinity of the discharge.

RFI (radio frequency interference)   Occurs when electrical equipment sends out radio waves that disrupt the electrical operations or communications of another device.

Wiring closet   Network infrastructure devices and wiring are secured in locked, monitored, dedicated, specially cooled closets.

Sample Questions

1. Which of the following are the best places to check for error records?

   A. Wiring closet

   B. EMI

   C. Log files

   D. RFI

   E. Error messages on screen

   Answer: C, E—Log files and on-screen error messages are the best places to look for records of errors. (A wiring closet is where equipment is stored. EMI and RFI are types of interference.)

2. What can cause disruptions of electrical devices via radio waves?

   A. DNS

   B. EMI

   C. SOP

   D. ESD

   E. RFI

   Answer: E—Radio frequency interference causes disruptions of electrical devices via radio waves. (DNS provides domain names for IP address resolution. EMI is interference caused by magnetic waves. SOPs are the procedures network administrators follow. ESD is an electrical charge that can damage equipment.)

3. What equipment should you use near computer equipment?

A. Central heating/cooling

B. Portable heater

C. Radio

D. Television

E. Raised floor

Answer: A, E—Centralized heating and cooling systems need to be installed and monitored. A raised floor adds ventilation space and minimizes the effects of floods. (A portable heater can overheat or adversely affect the humidity of equipment. Radios and televisions can generate RFI and EMI.)

Recognize visually, or by description, common peripheral ports, external SCSI (especially DB-25 connectors), and common network componentry, including:

- Print servers
- Peripherals
- Hubs
- Routers
- Brouters
- Bridges
- Patch panels

This objective requires that you know some of the common hardware devices found on a network. It is important that you have a basic understanding of what these components are, what they do, and their general appearance so you will recognize them when you are out in the field.

Critical Information

There are many devices on a network. The exam asks that you be able to identify, describe, and differentiate between the specific pieces of hardware often found on a network. You will see these devices when working on a network, so it is important that you know what they are and how they work.

Print Servers

In a typical production network, it is common to find servers with specialized duties. Specialized servers perform such duties as Internet proxy, SQL data inquiries, and remote access (via direct dial or the Internet). Today, the most common type of specialized server is the print server, which is the centralized device that facilitates network print services. It controls and manages all network printers. The print server can be hardware, software, or a combination of both. Some print servers are actually built into network printer network interfaces (like the HP JetDirect network interface cards).

Peripheral Ports

Network cabling and external devices connect via ports. When connecting or troubleshooting a computer, you will need to be able to identify each of its ports and plug the appropriate cables into their corresponding connectors. These ports are primarily on the back of computers, but connectors can also be built onto the back of the motherboard or can be part of an expansion card. This section will discuss four of the most popular data connectors, including BNC, RJ-series, IBM Data Connector, and SCSI connectors.

BNC Connector

The BNC connector is used to lock in a coaxial cable to a device. The channel and notch configuration provides a locking mechanism and prevents the cable from becoming disconnected. It is a twist-lock mechanism, which means that you must push the cable's connector onto the connector on the NIC and then twist the connector on the cable to lock it in place.

BNC connectors are most commonly used for 10Base2 Ethernet and ARCNet, but they can also be used on any network that uses coaxial cable. Figure 10.2 shows a BNC connector.

F I G U R E 10.2: A sample BNC connector

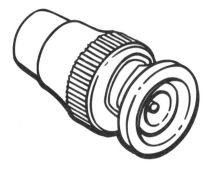

RJ Connectors

As has been discussed in a previous chapter, registered jack connectors are used to attach cables to telephones or computer network ports. The little clip connector that connects most phones to a wall jack phones is an RJ-11 connector. RJ-45 connectors, on the other hand, are most commonly found on both 10BaseT and Token Ring networks, but they can be found on any network that uses four-pair UTP cable. The physical difference between the RJ-11s and RJ-45s is that the RJ-11 is smaller than an RJ-45, and the RJ-11 uses four (or six) wires while the RJ-45 has eight connections housed in its case. Figure 10.3 shows an RJ-45 connector that might be used in 10BaseT Ethernet.

F I G U R E 10.3: A typical RJ-45 connector

IBM Data Connector

IBM Data Connectors are unique in many ways. They aren't as universal as the other types of network connectors, and there aren't male and female connector types; one connector is both male and female. Any two connectors can connect, as shown in Figure 10.4. But like the RJ-series connectors, the IBM Data Connector uses a tab to hold the connectors together. This connector is most commonly used with IBM's Token Ring technology and Type 1 or Type 2 STP cable.

F I G U R E 10.4: An IBM Data Connector

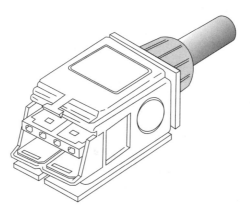

SCSI

Small Computer System Interface (SCSI) connectors come in one of three styles: DB-25, Centronics-50, and a special, high-density 68-pin connector. The DB-25 female is commonly found on the back of older Macintosh computers, allowing an external disk drive to be connected. However, these connectors haven't experienced widespread use in the PC world. Figure 10.5 (on the next page) shows a sample DB-25 female connector.

More commonplace is the Centronics-50 interface, which is considered to be the standard SCSI connector. Centronics-50 connectors have both male and female connectors and are typically seen with SCSI-1 implementations. Figure 10.6 (also on the next page) shows the male and female connectors of a Centronics-50 SCSI.

FIGURE 10.5: A sample DB-25 female SCSI connector

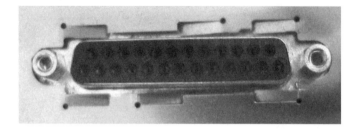

FIGURE 10.6: Male and female connector of a Centronics-50 SCSI

The high-density 68-pin connector has been dubbed the SCSI-2 or SCSI-3 connector by the industry. This is mainly because it was introduced on systems along with the introduction of the SCSI-2 interface. With this connector, a cable will typically connect to the 68-pin connector on one end and to either another 68-pin connector or a standard Centronics-50 connector on the other end. Figure 10.7 shows a sample high-density 68-pin connector.

FIGURE 10.7: A high-density 68-pin SCSI connector

NOTE   SCSI-3 is also now available. You will not need to differentiate between SCSI types on the exam, but you will need to be able differentiate between a SCSI port, an RJ-11, an RJ-45, and a BNC port.

Hubs

A hub regenerates the inbound electrical signal from one port and then distributes it out of all other ports. By using a hub, you can commonly connect from four to 24 computers and printers to each other. A hub is electrically powered and is considered to be active. If someone says you have a passive hub, you actually have a patch panel. Figure 10.8 shows a hub configured into a start format.

FIGURE 10.8: An example of a hub connecting four devices

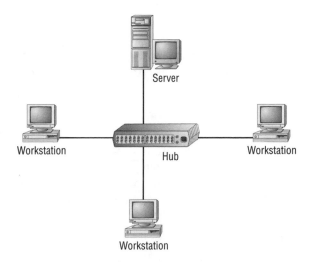

Routers

Operating on the third layer of the OSI model (the Network layer), routers direct packets from one network to another. They can perform all of the functions of repeaters and bridges, but with more intelligence. Routers can make decisions based on the cost of a link—in terms of both money and time lag. These devices can carry much higher network traffic loads than bridges are capable of.

Routers can communicate with other routers, but they are not used to communicate directly to remote computers. This is in addition to almost any number of physical network segments that they control. Routers usually have a serial connection to a computer for command information and setup with either Telnet or a terminal program. Finally, some routers are expandable with plug-in modules.

NOTE On the Network+ exam and, in fact, on most network tests, the classic definition of the router is used. This is important to note because some of today's modern routers can actually perform the functions of a gateway as well. New product designs and advancing technology can sometimes blur the lines that have separated the traditional functions of various network devices. Additionally, there are network devices that can be combinations of other network devices. For example, a brouter performs all of the functions of a bridge plus some of the functions of a router.

Configuring routers can be a very complex procedure. Do not work on a router's configuration without clear instructions and authority.

Bridges

A bridge can extend the total length of a cable run as well as join logical workgroups. Bridges forward packets based on their MAC addresses to LAN areas. It knows which computers are on which side of the bridge by learning and building a simple routing table. Should power be lost to a bridge, the simple routing table vanishes, requiring a rebuild when power is restored. Working on the Data Link layer of the OSI model (IEEE MAC sub-layer), it knows nothing about protocols and simply passes them on. Bridges offer better network performance, due in part to less network traffic being forwarded. Occasionally, two NICs will be placed in one computer to make it into a bridge of sorts. This is commonly called an internal bridge.

Brouters

A brouter is a combination of a bridge and a router. Brouters operate on the Data Link layer and the Network layer. The router functions allow it to route packets, such as IP packets and IPX packets. The bridge functions allow non-routable packets, such as NetBEUI, to go from one portion of the network to the other.

Patch Panels

A patch panel may be thought of as a physical converter. It connects the bare copper ends of the UTP cable into a RJ-45 jack. It is used as a central wiring point for multiple UTP cables. This makes upgrading or troubleshooting much simpler and avoids physical damage to the cabling. Replacing a cable in a wall is neither fun nor inexpensive, and a patch panel prevents cables from having to be moved around to make network changes.

Using a patch panel on a UTP network makes making changes much simpler because you use patch cables to make connections. A patch cable is any cable that connects from one network device to the main cable run. Patch cables are used to connect workstations to the main cable run, and they connect the main cable run through the patch panel to the hub. Instead of plugging the long run of cable directly into the hub, you connect it to a patch panel and then connect the patch panel port that represents that cable into the hub using a patch cable.

Exam Essentials

This objective stresses your ability to describe and identify connectors and other network hardware.

Know how to recognize SCSI and other common ports. SCSI ports use the most pins in a single connection. 25-, 50-, and 68-pin SCSI connectors connect to hard drives, tape drives, and similar devices. BNC connectors are round and lock into place for network connectivity. RJ-11 connectors are four-wire or six-wire ports used for telephones. RJ-45 connectors are eight-wire ports used for computer networks. Wires for all RJ connectors are contained in plastic blocks.

Know how to identify network infrastructure devices. Hubs are multi-port boxes that allow many computers to be networked together. Routers direct packets from one network to another. Brouters extend networks and allow packet routing, as with a router. Bridges connect two networks and make them appear as one. Patch panels are long rows of ports that computers are plugged into, managing the wires that come from the computers. Patch panels do not use electricity and are intermediaries between computers and hubs or switches.

Key Terms and Concepts

You will be asked to define network devices. The following terms are some of the network devices you will be asked to define.

Bridge   Extends your network and allows two segments to look alike on the Data Link layer.

Brouter   A router and bridge are combined into one product.

Hub   Multiple computers are connected via this powered device, which only regenerates signals to all ports.

Patch panels   Network cables are run from different computers, rooms, and floors to these intermediary, non-powered rows of ports before going to powered hubs or switches.

Peripheral ports   Provide external connection to devices such as hard drives, modems, scanners, and networks.

Print servers   A service that directs print jobs between the user, print queue, and print engine. It can be built into a printer or be in software format on a server.

RJ-11 jack   The four- or six-wire connector that is used for analog telephone connections.

RJ-45 jack   The four- or eight-wire connector that is used for digital computer connections. (Eight wires are normally used for networking.)

Router   Allows packets to be directed from one network to another.

SCSI (Small Computer System Interface)   Manages devices along a SCSI bus via a controller chip built into the motherboard or on an expansion card. Some of the managed devices are CD-ROMs, DVD-ROMs, hard drives, cameras, and scanners. SCSI ports are not for network connection.

Sample Questions

1. What type of cable connector is most often used to connect an external CD-ROM tower (without any network capability) to a server?

   A. RJ-11

   B. RJ-45

   C. Serial

   D. SCSI

   E. IDE

Answer: D—SCSI was invented for internal and external storage (e.g., hard drives, CD-ROM drives) or multimedia (e.g., scanners, cameras). (RJ connectors are used for network connectivity. A serial port is typically used for modems, mice, and cameras. IDE is an internal-only communications medium.)

2. What connector is used to attach an eight-wire (four wire pairs) network cable to a computer.

   A. RJ-11

   B. RJ-45

   C. Serial

   D. SCSI

   E. IDE

Answer: B—RJ-45 connectors can handle up to eight wires. (RJ-11 connectors can only handle a maximum of either four or six wires. A serial connector is used for locally connected devices that are run by computers. An SCSI connector is also used to connect devices to a computer, not a network. IDE connectors are used to connect internal computer devices.)

▶ Given an installation scenario, demonstrate awareness of the following compatibility and cabling issues:

- The consequences of trying to install an analog modem in a digital jack
- That the uses of RJ-45 connectors may differ greatly depending on the cabling
- That patch cables contribute to the overall length of the cabling segment

When installing a network, there are a few special conditions, covered in this section, that you must understand beforehand. These conditions are unique to network cabling and connectors. The Network+ exam will test your knowledge of these special situations.

Critical Information

It is important that you understand the three major cabling/connector issues that crop up from time to time when implementing networks, because the consequences of doing it wrong are network failure or hardware damage. The three major issues are:

- Analog modem in a digital jack
- RJ-45 usage
- Overall length of cable segments

Analog Modem in a Digital Jack

RJ-11 and RJ-45 connectors are both RJ-series connectors. They both share the same shape and are roughly compatible (the RJ-11 connector will fit into an RJ-45 jack, but *not* vice-versa). However, each connector has different uses. RJ-11 connectors are most often found in telephone-to-wall-socket connections. RJ-45 connectors, on the other hand, are most often used for digital connections of some sort (i.e., Ethernet or digital telephone connections). For both the Network+ exam and in real life, it is important that you be able to distinguish between the two. Plugging an analog modem into an RJ-45 digital jack can cause serious consequences.

Depending on factors outside a person's ability to directly observe, one of two outcomes is possible:

- The connection will not function
- The analog modem will never function again

Clearly, when an analog device gets a digital signal, there is no basis for a successful connection. However, the possibility for destruction of a modem arises when the higher voltage from the digital connection burns out the modem.

Some digital phone systems with modem-eating voltages can also be accessed by RJ-11 plugs and jacks. The only defenses are clear labeling and careful attention by end users, or a filtering/conversation third-party device.

RJ-45 Usage Variance

The RJ-45 is very popular, even outside of networking. Frequently, this same connector is used for digital phone systems in offices and motels. Relatively new office buildings may not have the legacy RJ-11 cabling that is best used for analog telephone traffic. Running just RJ-45 connectors throughout an entire building simplifies things. All the cables go back to a wiring closet, which will have telecommunications switches and computer network equipment. You can change the ratio of phone lines to computer lines by just changing where the plugs are inserted. Be sure to label each cable with a number or letter combination that corresponds to its room and location. Otherwise, you will be searching for a cable in the proverbial haystack.

Overall Length of Cable Segments

Patch cables contribute to the overall length of the cabling segment. Instead of plugging the long run of cable directly into a hub, you connect it to a patch panel and then, using a patch cable, connect the patch panel port that represents that cable into the hub. Be careful, though, because the total segment length of the network includes the patch cables at both ends. This can come back to hurt you later. For example, consider that you are using Ethernet over UTP in the 10BaseT configuration. The maximum segment length is 100 meters. That means the maximum distance from hub to NIC can be 100 meters. Some people who run network cables mistake this and put in a 100-meter cable running from patch panel to wall plate. Then they install a 10-meter workstation-to-wall-plate patch cable and a 3-meter patch-panel-to-hub patch cable. This brings the total distance to 113 meters, and the workstation using that cable run may not be able to communicate correctly with the rest of the network because the total length is longer than the maximum rated distance.

Be sure to match or exceed the rating for existing cabling. Putting a Category 3 patch panel on Category 5 cabling would make the network a Category 3 network.

Exam Essentials

The Network+ exam requires that you be familiar with cabling issues.

Know how to identify the consequences of connecting an analog modem to a digital telephone port. Either nothing will happen or, due to voltage inconsistencies, you will ruin the modem. Be sure to check and identify all equipment and ports before using them.

Know how to deal with an RJ-45 connection. All connections should be labeled to describe the intended use of the port. This will help you to differentiate between a network connection and a digital telephone connection. In addition, all ports should be labeled according to user location at both the wiring closet and at the user location.

Know how to figure the total length of a network segment. A cable segment reaches from the computer and includes the patch cable to the wall, the cable in the wall, the connection to a patch panel in the wiring closet, and the patch cable to the first electrically powered network device. Network devices include routers, hubs, gateways, bridges, switches, brouters, and repeaters.

Key Terms and Concepts

Know the concepts that relate to ports, jacks, and cable lengths for computer networks.

Analog modem A communications device that connects a computer to the Plain Old Telephone Service and allows different frequencies to encode transmissions.

Digital jack A jack port that allows binary traffic of zeros and ones. Computer networks and high-end telephone systems use digital equipment and jacks.

Overall length The total length from node to node, including all patch panels and patch cables.

Sample Questions

1. Your workstation is trying to talk to a NetWare server and a Windows NT server on a 100BaseTX network. You have a workstation that connects to the wall with a 7-foot patch cable. The cubicle structure reaches 60 meters to the wall of the building. The wall has 20 meters of cabling to the wiring closet patch panel. A 4-foot patch cable connects the patch panel to the switch. Another 80 meters of cabling goes to the NetWare server. The Windows NT server is 611 feet away.

   Required results Ensure that the workstation cabling is within specifications.

   Optional results Ensure that the NetWare server cabling is within specifications. Ensure that the Windows NT server cabling is within specifications.

Proposed solution Keep the 100BaseTX cabling for the workstation and NetWare server. Connect the Windows NT Server to the switch in the wiring closet with 10Base2 cabling and ports.

A. The proposed solution meets the required results.

B. The proposed solution meets the required results and one of the optional results.

C. The proposed solution meets the required results and both of the optional results.

D. The proposed solution does not meet the required results.

Answer: B—The workstation and NetWare server cabling is under 100 meters each. The Windows NT server is 611 feet, or 186 meters, away. 10Base2 cabling is only rated for 185 meters. The Windows NT server, second optional result, will not be covered.

2. Your are in another company's offices with your laptop. After getting permission to connect to an outside telephone line, you look at the port on the wall. Which port do you plug your analog modem cable into?

A. Round port with a thin copper wire in the middle

B. Four-wire port

C. Eight-wire port

D. 12-wire port

E. 16-wire port

Answer: B—A four-wire port is commonly used for telephones and analog modems. (A round port is generally used for 10Base2 computer networks or cable television. Eight-wire ports are used for digital telephones or computers. 12- and 16-wire ports are not used.)

CHAPTER

11

Administering the Change Control System

Network+ Exam Objectives Covered in This Chapter:

▶ Demonstrate awareness of the need to document the current status and configuration of the workstation (i.e., providing a baseline) prior to making any changes. *(pages 253 – 256)*

▶ Given a configuration scenario, select a course of action that would allow the return of a system to its original state. *(pages 257 – 259)*

▶ Given a scenario involving workstation backups, select the appropriate backup technique from among the following: *(pages 260 – 263)*
- Tape backup
- Folder replication to a network drive
- Removable media
- Multi-generation

▶ Demonstrate awareness of the need to remove outdated or unused drivers, properties, etc. when an upgrade is successfully completed. *(pages 263 – 265)*

▶ Identify the possible adverse effects on the network caused by local changes (e.g., version conflicts, overwritten DLLs, etc.). *(pages 266 – 269)*

▶ Explain the purpose of drive mapping, and, given a scenario, identify the mapping that will produce the desired results using Universal Naming Convention (UNC) or an equivalent feature. Explain the purpose of printer port capturing and identify properly formed capture commands, given a scenario. *(pages 269 – 275)*

▶ Given a scenario where equipment is being moved or changed, decide when and how to verify the functionality of the network and critical applications. *(pages 276 – 279)*

▶ Given a scenario where equipment is being moved or changed, decide when and how to verify the functionality of that equipment. *(pages 279 – 282)*

▶ Demonstrate awareness of the need to obtain relevant permissions before adding, deleting, or modifying users. *(pages 283 – 286)*

> **Identify the purpose and function of the following networking elements:** *(pages 286 – 295)*
>
> - Profiles
> - Rights
> - Procedures/policies
> - Administrative utilities
> - Login accounts, groups, and passwords

The *change control system* is the main system that a network administrator uses to administrate a network. The change control system manages all changes that occur, from performing installations and upgrades to adding users to the existing network. This system is designed to perform and keep track of all network changes so that there is a way of making network changes and determining the source of a network problem. The change control system encompasses many areas, including those in the following list.

- Documentation
- Backup procedures
- Network maintenance
- Standard administration procedures

Demonstrate awareness of the need to document the current status and configuration of the workstation (i.e., providing a baseline) prior to making any changes.

The most often overlooked procedure in network administration is network documentation. Network documentation is the set of documents that a network administrator creates to make notes about how a network is normally configured and how it normally operates. Documentation is a resource that an administrator can refer to when they think a network may be malfunctioning. The administrator can refer to the documentation and tell whether or not a condition is an error or just the normal functioning of the network. The Network+ exam will test you on your ability to understand network documentation.

Critical Information

There are many types of documentation. You need to find out what the normal performance of your network is. To do this, take performance readings at the start of the business day, at lunch, at the end of the business day, and at a random time during the day. This will give you a complete picture, not just a sense of when people log in. This will also give you a more complete picture of the normal performance of your network so you can quantify abnormal performance when it happens.

The Need to Document

Documentation, while not a key issue to the operation of a server, becomes more important as system failures occur. Without proper documentation, a simple rebuild or restore of a server can become a monumental task. System documentation should include:

- Configuration
- Network access configuration
- Backup procedures
- Restore procedures

You know your documentation is acceptable if a person with administrative server knowledge can rebuild your system, cookbook style, with no prior knowledge of the system.

Providing a Baseline

A *baseline* is the category of network documentation that indicates how the network normally runs. It includes such information as network traffic statistics, server utilization trends, and processor performance statistics. Baseline information helps to answer the question "Is this normal?" Another category of baseline information is general network documentation. These differ from standard operating procedures (SOPs) because baselines indicate how things normally are and not how they should be. General network documentation might include a cable map and server configuration documents. Cable maps indicate each network cable's source and destination, as well as where each network cable runs. As anyone who has ever had to trace a network cable can attest, the cable map is an important part of your network documentation. The server configuration documents include information such as the current hardware configuration (including I/O address, IRQ, DMA, and memory address information), current installed software packages, and any patches that are installed. Additionally, notes can be made as to any special settings, over and above the defaults, that have been made.

In addition to providing a current backup, creating and maintaining a collection of data that may be referred to can prevent a molehill from turning into a mountain. If, after making an upgrade, all heck breaks loose, knowing you have a reference will make the restoration to the previous state much easier. Even when an upgrade goes well, should the end user's workstation or a server suddenly experience a breakdown, having a reference point of how everything looked when it was working well will help you find out what happened.

Exam Essentials

This objective is based on your ability to document your network and prepare a baseline in order to spot system anomalies as they occur.

Know how to document your network.   Write simple, cookbook-style documentation for your system. Prepare network and system diagrams for total system rebuilds.

Know how to prepare a baseline.   Prepare a baseline for your system as a standard for system and network recovery.

Key Terms and Concepts

Know the key words that relate to system documentation. A couple of common terms are listed below.

Baseline   A snapshot of a network or server during acceptable levels of performance to which future performance may be compared.

Documentation   Written diagrams and instructions of server and/or network operations that can be followed for system and/or network reconstruction and day-to-day operations.

Sample Question

1. Which of the following is a good use for a baseline?

   A. Installing a network

   B. Documenting backup procedures

   C. Restoring a server/network to optimum performance

   D. Having a point of comparison between current and optimal performance

   E. Having a good list of network components

   Answer: D—A baseline is the point, usually selected by the customer, to which server/network performance is compared. (A network or server must be installed *before* a baseline can be established. Backup procedures are part of disaster recovery and would be unaffected by a baseline. The baseline is where a server or network would be *after* a restoration. A list of network components would be in the documentation.)

Given a configuration scenario, select a course of action that would allow the return of a system to its original state.

This objective tests you on your ability to prepare a system for a failure of some kind. When a system fails, you must have a way of quickly restoring it to its original state so your users will experience minimum of downtime. The Network+ exam will test you on your ability to return a system to its original state after a failure.

Critical Information

No matter how bulletproof network administrators try to make their systems, there is always the risk of a failure. How quickly you recover from these failures is dependent on how methodically you prepare emergency repair disks and do backups.

The Need for Recovery Disks

The importance of having a current emergency repair disk (ERD) cannot be overstated. While backups can recover data, the placement of that data, user profiles, registry information, user accounts, and passwords are all contained in the ERD. ERDs should be made as often as is feasible.

WARNING   If you use an ERD to recover a system, keep in mind that all user information contained in the ERD will revert to the time when the disk was made. This means, for example, that if someone changed their password since the ERD was made the recovered password will be the old password.

The Need for Regular Backups

Applying an ERD to a reconstructed system will prove fruitless if you cannot restore the missing data. While full backups may be impractical to do as often as most network administrators would like, a good schedule of incremental backups can ward off disaster in the event of a failure.

Exam Essentials

This objective is based on the ability to restore a system after a failure.

Know how to prepare and utilize an emergency repair disk. The ERD is created using the Emergency Repair Disk utility that comes with Windows 95/98. If your system fails, you can insert the disk to boot the system.

Know how to perform backups and restore from backup media. You should be able to perform regular, systematic backups and know how to use those backups to restore data and user files. All backup software is different, but you should know that backups are needed in order to guarantee that data will be available after a system failure.

Key Terms and Concepts

Know the acronyms that relate to system restoration. A couple of common terms are listed below.

Backup   Copying data to an alternate media to prepare for any failure of the primary media.

ERD (emergency repair disk)   Used to restore system parameter settings, user accounts, groups, and file structures in the event of a failure.

Restore   The process of copying data back from the alternate media to the main disk drive after a failure.

Sample Questions

1. When should an emergency repair disk be created?

   A. Only when you finish installing the OS

   B. After a major upgrade

   C. Before moving hardware

   D. When the system is created and as often as possible afterward

   E. Before shutting the system down

   Answer: D—The ERD should be made after installing the system and as often as possible thereafter. (The others are correct to a point but are not all-inclusive. Selection A is not correct because of the word *only*.)

2. What is the best way to make sure data is available after a hardware failure?

   A. Mirror the drives.

   B. Only store data locally on workstations.

   C. Do frequent backups.

   D. Store data in two locations.

   E. Keep spares.

   Answer: C—Frequent backups are the best way to ensure that data is available after a failure. (Mirrored drives can both fail together. You should never encourage people to store data locally. Sometimes it is space or cost prohibitive to store data in multiple locations. A spare, as in selection D., would not contain data unless it was a hot spare.)

Given a scenario involving workstation backups, select the appropriate backup technique from among the following:

- Tape backup
- Folder replication to a network drive
- Removable media
- Multi-generation

Backups are important, but, with advances in networking, it is rarely necessary to back up data on a workstation. All data are typically stored on the server and backed up from there. However, this objective discusses the different types of workstation backups available and the situations in which they are used. The Network+ exam will test you on the details of the types of workstation backups available and their uses.

Critical Information

Backing up your data is not as simple as copying everything to tape. Do you tell 10,000 users to copy their data onto a tape cartridge? No, you tell them to save their work to a network drive, and then, as the network administrator, you copy everything from the server to tape. This objective is about selecting the proper backup method, and the next objective covers the specifics of each type.

Proper Backup Techniques

With the improvement of workstation technology, servers and networks have become more stable, and sometimes backups and data integrity take a back seat to the hustle and bustle of network and server management. Data integrity is sometimes not thought about much until a hard disk fails. Then it can become a serious crisis. A well-planned backup procedure can save you much unnecessary stress when "old faithful" loses an entire department's directory tree.

Backup techniques can vary depending on the importance of the data. This is usually a level of integrity determined by the customer and established in your baseline. The backup and restore procedure should be well documented. And testing the validity of the backups and procedures from time to time may save you a spoiled vacation or workweek.

All computers are not typically backed up. Desktop workstations are not usually covered, and notebook and palm computer files are never backed up. However, data loss is still unacceptable to users. On the other hand, backing up all hard drives is impossible when you look at time and tape restrictions. A nice, but reluctant, compromise it to have users save all data to their home directories on a server.

Exam Essentials

This objective is based on your ability to prepare, implement, and test a backup procedure suitable for your site.

Know how to determine which type of backup is acceptable for your site. Poll your users. Determine the criticality of data. Use this information to determine whether or not individual workstations should be backed up and which type of backup technology to use.

Key Terms and Concepts

Know the acronyms and terms that relate to backup. Different types and common terms are listed below.

Folder replication A method of copying data to an alternate location within the server/network structure (preferably a redundant or isolated area).

Removable media A method employing removable or hot-swappable disk media, otherwise known as CD-R. Each type of removable media has its uses.

Tape backup A method of backing up data to a tape (cassette magnetic media); very useful in multi-generation backups.

Sample Questions

1. You perform tape backups on a server located in an area where there is a history of catastrophic events. Where should you store the tapes?

   A. Off site

   B. Near the server

   C. In a separate room

   D. On top of the tape unit

   Answer: A—The tapes should be stored off site. (Any of the other choices would place the backup media too close to a potentially volatile area.)

2. Which of the following is correct if you have a fully redundant RAID array and you do replication to another RAID drive on the server?

   A. You don't need to perform any backups.

   B. You only need to back up before and after upgrades.

   C. For true data integrity, you should perform backups on a regular basis.

   D. You only need to perform backups before and after major OS upgrades.

   Answer: C—You should perform backups on a regular basis. Any hardware-based redundancy, such as RAID, no matter how safe it seems, is still subject to failure. While it is certainly recommended to perform backups before and after *any* upgrade, you should still do removable media backups on a regular basis.

3. You have 60 workstations, all of which store critical, volatile data. What is the best way to back them up?

   A. Make sure each one has a tape drive.

   B. Have users copy files to a backup folder on their workstations.

    C. Use a network-accessible backup device.

    D. Use file replication to the server.

Answer: D—Automatic replication should be set up to a server that has a regular, scheduled backups. Answer A would be costly and an administrative nightmare. B won't protect the users' data if their workstations fail. C is incorrect because 60 users would be overloading a single network device.

  4. Which of the following is a way for an incremental backup to determine if a file is already on tape?

    A. Check the creation date.

    B. Check the modification date.

    C. Check the archive bit.

    D. Back up all files just to be sure.

Answer: C—An incremental backup will look for set archive bits and back up those files. (Doing date comparisons would be too time consuming, which is also the likely case for performing full backups each day.)

Demonstrate awareness of the need to remove outdated or unused drivers, properties, etc. when an upgrade is successfully completed.

When you upgrade software, it is considered good form to remove any unnecessary or outdated software and drivers. Outdated software and drivers can conflict with the updates and can interfere with the proper operation of the computer. The Network+ exam will test you on your ability to recognize that this procedure needs to be done.

Critical Information

The bug searches that are associated with old drivers and program components can plague software developers for hours. Users may also have problematic old components after the components are upgraded. This means that you sometimes have to go in by hand and delete old drivers.

Removing Outdated Drivers and DLLs

Begin the process for upgrading as you did earlier by getting a known baseline and having documentation before beginning an upgrade. Once a driver has been upgraded and testing has proven proper functioning, the old driver needs to be removed from the system. You can do this by first taking note of the version and date of the files being upgraded. Then, after the upgrade, perform a directory listing and see if there are duplicate files that were saved after the upgrade. The files and drivers that were upgraded may be placed in a directory with the .OLD extension. If you have removed a piece of hardware, you should remove the software driver for it so the operating system doesn't think the device is still there and end up reporting several errors.

Exam Essentials

This objective is designed to help you to know which drives to remove and when to remove them after an upgrade.

Know how to identify and remove unneeded drivers, DLLs, and old applications.   Use the Windows 9.x registry and the ODBC manager to check which vendor-installed drivers exist, as well as their dates and versions. After a hardware upgrade, remove any outdated drivers by deleting them from the Windows directory.

Key Terms and Concepts

You should know the following terms that relate to removing outdated portions of an OS or software.

DLL (Dynamic Link Library)   Small pieces of executable code that are shared by many Windows applications to provide similar functionality among all program.

Driver   A program that serves as an interface between hardware and software.

Sample Question

1. Which of the following should you do after upgrading a piece of application software?

   A. Move the old drivers to another location.

   B. Keep the old drivers in case the new ones fail.

   C. Remove all old drivers from the system.

   D. Test the new software with the old drivers for backward compatibility.

   E. Test data files for compatibility.

   Answer: C—Remove all old drivers from the system. (Answers A, B, and D are not correct because they could cause conflicts. While you should test data files, E does not answer the necessity for old drivers.)

Identify the possible adverse effects on the network caused by local changes (e.g., version conflicts, overwritten DLLs, etc.).

This objective is designed to illustrate that a change on a server can adversely affect the entire network. For example, installing new software can make it so that no one can communicate with the server. The Network+ exam will test you on your ability to recognize some of these changes that can possibly adversely affect the entire network.

Critical Information

Overwritten software components and version issues are hard to track down. ODBC files are often overwritten with the wrong version. ODBC files are an example of Dynamic Link Libraries (small pieces of executable code that programs share to allow sharing of certain functions) for programs. Another common problem is Java or ActiveX version conflicts. Why can the director of computing view a dynamic table via a Web browser in the Computing Department while someone in the Finance Department cannot? The reason is most likely that the Finance Department is running an old version of the Web browser. Be sure to maintain the latest corporation-approved versions of all software packages and operating systems.

Version Conflicts

Version conflicts have been part of computing since its beginning. When Microsoft first upgraded Windows, it created methods for programmers' to use to enhance and extend their operating systems. Upgrades like these have been both a bane and a blessing for the computer environment. It is completely possible that the new software or patch that you add to your system will conflict with other installed products. And when you install a patch to solve the problem, it might cause still other problems. It truly can become a computing version of Pandora's box.

Word processors, spreadsheets, and databases also have to worry about version conflicts. An inconvenience would be receiving a copy of a document via e-mail that your old word processor cannot understand. A major problem occurs when the document is on a server and many people access it.

A company runs its entire business on information. Consider that a particular company uses a database that is stored on its server. Everyone has the same version of the application that accessed the data. Then a department buys all new computers. These new machines have an office productivity suite included. Now a user with the new PC opens the database with the new software. The database is automatically upgraded to the new version of the user. This might seem great since there is increased functionality. But this is actually a disaster. The rest of the company that uses the old database application can no longer access their data. Either many, potentially thousands, users need to upgrade in one day, or a restore from tape needs to be done. This is an example of version conflicts that are across the network, not just on the local machine.

Overwritten DLLs

Perhaps the most infamous culprit of software upgrade problems is the Dynamic Link Library. Pondering the combined meaning of these words is sufficient to give any sane administrator chills down the spine. The word dynamic means fluid, changing. A link chains two or more processes together. And library refers to a collection of data. The good news for programmers is that they can create DLLs to add whatever functionality they desire. The difficulty in this for the administrator is that a freshly installed DLL can destroy a working DLL by overwriting it to yield the results the new program needs.

A classic example of this was a golf game that was free inside every box of 1.44-inch diskettes. It was fine as a game but frequently a disaster to a working system. Simply put, it trashed DLLs with reckless abandon. After a user would install this golf game, and the computer would no longer function as before, you can guess who got a call. To make matters worse, it is the very rare case that the end user would fess up to what they did.

Overwriting DLLs has been such a pervasive challenge that when Microsoft released Windows 98, it included an installation history file so administrators could track down any DLLs that were changed as a result of the installation of Windows 98.

Two common DLLs that may be overwritten during an upgrade are VBRUNx00.DLL (x is the version number) and ODBC.DLL. The former is the Visual Basic Runtime Library and is used to store many of the basic Visual Basic subroutines. The latter is the Open Database Connectivity DLL that is used to connect workstations to many different types of databases, including Access, SQL, and DB/2 databases.

It should be evident that version conflicts and DLL overwriting can be avoided only by detailed and vigilant tracking on your part. At the time you are doing this routine stuff, it may seem unproductive. However, the day will come when you will be very happy that you performed these tasks.

Exam Essentials

This objective is about the adverse effects of software and driver version conflicts.

Know how to identify the adverse effects of software and driver conflicts.   Software conflicts can cause a server to malfunction and deny service to network clients. For this reason, you must remove unused or outdated software after that software has been upgraded.

Sample Question

1. What might happen when one user upgrades their word processor and then sends e-mail to another user with an old version of the same word processor?

   A. The file corrupts the recipient's PC.

   B. The file opens without a problem.

   C. The file automatically downgrades to the previous version.

   D. The file opens, but the content is unintelligible.

   E. The file cannot be opened.

   Answer: D, E—The new version of the file will either open as garbage or will not open at all. (The file is not intelligent and will not cause itself to be returned or downgraded.)

Explain the purpose of drive mapping, and, given a scenario, identify the mapping that will produce the desired results using Universal Naming Convention (UNC) or an equivalent feature. Explain the purpose of printer port capturing and identify properly formed capture commands, given a scenario.

This objective tests you on your understanding of the use of drive mapping, including using workstation pointers for network resources (drives and printers), the use of Universal Naming Convention (UNC) paths, and printer port assignments.

Critical Information

Windows 9.*x* has its origins with MS-DOS, which uses drive letters and LPT ports to access hard disks and printers on local machines. Windows 9.*x* still uses these methods to access remote resources as well. Drive mapping and printer port captures are used to make the remote resources look as if they were locally connected. The Network+ exam is specific here. Knowing about the technology, as with other objectives, is not enough. You must also be able to properly format text-based commands that will get you access to these resources.

Drive Mapping

A hard disk storage unit is commonly referred to as a hard drive, or just a drive. When a remote network resource is linked to a local computer name, it is referred to as mapping. So drive mapping is when a remote network share is linked to a local computer by a drive name. A common scenario is to map the user's home directory to their H: drive on their local computer.

Windows NT

When you want to access network resources provided by either Windows 9.*x* or Windows NT computers, you will be accessing a directory that has been shared out by the administrator. Network shares are identified on Windows networks by the Universal Naming Convention. The Client for Microsoft Networks uses this format to connect to network shares. The UNC path specifies the name of the server hosting the share and the name of the share. The format of a UNC name is as follows:

```
\\SERVERNAME\SHARENAME
```

This format provides a universal network name that refers to any network resource.

A mapping to a share is performed with the NET USE command. The format is NET USE, a space, the drive letter for the drive you want mapped, a colon followed by another space, followed by the UNC name of the resource you want to access, like so:

```
NET USE g: \\servername\sharename
```

NOTE If you are using Windows 9.*x* or NT workstations on a Windows network (and most people are), and you have the Windows client software for that platform installed, you can use Explorer and Network Neighborhood to perform the mappings. Simply browse to the network device, right-click, and pick "Map network drive." A window will appear, allowing you to choose which drive letter you want to map to the device. Choose it and select whether or not you want the drive mapping to be permanent (meaning it is reconnected every time you start up). Then Click OK to map the drive.

NetWare

NetWare uses a slightly different naming convention—server names and volume names (or volume object names, if you're using NDS), directories, and subdirectories. When a server is not listed, the mapping goes to the user's preferred server. Things are getting more complicated, but the good news is that a user can have a mapping that goes directly to a subdirectory on a server that is on their home drive. The format is the map command, space, drive letter, colon, equal sign, server name with a backslash, followed by the volume name (or the name of the volume object), colon, directory, subdirectory, subdirectory, etc. Here are two examples—one using server and volume name, and the next using volume object name.

Server and Volume

```
MAP F:=SERVER\VOLUME:DIRECTORY\SUBDIRECTORY
```

Volume Object Name

```
MAP F:=VOLUMEOBJECTNAME:DIRECTORY\SUBDIR
```

Unix

Unix shares use the same special characters as NetWare, but they are reversed. A colon is used to separate the server name, and forward slashes are used for directory and subdirectory divisions. Lastly, case is important in Unix; the terms Data and data denote the same directory in Windows NT and NetWare, but they are different locations in a Unix file system. Mapping a share from one Unix workstation to another Unix workstation is detailed later in this chapter.

Perhaps an example will help clarify the matter. The structure is the mount command, space, server name, colon, forward slash, directory, forward slash, subdirectory, space, forward slash, and the local directory that the remote share will be mapped to, like this:

```
mount server:/directory/subdirectory /localDirectory
```

This command would mount the /directory/subdirectory NFS share to the /localDirectory directory mount point.

Printer Port Capturing

Remote printers, just like network shares, need to be mapped to a local equivalent. A Windows 9.*x* PC can have up to three locally configured printers—LPT1, LT2, and LPT3. Windows 9.*x* allows far more than that for remote printing. For DOS programs or non-network–aware applications, you need to grab the information from the local LPT port. This capture is then rerouted to a server-managed printer on the network. The three clients, Microsoft, NetWare, and Unix, use different syntax to map the ports. This process is typically called *capturing* a parallel port.

Windows 9.x and Windows NT

To capture a Microsoft-shared printer, the Client for Microsoft Networks uses the NET USE command—as was explained in the drive mapping section. This time, instead of a drive letter, an LPT (parallel) port is used. The format is the NET USE command, parallel port number, colon, space, and then the UNC name of the shared printer, like so:

```
NET USE LPT1: \\SERVERNAME\PRINTER
```

TIP As mentioned before, Explorer and Network Neighborhood can also be used to capture printer ports. Just choose the printer in Network Neighborhood, right-click, and choose "Capture print port" from the pop-up menu. Then pick which local port you want to associate with that printer and click OK.

NetWare

NetWare uses the CAPTURE command for printer ports. This is easy to remember; use the CAPTURE command to capture a printer port. You can select a print queue or a printer. The printer is the NDS object for the actual printing device, while the queue object manages print jobs and their order. NetWare 4.*x* and above allows you send a job directly to the printer. Stay away from this switch if possible. The operating system is slowed down as it searches for the first available queue attached to the printer. The command structure to print to your preferred server is: CAPTURE, space, forward slash, L, equal sign and lpt port number, space, forward slash, Q or P, equal sign, and then the printer or queue name.

```
CAPTURE /L=# /Q=QueueName
CAPTURE /L=# /P=PrinterName
```

Unix

Unix workstations use the lpr command to print directly to a remote Unix-managed printer. You do not need to map a network printer to your desktop Unix box. This is because Unix was created from the ground up to be a networked operating system. (A Windows 9.*x* client requires Unix servers to have special software to manage print jobs and to handle Windows 9.*x* print requests.) To print from one Unix box to another, use the lpr command, space, minus sign, P, printer name, space, and then the file name, like this:

```
lpr -Pprinter filename
```

Exam Essentials

This objective is based on connecting remote shares and printers to your local computer.

Know how to map a network share to a local name in Windows NT, NetWare, and Unix.   You can map network shares in

Windows 9.*x*, Windows NT, or Unix by opening a command prompt window (e.g., a DOS box) and typing in the following:

On a Windows 9.*x* or NT machine connecting to an NT server:

```
NET USE G: \\SERVER\SHARE
```

On a Windows 9.*x* or NT machine connecting to a NetWare server:

```
MAP F:=SERVER\VOLUME:DIRECTORY\SUBDIRECTORY
```

On a Unix workstation connecting to another Unix machine:

```
mount server:/directory/subdirectory /localDirectory
```

Know how to capture printer ports. On a Windows 9.*x* or NT machine connecting to an NT server:

```
NET USE LPT1: \\SERVERNAME\PRINTER
```

On a Windows 9.*x* or NT machine connecting to a NetWare server, enter:

```
CAPTURE /L=# /Q=QueueName
CAPTURE /L=# /P=PrinterName
```

On a Windows 9.*x* or NT machine printing to a Unix server, enter:

```
lpr -Pprinter filename
```

Key Terms and Concepts

Know the concepts that relate to accessing remote network shares and printers.

Drive mapping A remote network share is connected to a local directory labeled with a letter in Windows 9.*x* or NT.

Port capturing When a Windows 9.*x* or NT computer has its printer communications grabbed and redirected to a network printer.

UNC (Universal Naming Convention) Used to define a server name and network share. It is in the format \\server\share.

Sample Questions

1. What syntax connects a remote Windows NT server share to a local Windows 9.*x* computer? (The server name is Boxter, and the remote share is called ASH. You want to connect the remote share to the local G drive.)

   A. NET USE G: \\Boxter\ASH

   B. NET USE G: //Boxter/ASH

   C. MAP G:=Boxter:ASH

   D. MAP G:=ASH:Boxter

   E. MAP G: \\Boxter\ASH

   Answer: A—The NET USE is for mapping to Windows 9.*x* or NT servers. The format used is NET USE DRIVE LETTER: \\server\share. (The MAP command is used to connect to NetWare servers.)

2. What command is used to directly print to a Unix print server.

   A. lpr

   B. lpq

   C. lpd

   D. plr

   E. plq

   Answer: A—lpr is the command used to send a print job to a Unix-managed printer. (lpq looks at the print queue. lpd works with the print daemon—Unix speak for print server.)

Given a scenario where equipment is being moved or changed, decide when and how to verify the functionality of the network and critical applications.

This objective tests your knowledge of the procedures necessary to prepare for a move and to verify that hardware and software is functional after a major network change or network move.

Critical Information

This objective stresses software functionality. The exam will test your awareness of pre-move and post-move testing. You must test your network hardware and software before a move or major change to ensure that it is functioning. Then, after a move or a major change, perform the same test to ensure the network is functioning properly.

Verifying Software Functionality before a Move

All software applications and network connectivity should be tested before a move. Here are some commonly checked items:

- Software configuration
- Network connectivity
- Web browser functionality
- Network applications
- Remote database functionality
- Internet access
- IP settings
- E-mail access

- Network share access

- Home directory access

- Printing access

Before testing, log in to the computer. This establishes that the operating system allows local logins. Attempt to view the network; this will establish network connectivity. Open a Web browser and go to an internal corporate Web site as well as an external site. Be sure to clear the browser's cache or reload each Web page. (Many Web site pages are stored on the local hard drive, and seeing those pages will not verify the operation of the Web browser.) Attempt to run a network-based application. This might be a word processor that is run off the network and opens its documents from the network.

Verifying Software Functionality after a Move

After you move equipment, it is important to check for hardware functionality. (Hardware functionality is discussed in the next section.) When the hardware is confirmed as being operational, move on to check the software. Have a checklist next to you when the system powers up. The checklist should be the same one that was used during the pre-move functionality check.

It would be foolhardy to simply return power to the system and check the System tab in Windows 9.x and be satisfied with the fact that no errors are showing on the NIC. This does not tell you that the domain or context tree for attaching to the server is entered correctly. Nor will it tell you that a proper user account has been created at the server.

The only way to be sure everything went as planned is to actually log in to the new server and create a file with an application. It can be as simple as opening Notepad, entering the words "Testing station 127 for George in Accounting. Functioning at Date/Time." Save, close, and then reopen the file to make sure you can read it. One more line stating your success of reopening the file will go a long way to document your work.

Performing this step on an actual user's account may be cause for a security violation in some firms. Depending on the company policies found in standard operating procedures, you might need to either enter the employee's password in a log or have it so only the employee knows their password. Changing a password in NT4 is done with User Manager for Domains, while in Netware 3.*x* and 4.*x* you can use the DOS-based SETPASS.

Before wrapping up and moving on to the next challenge, if the end user is available, ask them to test some of their work. Ask the user about their system's performance, and take note of any errors they may have uncovered that you may have missed. Perhaps permissions are not correctly set for the entire folder the user needs access to in order to accomplish their work.

Finally, following best practices on the client side, enter in the paper logs what happened with each upgrade or move. You will not necessarily be the same person who has to troubleshoot this station at a later time, so someone following in your footsteps will greatly appreciate this log—just as you would if you walked into a new scenario.

Exam Essentials

This objective is based on confirming software operation before and after a move.

Know how to verify the functionality of software and network connectivity when equipment is moved. Use a checklist of the software and the network that needs to be checked before and after the move. Check network functionality before the move or change, and then check it after the move or changes have been completed.

Sample Question

1. How do you verify network connectivity after a move?

    A. Try to ping the router.

    B. Log in to the network.

    C. Log in to the local PC.

    D. Try to ping a remote host.

    E. Print to a local printer.

Answer: A, B, D—Pinging the router will check connections to your router on the network. Logging in to the network checks your network card as well as connectivity to the authenticating server. Pinging a remote host checks connectivity on another network, such as the Internet. (Logging in to the local PC does not test anything network related, and neither does printing to a local printer).

Given a scenario where equipment is being moved or changed, decide when and how to verify the functionality of that equipment.

Like the previous objective, this objective was designed to test your knowledge of procedures that should be followed before and after moving network equipment. The exception is that this objective tests your ability to test the functionality of the equipment being moved.

Critical Information

Depending on the scenario, equipment may be moved daily from one cubicle to the next, one building to the next, and even between companies. Care needs to be taken when you move equipment. You are accountable for any unintentional changes or damage that occurs, so understanding how to verify hardware functionality after a move is crucial.

Verifying Hardware Functionality before a Move

Verifying hardware functionality after a move can reduce downtime as well as frustration on your part. Among the things that you should check out at the new location before a move are proper power, cable placement and functionality, and proper environmental conditions. Few things are more frustrating than finding out that your cable from the computer to the wall plate is 25cm too short or that the network connection is dead.

Realize that great care needs to be taken when moving network equipment. The following items should be checked before moving a workstation.

- inventory hardware
- Monitor powers up
- Computer powers up
- Monitor displays video
- Lights flash for each storage device on power-up
- No pins are missing or damaged on any connector, port, or cable
- No DIP switches or jumpers are changed or missing
- Exterior equipment cases are undamaged
- All internal cabling is securely attached to each component

This list will obviously change if you have to move a router. But, for the most part, the same basic procedures are used regardless of the equipment.

Protecting Equipment during Transport

Various steps should be taken when moving equipment. Power down all electrical equipment. Unplug all electrical cables and secure them with their devices. A box or bag is needed to contain everything during the move. Put the equipment in a padded container, or secure it safely to a hand truck or cart. Label every container with the user's first and last name, old location, and new location. Equipment can be lost even when you move from one floor to another. Machines can be damaged and cables can be lost.

When you move equipment, several issues need to be addressed. If you work for a union shop, the network staff may not be allowed to physically move any equipment. If you take action without knowing the rules and a union rule is broken, you could be in deep trouble. This is true even if the movers are union members and you are not. A union grievance is a serious matter and should be avoided. Make sure that you learn and follow corporate policy before moving any equipment.

Verifying Hardware Functionality after a Move

Ensure that all equipment makes it to the correct location. After that, unpack the equipment, connect it to the network, and verify all settings. Check each of the hardware items listed earlier in the section called "Verifying Software Functionality after a Move."

Exam Essentials

This objective is based on moving network equipment properly and then verifying its functionality.

Know how to verify the functionality of equipment before a move.   Test the equipment for network connectivity and proper operation. Take a full inventory, and label everything with both the original location and the new location.

Know how to protect equipment during transportation.   Make sure the equipment is padded, boxed, strapped down, and that all measures are taken to minimize breakage or loss. Realize that, in certain instances, only designated people are allowed to move equipment.

Know how to unpack and finish a move.   Check the inventory. Ensure that all equipment made it to the right location. Connect everything, power it up, and test network connectivity.

Sample Questions

1. If you need to move a 15-inch computer monitor from one side of an office to another, which of the following should you do?

   A. Fill out a work request.

   B. Call a union representative.

   C. Pack the monitor into a shock-proof box.

   D. Move the monitor yourself.

   E. Call your secretary.

   Answer: D—Moving the monitor yourself is the best answer for this scenario. (A work request is not needed for a minor move from one side of the office to another. A union-sanctioned move is normally only required when something leaves an office. A box is only needed when an item moves a long distance, such as from one building to another. And your secretary will probably only laugh at you.)

   WARNING   The previous question assumes that you can safely lift a 15-inch monitor without assistance.

   ---

2. What should you do to prepare for a move of your own equipment?

   A. Power down the equipment.

   B. Inventory everything.

   C. Let someone else move your equipment.

   D. Move everything while powered up.

   Answer: A, B—A complete inventory is important even if you will move the equipment yourself. Power down the equipment to prevent electrical damage when you disconnect the equipment from the wall outlet or power strip. (Do not pawn the move off onto another person, and never move something that is still powered.)

Demonstrate awareness of the need to obtain relevant permissions before adding, deleting, or modifying users.

This objective is designed to test your awareness of the need to obtain network rights and permissions before doing network maintenance. If you don't obtain the correct permissions, you may have difficulty completing some network maintenance operations, or you may not be able to do them at all.

Critical Information

Permission needs to be obtained before you make changes to user accounts. Just because you have the power to delete or change accounts does not mean that you should do it without consulting those who are affected.

Every person in Management Information Services will often have administrative rights. These rights include the capability to add new network administrators. You should not give someone these high-level rights without specific criteria being met first. The group manager, or a central administration unit, needs to authorize this. The standard is to have the appropriate manager add the new person to the administrative group on the network. An alternate method is for the manager to delegate the task with an order. This can be tedious and may take several days or weeks, so you may be tempted to take five minutes to create and add the new account to the administrator's group. Before doing that, remember that being a Network+ certified administrator involves restraint and compliance with company policies.

Another issue, although it may appear less serious, is that of managing user accounts. You also need to get the appropriate required permission in order to change a user's account, which may be obtained from one of the following sources.

- Manager of your Information Services Group

- Human Resources

- Personnel

- Legal Department

- Other designated manager or administrative body

Notice that other network administrators are not listed. You personally, as the network administrator, are not listed. That is because these administrators do not normally have approval to make management decisions. Only administrative units will know the full details necessary to making an informed decision.

WARNING   Do not have your administrative unit or manager send an e-mail message to a distribution list requesting that an account be deleted. Where there is no central authority, no work gets done, or a duplication of effort results. Assign the work request to a specific person. When the assignment is done, the network administrator then logs it as completed in a database.

Exam Essentials

This objective requires you to obtain relevant permissions before changing user accounts.

Know how to follow corporate policy when modifying accounts. Do not add, delete, or modify accounts without a prior directive for each. Modifying any account requires a new work order, either verbal or written, as specified by corporate policy.

Sample Questions

1. You work in the Global Services Department, which provides network administration for your company. A new network administrator is hired with extensive NetWare experience and certifications. The new employee also has some Unix but no Windows NT experience. What level of administrative rights should you assign this new administrator?

   A. No access

   B. User-level access only

   C. Network administrator rights on the NetWare network

   D. Network administrator rights on the Windows NT network

   E. Network administrator rights on the Unix network

   F. Network administrator rights on the NetWare and Unix networks

   G. Network administrator rights on all networks

   Answer: A—No directive from a recognized administrative unit or manager has been issued to take action. Experience, certifications, and even designated job duties and titles have no bearing on whether you assign rights or privileges to another.

2. An employee resigns from your company. Which of the following is authorized to order you to delete or move the user account and its associated data?

   A. Department secretary

   B. Personnel department

   C. Yourself as the network administrator

   D. Another network administrator

   E. Coworker of the former employee

   F. Your manager

Answer: B, F—Only recognized administrative departments or managers are authorized to give an order to modify, add, or delete accounts and data. (Neither the department secretary, you, another network administrator, nor a coworker have the necessary authority.)

Identify the purpose and function of the following networking elements

- Profiles
- Rights
- Procedures/policies
- Administrative utilities
- Login accounts, groups, and passwords

This exam objective is designed to test your knowledge of the various networking features used to make network administration easier. Each element provides a way to make the process of network administration more efficient and keep the network running.

Critical Information

Users are managed with many settings, organizations, and utilities. This is important because a degree of uniformity and standardization is needed to handle any number of users. Profiles, such as icons on your desktop, are used to define user environments. Rights allow the user to access or manage network resources. Policies set standards for the way networks are to be run. The various network administration utilities make network administration possible, and login accounts, groups, and passwords are what you administrate with these utilities.

Profiles

Profiles are used to define the users' computing environment. A user's desktop colors and icons, program groups, Start menu settings, and network connections are remembered in their profile. In Windows NT, profiles are automatically enabled. Each user's profile is stored in the \winnt\profiles folder. The Default User and All Users profiles are added during installation. Additional folders are created each time a user logs in for the first time on any machine.

Windows 9.*x* does not have profiles turned on by default. To turn them on, go to Start ≻ Settings ≻ Control Panel. When the control panel window opens, click the Users applet. The Enable Multi-User Settings wizard will appear and guide you through the process of activating profiles. Profiles are stored in the windows\profiles folder on Windows 9.*x* machines.

WARNING   NetWare also has an NDS object called Profile. It is not the same thing as a profile. The NDS Profile object has users assigned to it. This allows the users to use the same login script. (NetWare also has support for Windows NT profiles using its Z.E.N. works product.) The Windows profiles can be stored in NDS, allowing for Windows client and NetWare server integration.

Administrators or users may want to control profiles. There are two types of profiles for Windows NT users: roaming and mandatory. Roaming profiles are downloaded from a server at each login. Desktop changes are made and icons are moved around, among other things, with roaming profiles. When you log out, the changes are loaded back up to the server, ready for your next login. A mandatory profile can be for an entire network; it can be a roaming profile, or, for a single computer, standard. The difference in a mandatory profile is that changes are not loaded back up to the server on logout.

Unix uses a GUI overlay called X-Windows. To set a personal profile, the user needs to add the xset command to their login script. Various switches are used to customize displays. The Unix xdpyinfo is a helpful utility. It is used to display the characteristics of your X-Windows installation.

Rights

You need to have the proper rights to access files and complete administrative tasks. The words *rights* and *permissions* are often used interchangeably, but Microsoft makes a distinction between the two. In the Microsoft world, rights apply to file manipulation, and permissions apply to the ability to do administrative tasks. For the Network+ exam, and in other networking environments, no differentiation is made.

Procedures

Proper documentation is required to run a network. Every time you move locations, upgrade the network, and recover from a disaster, you need to know how things are to be set up. A logbook should be kept near the servers to record changes that are made in software, as well as any crashes that occur. You may be tempted to put the data into a text file. That is fine. Just remember to keep a hard copy. The file is of no use when a software bug hangs the server.

The physical aspects of your network need to be recorded. This includes all network cabling, routers, hubs, switches, workstations, servers, and their locations. Using a graphical representation is best.

TIP You can use network mapping software to make a map of your network, but it's usually simpler (and cheaper) to use a commercial drawing or graphics package. (Visio software has a network version with graphics for common network hardware topologies.)

All hardware settings need to be recorded. This should be done for servers *and* workstations. Write down the IRQ, DMA, memory, and I/O information for all peripherals installed. This process will be much simpler if you standardize on a common IRQ for your network interface cards. (Common settings are 10, 11, or 15.)

Software settings need to be stored as well. The version numbers of your operating system, service pack, patch, and options are all very important. Also standardize on a certain version of service pack after it has been internally tested. IP address, machine address (MAC address), file/print server, e-mail server, and owner need to be collected in a searchable database. When you have a MAC address that is causing conflicts on the network, you need to be able to cross-reference that with a location and user.

Policies

Users sometimes need to be restricted as to how or when they can access network resources. Contractors, interns, and temporary employees all can be managed by policies. You can set their account to automatically expire at the end of a semester or the end of a contract. A user can be limited to which computers will allow a login with a particular account. Late night work is often restricted corporation-wide. At midnight, for example, a company might have a policy that forces all users off of the network until 6:00 am. This would allow the backup procedure to copy all data and not be restricted by open files. Lastly, you might restrict the remote access right for people you do not want working at home. These are just a few examples of the policies you can implement.

Administrative Utilities

Network administrators need applications to help facilitate their jobs. Accounts need to be created, changed, and deleted. Network shares, groups, printers, and other resources all need to be managed. This is done through administrative utilities.

Windows NT

Windows NT has the User Manager and User Manager for Domains utilities. The User Manager is a program used to manage accounts on a single workstation or server. When you want to administer an entire network of servers in Windows NT Server, use User Manager for Domains (shown in Figure 11.1).

The User Manager for Domains utility is available on the Windows NT Server CD and in the Windows NT Server Resource Kit. (Resource kit CDs often contain many essential utilities.)

FIGURE 11.1: User Manager for Domains

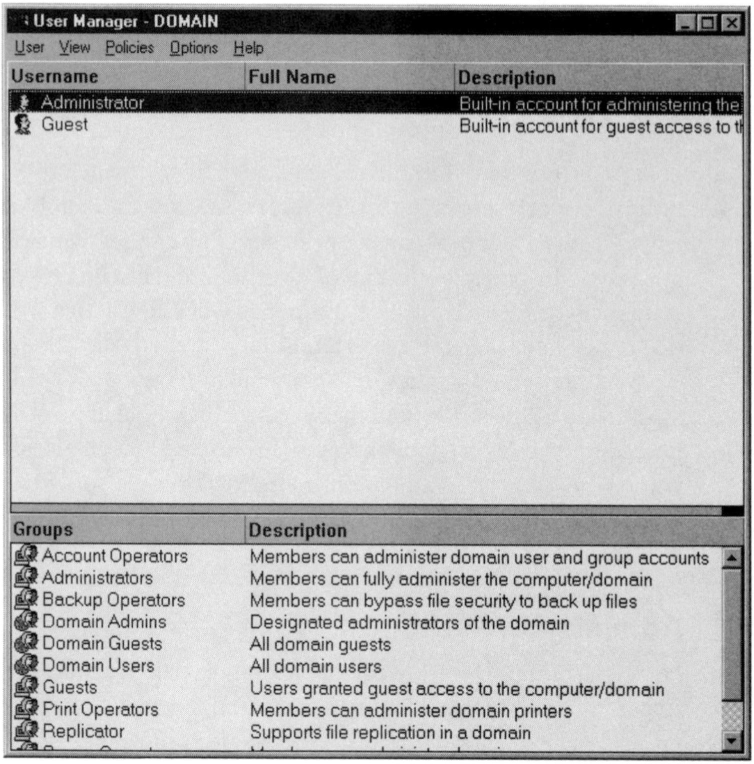

To start the User Manager for Domains on a Windows NT server, go to Start ➤ Program Files ➤ Administrative Tools ➤ User Manager for Domains. To create a new account, select User ➤ New User.... The window shown in Figure 11.2 will appear.

TIP The Server Manager utilities manage servers' shares and actively connected users. This utility complements the User Manager for Domains.

FIGURE 11.2: New User window

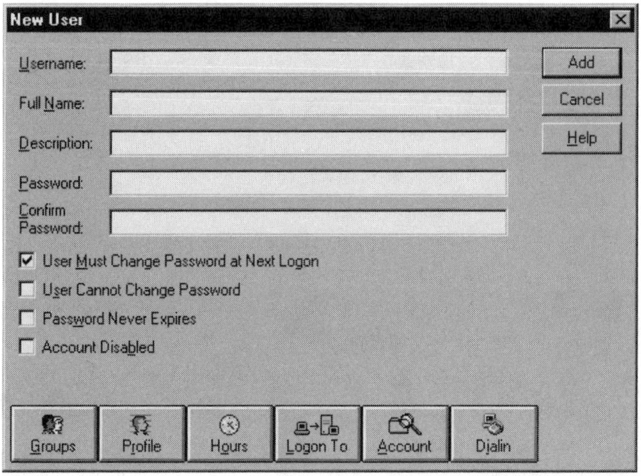

NetWare

Novell NetWare servers are now managed by the NetWare Console One or the NetWare Administrator utilities. The Console One is used in NetWare 5 and is not tested on the Network+ exam. The NetWare Administrator is used in both NetWare 4.*x* and 5, so it is covered on the exam.

The NetWare Administrator utility is located on NetWare servers, the NetWare CD, and it can be copied to local Windows 9.*x* or NT machines. This utility cannot be run from the server console. Accounts, groups, network resources, and their relationships can all be managed through the NetWare Administrator. This is truly the most advanced and integrated single utility for network management.

Unix

There are several flavors of Unix. The two major ones are System V, developed by AT&T Bell Laboratories (now Lucent Bell Laboratories), and BSD, developed at the University of California at Berkeley. System V is a commercial product, and Bell Laboratories is one of the most famous research labs in the United States.

A specific Unix utility is not tested for administrative functions. However, all Unix utilities manipulate certain text files. The knowledge of these text files can be tested. For instance, The RedHat Linux 5.1 User Configurator is a window-based utility that changes the passwd file to manage user names and passwords. For the exam, you are expected to know that the passwd file controls users (this is true for most implementations of Unix). The User Configurator is a specific RedHat utility, so it will not be on the Network+ exam. The passwd file is located in the /etc/ directory and is shown in Figure 11.3.

F I G U R E 11.3: /etc/passwd file

Some common administrative files are included in the following list.

passwd: A plain text listing of Unix usernames, and an encrypted listing of all passwords.

hosts: The Unix file that stores all Internet addresses and their corresponding IP addresses for your computers.

group: Every Unix group is located in this file.

services: The Unix file that defines services such as FTP, HTTP, NNTP and others; their respective port numbers are also listed.

alias: A Unix file that maps short, memorable names to the longer physical names and directory structures.

Login Accounts, Groups, and Passwords

Login accounts are created to uniquely identify users or
Each user can then be individually managed and given r.
or the ability to use certain administrative utilities. Login accounts
need to be restricted to a single user. To do this, a secret combination
of letters, numbers, and special characters are used, which secures the
account. This special combination of characters is called a password.
Passwords must never be given to another person, because they could
then impersonate you on the network and through e-mail. When
administrators need to test something for a given user, they must use
a test account or reset the user's password.

NOTE   Chapter 9 covers passwords in detail.

Network administrators cannot individually manage thousands of
users. This could consume your entire job. Instead, assign people to
groups, which are a collection of users that are given like privileges
and rights. Then you can assign access to certain files or management
utilities only once to the entire group. You might have a group for the
fourth floor of a building, for example, so you can then give the group
the right to use all of the printers on that floor. This saves you the time
of individually assigning each user to each printer.

TIP   Global groups are used network-wide, as in an NT Domain or
Novell Tree. Local groups only work on a single server. Be sure you
know which one is being used, along with its limitations.

Exam Essentials

This objective is based on automating and simplifying user management. You will need to identify the purpose and function of several
networking elements.

Know how to define profiles and rights.   Profiles manage a user's
environment, such as desktop layout, window colors, and icon

placement. Rights restrict and allow a user access to specific network resources.

Know how to differentiate between procedures and policies. Procedures are used to guide the network administrator in the daily management of tasks. Procedures are normally written steps that walk a network manager through administrative tasks in a company-specified way. Policies restrict user network access by the time of day, status of the employee, or other criteria.

Know the main administrative utilities for each network operating system. Windows NT 4 has User Manager for Domains. NetWare 4.*x* has NetWare Administrator. Unix has text-based files such as the passwd, hosts, group, and services files.

Know how to uniquely identify, secure, and group users. A login account identifies the user on the network. The user's password secures the account to a single user. Groups are a collection of users that are combined to ease network administration tasks.

Key Terms and Concepts

Know the concepts that relate to the functions of network administration.

alias file   Common, easily remembered names are mapped to actual directory structures in this Unix file.

Group   Users combined together so the collection can be administered as a whole.

hosts file   Domain names are resolved to IP addresses in this Unix file. (Other operating systems now use host files as well.)

Login account   Login name that uniquely identifies each user on a network.

NetWare Administrator   Novell NetWare 4.*x* and later versions use this utility for administration tasks.

Password A hard-to-guess combination of letters, numbers, and special characters, used to secure an account to a single user.

passwd file A text-based document that is used in Unix to store user accounts, encrypted passwords, and demographic information.

services file Server-provided applications and their TCP/IP port numbers are listed in this Unix text file.

User Manager A Windows NT administration utility that only controls accounts on the servers that users are logged into.

User Manager for Domains Windows NT tool that manages user accounts, passwords, and groups for the entire Microsoft network.

Sample Question

1. What administrative utility or file is used to manage Unix accounts, passwords, and user demographics?

   A. passwd

   B. Passwd

   C. group

   D. Group

   E. user manager

   F. User Manager for Domains

   Answer: A—The passwd file is used in Unix to store user accounts, passwords, and demographics. (Uppercase Unix file names are not used. The User Manager and User Manager for Domains utilities are Windows NT based.)

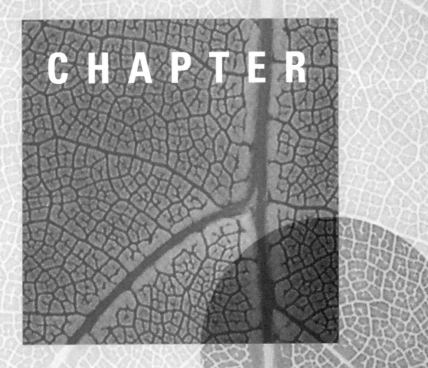

CHAPTER

12

Maintaining and Supporting
the Network

Network+ Exam Objectives Covered in This Chapter:

▶ **Identify the kinds of test documentation that are usually available regarding a vendor's patches, fixes, upgrades, etc.** *(pages 298 – 301)*

▶ **Given a network maintenance scenario, demonstrate awareness of the following issues:** *(pages 302 – 315)*
- Standard backup procedures and backup media storage practices
- The need for periodic application of software patches and other fixes to the network
- The need to install anti-virus software on the server and workstations
- The need to frequently update virus signatures

This chapter is all about patches and disaster recovery. Network administrators need to ensure data integrity. This entails more than handling a hard drive failure. Active measures, such as the installation of virus protection software and other new software, as well as hardware and software upgrades, need to be taken to keep networks functioning. The exam has several questions on this topic.

Identify the kinds of test documentation that are usually available regarding a vendor's patches, fixes, upgrades, etc.

Test documentation is information about what exactly is contained in updates and patches as well as what problems they are going to fix. Updates should never be done unless you know what they do and don't fix.

Critical Information

Patches, fixes, and upgrades all have documentation, which tells you how to install, test, and run the fixes. Hot fixes, regular fixes, updates, and patches are all basically the same thing; they are repairs and minor enhancements. Large enhancements warrant a new product version and an upgrade. Be aware of the difference between updates and upgrades. Updates simply fix known problems with a particular piece of software. Upgrades may also fix problems, but they also include several new features of that software. You can find documentation of varying types and in different locations. All the following types can be found by consulting a vendor's Web site, CDs, books, or e-mail newsletters.

Types of Documentation

White papers are documents that are used to list solutions and test methods. A white paper is basically a written record of the steps to fix a problem. White papers also define the theory behind a certain technology. An example of a white paper would be a document that walks you through configuring a Web browser installation for an obscure feature.

Technical specifications are short listings of the specific components in a software or hardware product. A SCSI card's specifications will tell the types of SCSI components that can be attached, the pins on the connectors, chip model, operating speed, number of devices supported, and other details.

Readme files are commonly called readme.txt or readme.doc. These files are on the distribution media (floppy, CD, or DVD) and in the directory of the software after installation. Normally, when you finish the installation, a window will appear asking if you want to open the readme file. You should always open and look through the file. Late-breaking tips and changes that have occurred between the time when the company printed the software's manual and the actual shipment of the software are included in the readme.

Manuals are traditionally paperback books. The desire to save money has caused a trend of transferring them to CD and to the vendor Web pages. You may be required to have a text editor, Microsoft

Word viewer, or Adobe Acrobat Reader to look at soft copy versions of manuals. Directions for installing products are usually at the beginning of most manuals. Troubleshooting advice is usually in the back. Be sure to familiarize yourself with the contents and layout of manuals.

News releases are often located on the manufacturers' Web sites and in e-mail newsletters. When you need to run tests and check upgrades and beta products, this quick type of communication can be invaluable.

Exam Essentials

This objective is based the types and locations of documentation for network patches and updates. This information should be consulted before doing a software patch or an upgrade. It is considered to be reference information for the patch or upgrade.

Know how to identify the different types of documentation for patches and fixes.   Types of documentation differ from types of distribution mediums. Web sites, CDs, and bound books are distribution mediums, and types of documentation include white papers, technical specifications, readme files, manuals, and news releases.

Key Terms and Concepts

Know the concepts that relate to network patches and software update documentation.

Manual   A hard-copy or soft-copy book that has chapters about installing, using, and troubleshooting a particular product.

News release   Presents events and news, usually on behalf of a product or a company.

Readme file   A text-file document located on distribution media that provides late-breaking news and other important information; ships with the product.

Technical specifications   Short listings of the specific components and operating environment for a software or hardware product.

White paper   A technical document that describes some obscure fact or bug fix.

Sample Questions

1. You think that a bug fix has come out since the last release of your software. What source(s) would mention this?

   A. Manual

   B. Readme file

   C. News release

   D. White papers

   E. Technical specifications

   Answers: C, D—News releases and white papers come out after products ship, so they would have current information. (Manuals and readme files are shipped with the product, so they would not have news since its shipment. Technical specifications list the components of the product and do not change, regardless of where they are located.)

2. What software packages will normally allow you to view documentation files?

   A. Word processor application

   B. Spreadsheet processor application

   C. Photo manipulation software

   D. Document viewer

   E. Image enhancement plug-ins

   Answers: A, D—A word processor application, such as Microsoft Word or Corel WordPerfect, as well as a document viewer, can view text and other document types. (A spreadsheet processor is designed for number crunching, not document viewing. Photo manipulation software is designed to work with photographs, not documents. Image enhancement plug-ins are for images and photos.)

Given a network maintenance scenario, demonstrate awareness of the following issues:

- Standard backup procedures and backup media storage practices
- The need for periodic application of software patches and other fixes to the network
- The need to install anti-virus software on the server and workstations
- The need to frequently update virus signatures

This exam objective is designed to test your knowledge of the various methods used to protect a network against downtime. Downtime can be caused by almost anything, but the Network+ exam will test you specifically on your ability to recover from and protect against network downtime caused by software problems and viruses.

Critical Information

Your data are the most important part of your network. A network is just an efficient means of transferring and storing the data. To ensure data integrity, network administrators need to back up data to tape, protect data from viruses, and update software packages when patches come out.

Backup

You know that data, when backed up, are actually retrievable from tape. If a real restore is not done by user request every month, you should do a test restore. Full backups, differential backups, and incremental backups are all tested on the Network+ exam, so you should know the difference between them.

Full Backup

Full backups copy all files from server hard disks to tape every day. This system is easy to use because there are no configurations, special settings, or even databases to search. Say a user corrupted a file on Tuesday afternoon. With a full back up, you know that every tape has the entire server's hard disk on it. Just put Monday night's tape in and pull up the file. With a full backup, you need not search for which tape the file backed up on. With other tape backup schemes, a database needs to be checked for which tape has the file. Figure 12.1 shows the amount of data backed up each day in a full backup scheme. Note that if you are regularly working with 20GB of data, each night 20GB are stored onto a new tape, along with any additional data from that day.

FIGURE 12.1: Amount of data backed up by a full backup

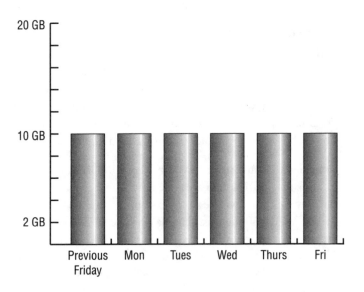

An archive bit is attached to every file, denoting its backup status. If the archive bit is set, the file needs to be backed up. Otherwise, the file is overlooked during the backup process. The archive bit is cleared during a full backup. All files are duplicated to tape every night regardless of the archive bit status on each file.

NOTE   Righ-click a file in Windows 9.*x* and click Properties. The archive attribute will have a check mark in its box if the file needs to be backed up. In binary terms, a set bit is one and a clear bit is zero.

It takes a long time to do nightly full backups. Consider that standard drives are at least 10GB each, and a file and print server for an average department would have five disk drives, with one drive (one-fifth of the capacity) used for parity. This means that you have a maximum 40GB of data from one server to back up nightly. You can assume that the server is half full and that 20GB must be archived. Most backups are run during the night and must be completed by the time the next morning's workers begin coming in. A high-quality single tape unit can back up 40MB per minute, or 19.2GB in eight hours.

Differential Backup

Differential backup allows a maximum of two backup sessions to restore a file or group of files. A single full backup is still typically performed once per week. The archive bit is cleared during the full backup to denote that everything is on tape. Then each night the backup program copies every item that has changed since the last full backup. The archive bit is not touched during each nightly differential backup.

Consider a file and print server that has 100GB stored on it on Friday. Assume that 2GB of data are added each business day. The backup from the previous week will be a full session, or 10GB to tape. Monday night will be 2GB in 50 minutes. Tuesday will be 4GB in an hour and 40 minutes, and so on, ending with 8GB in three hours and 20 minutes on Thursday. On Friday, you back up 20GB but are not worried about the downtime because your company is closed on weekends. Figure 12.2 (on the next page) presents further detail about differential backups.

Two tape sessions are used to do a restore for differential backups. This will give you everything on the server. The full session tape covers everything that was on the server on Friday. The second tape contains the data that has changed since the last full backup. This is a compromise in backup and restore times. The backup times are greatly reduced, but they grow daily. The restore time requires multiple tapes and backup databases, but it is restricted to two.

F I G U R E 12.2: Amount of data backed up daily with a differential backup

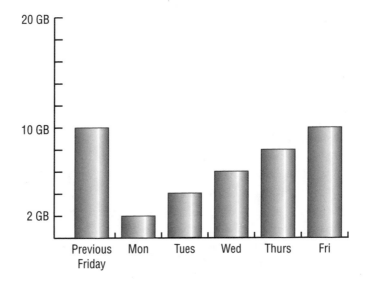

Incremental Backup

An incremental backup works with a full backup session but is different from a differential scheme. Data that have the archive bit set are backed up. After the data are copied, the archive bit is cleared on every file. Consider the previous backup scenario. This means that the previous Friday has 10GB stored. On Monday, 2GB are stored and the bit is cleared. On Tuesday, two more gigabytes of data are added. The new data from Tuesday are the only data with an archive bit, signaling a backup requirement. On Tuesday, 2GB are stored on tape. Each backup continues to be 2GB and take 50 minutes until the next full session. Each incremental session only stores what changed or was added that day.

Incremental backup is the fastest method to store your data. However, the network administrator does pay a price for shortened backup sessions. The restores take the longest of the three methods. The full backup tape plus every tape from the day in question back to the proceeding Friday are retrieved. Figure 12.3 (on the next page) shows the incremental backup scenario.

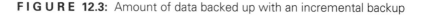

FIGURE 12.3: Amount of data backed up with an incremental backup

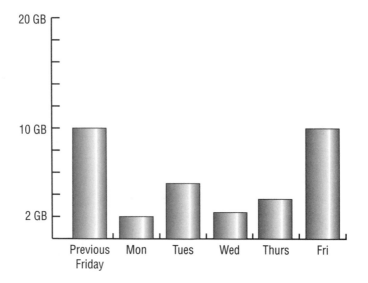

Multi-Generation GFS

A standard rotation scheme for tapes is the Grandfather-Father-Son (GFS) method. Daily backups are differential, incremental, or full. Full backups are done once per week. The daily backups are known as the Son. The last full backup of the week is known as the Father. The daily tapes are reused after a week, so they only age five days. The weekly tapes stay around for a month, watch five cycles of Sons and grow as old as Fathers. The last full backup of the month is known as the monthly backup, or the Grandfather backup. The Grandfather tapes grow the oldest and stay around for a year before they are reused.

Media Storage Types

There are dozens of types of removable media. Small removable disks are best used for personal files. If you have a picture from the company picnic that you want to print on your color inkjet at home, a Zip Disk or SuperDisk works great. If you are a publisher and you need to send photos to the printer, then Sharq and Jaz cartridges work great. CD-R and DVD-RAM disks are great for near-permanent storage. Tapes are the best, cheapest media for doing high-volume nightly backups.

Small Removable Disks   PCs have enjoyed low costs and continued improvement of performance in hardware. This is true in the small hard disk area as well. SyQuest drives started out in the early 1990s, stored up to 40MB, were large, and cost $80 each. Today, the Iomega Zip Disk 250MB is coming out and is slightly larger than a 3.5-inch floppy diskette. Sony is also touting small, portable media in the form of a high definition floppy. The HD floppy is compatible with regular floppies and Sony's high-definition diskette.

All of these small, removable disks are good solutions for personal storage. Many new personal computers and laptops have these drives preinstalled. However, they have no place on a server. When you are looking at hardware that must be compatible for Windows NT, NetWare, and Unix, you must be very careful. These products replace the floppy drive and can use a floppy controller or IDE controller. NetWare and Unix both expect to see a floppy drive during the installation of the network operating system. Without a floppy disk, neither Unix nor NetWare can be installed properly. Currently, Windows 9.*x* has the most support for these specialty products.

Large Removable Disks   The Sharq 1.5GB drive and Jaz 2GB drive are large, removable hard disks in cartridge format. You can use these as regular hard drives and boot from them. The cartridges cost approximately a dollar a megabyte. Think of the possibilities. You could have a Jaz drive on a test server, for instance. Depending on which cartridge you install, you get a different operating system. With six cartridges, you could test several operating systems: Windows NT Server 4.0, Windows 2000 Server, NetWare 4.11, NetWare 5, RedHat Linux, and Caldera OpenLinux. These media are good for exchanging large images with your printing department and for running test servers. But even with 2GB, you do not have enough storage space to back up a server or an entire network of servers.

Optical Disks   Optical disks use lasers to change the magnetic setting on a portion of a diskette. They share the magnetic diskette media of floppies and hard disks, along with the lasers of CD and DVD technology. One example is an Imation and 3M product called the SuperDisk, or LS-120. The SuperDisk drive is versatile—it can accept floppy disks and SuperDisks. The increased capacity disks can store 120MB, hence their alternate name LS-120. Like Zip Disks and high definition disks, they are great for your users to have on their desktops but are too small for a network administrator's servers.

CD-R, CD-RW, and DVD-RAM   Near-permanent records should be stored on media that you cannot erase. If you want to store a yearly financial statement going back 30 years, then compact disk media are a good solution. A common compact disk can store 640MB of data and can be burned either once or in multiple sessions. A CD-R has data burned into it by a CD writer laser. Opening and closing each additional session takes several megabytes of additional space. This reduces the total space available for data. If you wish to erase and reuse the media, use CD-RWs, as CD-Rs cannot be erased.

DVDs are known as digital versatile disks, or digital video disks, depending on whom you ask. A good thing about DVDs is that they have reached an initial standard of 4.6GB. Entire movies or large computer games can fit onto one DVD. DVD-RAMs are for computers only and come in protective cartridges.

Both CDs and DVDs hold the most data of any medium, but they come with the drawback of being the slowest medium to use. They are best relegated to special projects and kept off the nightly backup rotations.

Tapes   Digital Equipment Corporation (DEC) pioneered digital linear tape (DLT) technology. DLTs were originally used for backing up VAX mini computers. The cartridges are much larger than digital analog tapes, but they still can fit in the palm of your hand. The increased width and length of tapes add to increased storage capacity. DLTs commonly have 15GB and 35GB of native storage per cartridge. Normally, tapes have two spools inside, as well as outriggers that allow the tape to be read off of the central spool.

Digital audio tapes (DAT) come in 4mm and 8mm widths.

TIP   Native storage is when data are stored without compression. Tape drives are advertised with their native and compressed storage capacities. Compression amount varies with the type of data being stored. Because of this variance, only native capacities are discussed here.

Quarter-inch cartridges (QIC) are used in the home computer market. Several companies make these drives. A large QIC drive can store 5GB of native data per cartridge and copy approximately 30MB per minute. (Travan cartridges are similar to QIC. Check the specifications of your drive to see what it is compatible with.)

Advanced intelligent tapes (AIT) were invented by Sony. The tapes use media that are 8mm wide, like DATs, but that is where the similarity ends. AITs incorporate a memory chip in each tape. The chip stores the table of contents and the location of all files on the tape. This makes restores much faster because you do not need to hunt through databases that may or may not be on your hard drive. Native storage is currently up to 25GB. This technology is advanced, just like the name implies, and it carries a large price tag. The drives and tapes are the most expensive of the type described here.

NOTE Some tape backup programs call their databases trees or sets. When the size of the database gets beyond the limit you set, old records are deleted, or "pruned."

Periodic Patches and Fixes

Patches, fixes, service packs, and updates are all the same thing—small, free revisions for your software. These are intermediary solutions until a new full version of the product is released. These packages do everything from solving something particular, such as with a security patch, to changing the way your system works, as with an update. Hot fixes are considered to be hot because they can be applied without rebooting your computer. Other changes require you to schedule the server to go down for maintenance. Not all patches are necessary. You can get the patches from different locations, and there are different methods for applying different updates.

Is Patching Necessary?

Patches are available for everything from word processors to Web browsers to operating systems. You should not apply every patch that is out there. If the patch can never apply to your system, then skip it. If the patch hangs computers, then skip it. If you do not understand the changes that a patch will introduce, hold off until you do some research. Find out if the patch applies to you. Multi-CPU patches are not necessary if your computer is only capable of one CPU. A Net-BEUI fix is not needed if you only run TCP/IP. Security patches are the kind most often needed. If your laws allow it, install a strong encryption service pack. When a Web–server bug is found that opens your file system to anyone, you should obviously install the fix.

Where to Get Patches

Patches are available from the following locations:

- Manufacturers' Web sites
- Manufacturers' support CDs or DVDs
- Manufacturers' BBSs (less frequently used)
- Original equipment manufacturer (OEM)

Do you notice anything about the list above? All sources are directly from the manufacturer of the product you own. This is important. Online magazines, other companies, and shareware Web sites are not verified as being safe. That does not mean that the sites are dangerous but just that you cannot be sure that files you obtain from them have not become accidentally corrupted or intentionally altered. The exception is prepackaged patches with a new purchase from an original equipment manufacturer. Just as you trust that the operating system bundled with your new computer is safe, you can trust that the patch bundled with it has not been tampered with either.

How to Apply Patches

Upgrades—and that is what patches are—should always be approached systematically. Do not install patches on production equipment right away. That does not mean that you should only steer away from servers. Even your desktop is considered a production system. How much time and work is lost if a user's computer is down? Magnify that by downing a machine that is used by the IS staff to support the network.

Follow these steps to apply a patch:

1. Research the enhancements and changes that the patch provides. Use the manufacturer's Web site or official documentation.

2. Download the patch and related documentation to an isolated test network.

3. Decompress any documentation files and read them. (Yes, the manual is something you read before installation, not after things crash.)

4. Note the changes and define a way to test the new features.

5. Install the patch on a test workstation.

6. Select the installation method that allows you to save previous configurations to allow an uninstall.

7. Record any options and your selections, such as keeping or replacing drivers.

8. Reboot the computer.

9. If the operating system does not load or work properly, start over with a clean test machine. Choose to keep your original drivers. (NIC drivers are commonly updated and may not work.)

10. Try out the new features. Test all security patches to see if they do what is advertised.

11. Run the test workstation for two weeks. Reboot it and try different tasks during this time.

12. If all goes well, install the patch on a test server.

13. Repeat steps 5 through 12 on a test server.

14. If all goes well, do a limited rollout of the update to your support staff's personal computers, and have them test the patch.

15. After the IS support staff determines the product is safe, do a limited rollout to your users' workstations.

16. Roll out the patch to your production servers and all workstations via an automated procedure.

17. Ensure proper revision control. Make sure that all equipment has the same approved patch.

Installation of Anti-Virus Software

There are tens of thousands of viruses that your computer can contract. Known viruses that are out in the open are referred to as being in the wild. Research laboratories and universities study viruses for commercial and academic purposes. These viruses are known as being in the zoo, or not out in the wild. The number of viruses in the wild increases every month.

Viruses can be little more than hindrances, or they can shut down an entire corporation. The types vary, but the approach to handling them does not change. Where possible, you need to install virus protection software on all computer equipment. This is similar to vaccinating your entire family, not just the children who are going to summer camp. Workstations, servers, and firewalls must have protection. This is not overkill. A computer may never connect to your network. The stand-alone PC will not benefit from the server protection. Firewalls also need protection. If a virus is sent out to another corporation, then your network can possibly be harmed.

Updating Virus Signatures

Every month, you need to update your list of known viruses and how to protect yourself from them. In other words, you need to update your definition files, which are sometimes known as DAT files. Originally, you had to download zipped files manually. Then you would open the zip file, extract the contents, and copy them into the program directory of your virus scan software. Now you are able to use graphical utilities that are able to manually and automatically update your definitions. You can use a staging server within your company to download and then distribute the updates, or the computers can each do it individually. Windows 98 comes with Network Associates' McAfee AntiVirus.

When you start McAfee VirusScan Central, the virus definitions and their dates are listed. In previous versions of VirusScan, and in other manufacturer's products, you need to look elsewhere. The Help ➤ About button in McAfee VirusScan will also bring up a window showing you the version number of your newly updated engine and the date of your virus definitions. VirusScan Central in Figure 12.4 (on the next page) shows virus definitions that were created on 11/20/1998. They need to be updated.

FIGURE 12.4: Virus definitions need updating

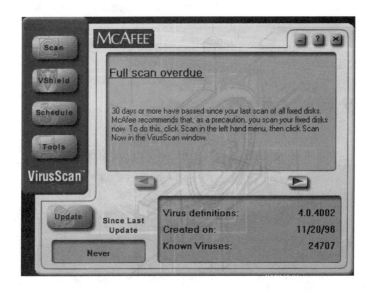

Exam Essentials

This objective is based on maintenance of a network. Backup methods, patch applications, and anti-virus software are all tested in this objective.

Know how to identify different backup procedures and media storage practices.   A full backup copies all data and clears the archive bit. A differential backup copies all data changes since the last full backup and does not clear the archive bit. An incremental backup copies changed data since the nearest incremental backup or full backup. Removable media are used to store and transfer data from one person to another. Tapes are the most common backup media. (See the Critical Information section for other removable media and their uses.)

Know how to update software with patches, fixes, and updates. Patches should only be installed after reading their documentation and testing them on non-production equipment.

Know how to identify the need to install anti-virus software and update virus signatures. Anti-virus software needs to be installed on all servers and workstations. The accompanying virus definition signatures need to be updated every month.

Key Terms and Concepts

Know the terms that relate to viruses, backup software, and patches.

Anti-virus engine A software package that runs the scans and cleans viruses by checking the computer storage with the virus definition files.

Differential backup All files that have changed since the last full backup are copied to removable media. The archive bit on each file is not cleared.

Full backup All files are copied to removable media. The archive bit on each file is cleared.

Incremental backup All files that have changed since the last incremental backup are copied to removable media. If no incremental backup has been done, all files that have changed since the last full backup are copied to removable media.

Patch All updates, fixes, and minor repairs and enhancements are considered to be patches, which are typically free additions or repairs for software.

Removable media Data are transferred from one person to another or stored for archive purposes on hardware that can be taken out of the computer. These data storage items are normally small and easily transportable, such as floppies, disks, cartridges, and tapes.

Virus definition files This is a list of all known viruses and how they can be cleaned from the system.

Sample Questions

1. What type of backup procedure copies data since the last full backup only?

   A. Supplemental backup

   B. Incremental with clearing the archive bit

   C. Incremental without clearing the archive bit

   D. Differential with clearing the archive bit

   E. Differential without clearing the archive bit

   Answer: E—Differential backups do not clear the archive bit. They also copy everything since the last full backup. (Supplemental is not a type of backup procedure. Incremental backs up data that changed since the last full or incremental backup.)

2. How often should you update virus signatures?

   A. Daily

   B. Weekly

   C. Monthly

   D. Quarterly

   E. Yearly

Answer: C—Manufacturers release virus signature updates on a routine, monthly basis.

CHAPTER

13

Identifying, Assessing,
and Responding to Problems

▶ Given an apparent network problem, determine the nature of the action required (i.e., information transfer vs. handholding vs. technical service). *(pages 318 – 322)*

▶ Given a scenario involving several network problems, prioritize them based on their seriousness. *(pages 322 – 328)*

Every network has problems from time to time. This chapter addresses how to handle certain network problems. This section of the Network+ exam covers the various topics involved in troubleshooting network problems and finding solutions to those problems.

Given an apparent network problem, determine the nature of the action required (i.e., information transfer vs. handholding vs. technical service).

The quick detection and diagnosis of network problems is important, but the steps that are taken to solve these problems are even more important. The three main methods that network administrators rely on to ascertain and resolve network issues are information transfer, handholding, and technical service. Information transfer consists of giving the user a set of instructions that they complete on their own. Handholding is normally done over the telephone or through remote management software. And technical service is an on-site visit that requires a hardware service technician for hardware failures or a network administrator for software issues. Each of these methods is discussed in detail in this section.

Critical Information

When troubleshooting network problems, you must determine what level of service is required to solve the problem.

Information Transfer

Information transfer is when you explain a solution to a user and have them solve their own networking problem. An example of this would be when the user is told that they should use Microsoft Word for their memos instead of Power Point. You are transferring the knowledge that Word is for documents and Power Point is for presentations. And, by transferring that knowledge to the user, you have solved the problem.

Handholding

Handholding is when you help a user step-by-step through a problem. At times, the solution to a problem is beyond the technical grasp of a user. Users forget how to perform some tasks, or the attempt at information transfer just fails. Sometimes even the most experienced network gurus need to humble themselves, ask for assistance, and be taken methodically through the steps for resolving an issue.

Technical Service

Technical service falls into the two distinct categories of hardware and software issues. Hardware technical service calls involve, as it sounds, problems with computer hardware. With these problems, it is important that the network administrator know the following about the desktop in question:

- Model number
- Serial number
- Description of problem
- Part number
- Manufacturer warranty information

Armed with this information, the network administrator can swap out defective parts and get machines up and running with minimal down time. Provided that there are service contracts and/or manufacturer warranties, the administrator should call to obtain a return authorization number and a tracking number so repairs can be made.

With software technical service issues, the problems that arise are, unfortunately, not as simple to fix as merely swapping out bad components. With the growing complexity of new software, the issue of support is a difficult one for many different packages. Typical software technical issues are usually related to the following scenarios:

- Upgrading an operating system

- Upgrading a software package

- Updating a patch or fix

- Reinstalling a software package

- Checking the network connection

- Reconfiguring a computer due to incorrect user configurations

- Fixing security bugs

- Reapplying a Corporate Standard Workstation Disk Image

When a Corporate Standard Workstation Disk Image is put on a machine that is beyond repair, you should beware that all user data that are not on a user-designated, periodically backed-up drive will be lost. If the user has data stored on that workstation, the data should be backed up before the image is done; otherwise, the data will be permanently lost.

Exam Essentials

This objective discusses the actions that need to be taken after a network problem presents itself.

Know how to determine if information transfer is the best course of action to resolve a particular problem. When users have moderate to high computer knowledge, support personnel can direct them to perform software upgrades, configuration, or other fixes on their own.

Know how to determine if handholding is the best course of action to resolve a particular problem.   When users with low to moderate computer knowledge have computer problems, you may have to walk them through each step. Specific directions need to be given.

Know how to determine if technical service is the best course of action to resolve a particular problem.   When you cannot resolve a problem remotely, technical service is warranted.

Know how to determine what type of technical service is needed. Hardware failures can generally be detected when a computer fails to power up or a device (like a floppy drive) does not write. Software failures involve applications that stop working, or related problems. Hardware failures are easier to identify.

Key Terms and Concepts

You should know the acronyms and terms that relate to resolving network issues.

Handholding   When users are walked through, item by item, how to resolve a particular computer problem.

Information transfer   When a network administrator passes knowledge about fixing an issue to a user and has them solve it on their own.

Technical service   When a network administrator, either by way of hardware replacement or software upgrade, intervenes to solve a particular user issue.

Sample Questions

1. What action should be taken when a hard drive does not spin?

   A. Handholding

   B. Support call

   C. Technical service

   D. Software reset

   E. Information transfer

Answer: C—Ultimately, a hard drive that is damaged to the point of not spinning needs to be replaced by a certified hardware service technician. (Handholding is one-on-one support. A support call is one method to get information transfer, handholding, or technical service. Information transfer is when the user gets instructions for how to solve their problem.)

2. Which of the following best describes handholding?

   A. Knowledge related about how to resolve an issue

   B. Direct intervention by network administrator to swap out hard drives

   C. A user is walked through how to resolve an issue

   D. Direct intervention by network administrator to upgrade software

   E. All of the above

Answer: C—Selection A is information transfer. B is the hardware aspect of technical service. D is the software aspect of technical service.)

Given a scenario involving several network problems, prioritize them based on their seriousness.

This objective is designed to test your ability to think on your feet and to prioritize problems so the problems that affect the most users are solved first and those that aren't as critical are solved as resources become available. The Network+ exam will give you several scenarios and ask you to pick the item with the highest priority.

Critical Information

When you encounter a network problem, you need to be able to establish its seriousness and rank it among other work assignments. This will allow you to keep the largest part of the network functioning for the longest amount of time. Higher priority should be given to problems that affect greater numbers of users.

Narrowing Problems Down

Troubleshooting a network problem can be a daunting task. That's why you must try to narrow problems down in a few key areas to make the task of troubleshooting them easier. The troubleshooting tips discussed in this chapter are only a short list of things to check, and as you become a better troubleshooter, you will develop your own list.

Prioritizing Network Outages

Regardless of what you call the levels or where you work, the following basic divisions of network outages are used:

- User(s) inconvenienced
- User(s) down
- Site(s) down
- Network(s) down

When users are inconvenienced, they might complain or be delayed in their work. However, users can still work on the network. This might mean that the nearest printer is out for repair, But users can still walk to another group's printer. Or perhaps the user can work on another machine if their computer dies.

The term *users down* refers to when a single person or small group of people cannot get access to the network. This could be because a user has forgotten their password or that several users have become locked out of the network due to a hardware failure in the network infrastructure.

A *site-down* situation is a serious problem. All users in a building or campus may have lost network connectivity. Your only router may have failed. The power may be out for that section of town or your whole city. A computer virus may have taken over all of your computers. Site-down emergencies warrant management intervention.

A *network-down* situation is the worst thing that can happen. When a network is in this condition, all users on the network are affected and no one can get access to their data on the server or access any other network resource.

Regardless of the situation, there is no reason to panic. Act the same in all situations; be calm, cool, levelheaded, and systematic. If you panic in a crisis situation, you will be useless. As a network administrator, you may even cause more damage. Realize that you can get more work done and think more clearly when you concentrate on the problems at hand and not about the anger and frustration of everyone around you is feeling.

Simple Stuff

Whenever there is a problem, the first thing to check, as most people will tell you, is the simple stuff. For computers, it's rather hard to categorize what simple stuff is, because what's simple to one person might be complex to another. Simple stuff, as it relates to troubleshooting, can be defined as those items that you may not think to check but appear obvious when you do. There are a few items that almost everyone can agree would fall into this category, including:

- Whether the problem is reproducible?
- Correct login procedure and rights
- Link lights
- Power switch
- Operator error

Can the Problems Be Reproduced?

The first thing you should always ask anyone who reports a network problem is, "Can you show me what 'not working' looks like?" This way, the user will be forced to reproduce the problem. This is an important thing to try because, if you can reproduce the problem, you can notice the conditions under which the problem is happening. If you can determine the conditions, you can start to determine the source of the problem.

Unfortunately, not every problem can be reproduced. The hardest problems to solve are those that can't be reproduced because they appear randomly and without any pattern,. This makes the source of the problem more difficult to detect.

Correct Login Procedures and Rights

In order to gain access to a network, users must follow the correct login procedure exactly. If they deviate from the norm, they will be denied access to the network. There are several items that can prevent a user from gaining access, and there is only one way to gain access.

The first, most basic item a user must do in order to log in correctly is to enter their username and password correctly. As easy as this sounds, there are many incidents where the username and password are entered incorrectly and the user wrongly interprets it as if there is a problem with the network. The most common problem is accidentally having the Caps Lock key pressed when trying to log in. The Caps Lock key causes a keyboard to type only in capital letters. Network operating systems can be case sensitive, so users will not be able to log in unless their passwords are typed on login as they were when originally entered.

Additionally, many network operating systems (like NetWare and Windows NT) can put restrictions on the times and conditions under which you log in. If you aren't logging in at the right time or from the right workstation, the network may reject your login request, even though it might be a correct request. A user could also see this as a problem to report, even though the network is doing what it should.

To test for this type of problem, you should first check the network documentation to see if these kinds of restrictions are in place. Then, if the user passes the restrictions, you should check their username and password by trying the login yourself from another workstation (assuming that doesn't violate any security policy). If it works, you might try asking the user to check to see if the Caps Lock light on their keyboard is on (indicating that the Caps Lock key has been activated).

TIP   If the user unsuccessfully attempts to log in too many times, this may trip the network's intruder detection, which will then refuse all attempts to login with that username until the administrator resets the account.

Link lights are the lights on NICs and hubs that indicate that a physical connection exists between the NIC and another device. If either link light doesn't light when a cable is connected between two devices, it means that the connection is faulty. Similarly, if you can't log in to the network, check for the link light on the NIC; if it is not on, the NIC is not making a connection to the rest of the network.

Power Switch

Almost every network device is powered. It seems obvious and almost ludicrous to mention, but the power switch must be turned on in order for the device to function properly. Check the power switch to make sure that it is in the On position so the device in question can receive power.

Operator Error

When a user reports a problem, one other simple check is to make sure they are correctly performing the operation in question. This possible source of problems is not always considered, but a user could be doing the operation incorrectly. A good way of checking is to have the user perform the operation for you. If it turns out that they were making some sort of mistake, you can then show them the correct way to do the operation.

Exam Essentials

This objective is based on narrowing problems down and establishing priorities based on scenarios. Each scenario is different, but, for the most part, you should prioritize items based on their seriousness. Those issues that affect the most users for the longest amount of time should be handled first, followed by those that affect smaller numbers of users, and then those that affect the lowest number of users (including just a single user).

Know how to prioritize network problems. Prioritize network problems based on the number of users affected by a particular problem. The more users who are affected by a problem, the higher the problem's priority should be.

Sample Questions

1. Users at your New York site are not able to access the Internet. A few interns in Canberra developing a demo cannot get the servers to work. An engineer in Mykonos cannot print to the laser printer, but the inkjet printer is working. In what order should you address these issues?

   A. Mykonos, New York, Canberra

   B. Mykonos, Canberra, New York

   C. Canberra, Mykonos, New York

   D. Canberra, New York, Mykonos

   E. New York, Mykonos, Canberra

   F. New York, Canberra, Mykonos

   Answer: F—The New York users are experiencing a site outage, which is considered a high priority. (The interns cannot get a server going for a demo, but they are not presenting, only developing. The engineer is able to print even though the laser printer is not available, so the engineer is a low priority. The importance of the user is a factor, but it is not the only one. The priority of regular users can outweigh that of an engineer, depending on their problems.)

2. A manager cannot access e-mail in Canberra. A boot sector virus has broken out among your Mykonos users. Users in New York are experiencing a longer-than-normal response time to connect to Web-based databases. In what order do you address these problems?

   A. Mykonos, Canberra, New York

   B. Mykonos, New York, Canberra

   C. Canberra, Mykonos, New York

   D. Canberra, New York, Mykonos

   E. New York, Mykonos, Canberra

   F. New York, Canberra, Mykonos

   Answer: A—The virus outbreak affects the most users and brings their system down. A boot sector virus has the potential to completely down all users. (The Canberra manager has a real problem, but it has only brought one user down. The New York users are currently only inconvenienced.)

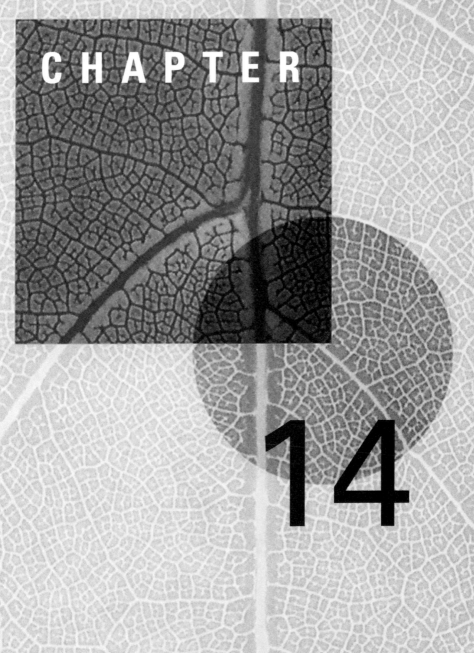

CHAPTER

14

Troubleshooting the Network

Network+ Exam Objectives Covered in This Chapter:

▶ **Identify the following steps as a systematic approach to identify the extent of a network problem, and, given a problem scenario, select the appropriate next step based on this approach:** *(pages 332 – 338)*

1. Determine whether the problem exists across the network.
2. Determine whether the problem is workstation, workgroup, LAN, or WAN.
3. Determine whether the problem is consistent and replicable.
4. Use standard troubleshooting methods.

▶ **Identify the following steps as a systematic approach for trouble-shooting network problems, and, given a problem scenario, select the appropriate next step based on this approach:** *(pages 339 – 345)*

1. Identify the exact issue.
2. Re-create the problem.
3. Isolate the cause.
4. Formulate a correction.
5. Implement the correction.
6. Test.
7. Document the problem and the solution.
8. Give feedback.

▶ **Identify the following steps as a systematic approach to determining whether a problem is attributable to the operator or the system, and, given a problem scenario, select the appropriate next step based on this approach:** *(pages 346 – 348)*

1. Have a second operator perform the same task on an equivalent workstation.
2. Have a second operator perform the same task on the original operator's workstation.
3. See whether operators are following standard operating procedure.

▶ **Given a network troubleshooting scenario, demonstrate awareness of the need to check for physical and logical indicators of trouble, including:** *(pages 349 – 369)*

- Link lights
- Power lights

- Error displays
- Error logs and displays
- Performance monitors

Identify common network troubleshooting resources, including: *(pages 370 – 374)*

- Knowledge bases on the World Wide Web
- Telephone technical support
- Vendor CDs

Given a network problem scenario, including symptoms, determine the most likely cause or causes of the problem based on the available information. Select the most appropriate course of action based on this inference. Issues that may be covered include: *(pages 375 – 381)*

- Recognizing abnormal physical conditions
- Isolating and correcting problems in cases where there is a fault in the physical media (patch cable)
- Checking the status of servers
- Checking for configuration problems with DNS, WINS, and HOSTS files
- Checking for viruses
- Checking the validity of the account name and password
- Rechecking operator logon procedures
- Selecting and running appropriate diagnostics

Specify the tools that are commonly used to resolve network equipment problems. Identify the purpose and function of common network tools, including: *(pages 382 – 388)*

- Crossover cable
- Hardware loopback
- Tone generator
- Tone locator (fox and hound)

Given a network problem scenario, select appropriate tools to help resolve the problem. *(pages 388 – 390)*

Users will inadvertently damage their PCs. Hardware fails. Administrators accidentally corrupt files. Your job as a network administrator is to find the problems, avoid getting pulled in by red herrings, and implement solutions. Hardware and software problems can be confused. People will not always give you a clear view of the problem.

You will need to look to isolate the severity of the problem. Is there a network outage on one workstation, one LAN, or all over the WAN? Using eight systematic steps, you can isolate the problem. Error logs and screen messages are a good starting point for troubleshooting. Remember to keep a cool head. Being in a panicked state will slow your troubleshooting skills and add to uncertainty among the users.

Identify the following steps as a systematic approach to identify the extent of a network problem, and, given a problem scenario, select the appropriate next step based on this approach:

- Determine whether the problem exists across the network.
- Determine whether the problem is workstation, workgroup, LAN, or WAN.
- Determine whether the problem is consistent and replicable.
- Use standard troubleshooting methods.

The first part of network troubleshooting is to narrow given problems down so you aren't looking everywhere on the network for a problem. This process involves testing various aspects of the network to find which part of the network is the source of the problem.

Critical Information

When you are looking at a problem, isolate the extent of its effect. Is more than one person having the problem? Is more than one building affected? Once you have determined how far-reaching the problem is, look toward replicating the problem. Does the workstation fail when any person logs in or just a particular person does?

To find a given problem and solve it, do not take random steps. Options cannot be eliminated unless a systematic approach to troubleshooting is followed.

Determining Whether Problems Exists Across a Network

One of the first things to do is to determine how widespread a problem is. Is the whole network experiencing the problem? Just one or two segments? Or only a single workstation or workgroup? If you don't know the extent, the first thing to do is to try to connect to other areas of the network, perhaps by pinging different nodes in different areas. After finding out how widespread the failure is, you might find out what it is affecting. Is it an application that is down? Is it data that is inaccessible, or perhaps just a connectivity issue? This step will assist you in narrowing down the problem to a particular segment, server, or application.

Use a top–down approach to network troubleshooting. Always look at the component highest up in the affected area first. For example, you have a router or switch feeding several hubs, which connect to several departmental servers, which connect to hubs, and then departmental workstations. If the entire network is down, start with the router. If one segment is down, start with the switch or hub for that area. If one departmental area is down, look at the departmental server and then the departmental hub. If you have made it that far down the chain, the problem probably originates on a single workstation.

In a large company that relies heavily on network operations, you can usually tell the extent of a problem by the number of phone calls that you receive. While being an inconvenience, these calls, especially the areas that they come from, may put you well on your way to discovering the extent of the problem. Are the problems similar? One person who can't connect to a server and another who can't boot their machine are not *necessarily* indicative of a widespread problem.

Determining whether Problems Are Workstation, Workgroup, LAN, or WAN

This is the next logical step when narrowing down the source of a problem. Once you have determined whether the problem exists across the entire network, you must determine whether a problem exists on a particular workstation, within a workgroup, or if the problem can be localized to either the LAN or the WAN.

Problems with Particular Workstation or Servers

This step in narrowing down a problem involves determining if the problem is related to a particular workstation or server. The symptoms will be whether one person or a group of people is affected. If only one person is affected, the problem might be related to just their workstation. If a whole group is affected, an entire server may be experiencing the problem.

The quickest way to determine this is to try and log in from another workstation within the same group of users as the user who is experiencing the problem. If they can log in fine from that workstation, the problem is related to their workstation. There may be a cabling fault, bad NIC, or some other problem with that workstation.

On the other hand, if several people in a workgroup (like a whole department) can't access a server, the problem may be related to that server. To check if the problem is related to the server, go to the server that people are having trouble logging in to and check for user connections. If everyone is logged in, then the problem could be related to something else, like individual rights or permissions. If no one can log in to the server, including the administrator, the server may have a communication problem with the rest of the network, or it may simply have crashed.

Determining Affected Segments

This step can be tough. Narrowing down the problem can also include determining which segment or segments of the network are affected.

Is the whole network having this problem, or just a certain segment. If it's just a particular segment, the problem might be an addressing or routing issue. If multiple segments are affected, the problem could result from a network address conflict. You might remember from Chapter 4 that network addresses must be unique across an entire network. If two segments have the same IPX address, for example, all of the routers and NetWare servers will complain bitterly by sending out error messages, hoping that it's just a simple problem that a router can correct. This is rarely the case, however, and this extra traffic can burden the two segments as well as slow down the entire network.

If the whole network is experiencing the problem, it could be located with a different device, like a particular server that everyone accesses. Or a main router or hub could be down, making network transmissions impossible.

Determining whether Problems Are Consistent and Replicable

When it comes to network operations, the word *intermittent* can strike fear in the hearts of the most seasoned engineers. If a workstation cannot connect to the mail server, can you connect from another workstation? Or can you connect the workstation from another segment?

The most overlooked and insignificant things can cause intermittent problems. The overlooked problem is most likely at the head of the affected area. Many a large WAN has been taken down by an over-crimped wire in an RJ-45 connector, for example. Consistent problems are much easier to spot. Does swapping ports help? If you swap ports and the problem follows the workstation or hub, you are close to resolving it. Be familiar with your network. Know the topography. Knowing where to start is the first hurdle.

Using Standard Troubleshooting Methods

You really must be careful to identify the *exact* issue. How many days would you spend troubleshooting a problem like "the network is slow," or "I can't get to my files"? Users can be pretty nebulous when it comes to pinpointing a problem. Ask as many questions as you can think of to help. Every problem has a root cause, and that is what you are out to eliminate. Once you discover what caused the problem, the only way you can be sure is to replicate it. For example, your network is flaky and you discover that that's because a custodian tripped over an extension cord and pulled out a plug in your computer room. You plug it back in and that solves the problem. However, you may want to pull that plug again and see if the problem repeats itself. It may have just been a coincidence that the cord was tripped over just before your network went into the ozone.

You also need to isolate the causes of problems. Why do people keep tripping over this cord? Because it is right in the middle of the floor! Formulate a solution, figure out how to move it out of the way, and then implement your plan. Get an electrician to move the outlet or install a new one out of harm's way. Then you should test it out, ensuring that you can walk around the room without having the cord in your way.

If your problem has been resolved, document both the problem and the solution. You might describe what happened and add a paragraph to the building's procedures manual about, in this case, the proper places to install outlets. Feedback is also very important here. For instance, make sure people know that if this particular problem manifests itself again they should check to make sure that no one has plugged the cord into the old outlet. A cord being tripped over is an example of a very simple problem, but your methodology should be the same in all cases, even for very complex problems. In other words, identify, re-create, isolate, formulate, implement, test, document, and supply feedback.

Exam Essentials

This objective is based on your ability to know and utilize true troubleshooting methodology.

Know how to follow a set troubleshooting methodology. Know your network. When trouble breaks out, know exactly how you are going to handle your troubleshooting. During a network-down, crisis situation, it is not a good time to be wondering where you should start.

Know how to isolate causes.   Know common points of failure in your network, and know how to identify which might cause the particular problem that you are experiencing.

Know how to follow up.   Too many people get the network up and running and then head for a break or the neighborhood pub. Make sure that you perform a sufficient postmortem on a problem so you decrease the likelihood of the problem reoccurring in the future.

Key Terms and Concepts

Know the acronyms and terms that relate to troubleshooting your network. A couple of different common terms are listed below.

Network topography   A wireframe diagram of your network that is used as a roadmap during troubleshooting operations.

Postmortem   A discussion that takes place after a failure, documenting the cause of a network failure and planning corrective action to prevent reoccurrence.

Sample Questions

1. When one out of five workstations on a segment cannot reach the mail server after booting, how might troubleshooting begin?

   A. Reboot the workstation.

   B. Replace the NIC card.

   C. Ping the workstation from another segment.

   D. Switch the port used with a functioning workstation on the segment.

   E. Reload the mail software.

   Answer: D—Switch the port used and see if it connects. (A and B could be correct, but they require more time than D. You will usually start with the quickest possible solution. C would be unnecessary since you could ping the station from another station in the same segment. And with E, if the mail software was functioning, while not impossible, it would be unlikely that it would cause a network to disconnect.)

2. You have a basic network with a server connected to a router and Category 5 wiring to the segment hubs. Segment C is down. The workstations can ping each other within segment C. Where might be a good place to start troubleshooting?

   A. At the router

   B. The cable between router and segment C hub

   C. The hub

   D. The workstation

   Answer: A—Always use a top–down methodology. While B would be the second thing you would check, you should start with the router and router port. (Since the workstations can ping each other, that would eliminate C and D.)

3. Workstation 7 in segment A and workstation 4 in segment D cannot reach the file server. All other workstations are experiencing normal intranet and Internet connections. Which of the following is the most likely cause?

   A. A bad NIC card at each station

   B. A bad hub

   C. A bad router port

   D. A segment link between the router and segment A and segment D

   Answer: A—While not the only possible cause, this is the most plausible choice since all other workstations are functioning normally. (More than one workstation in each segment would be affected with the other choices.)

Identify the following steps as a systematic approach for troubleshooting network problems, and, given a problem scenario, select the appropriate next step based on this approach:

- Identify the exact issue.
- Re-create the problem.
- Isolate the cause.
- Formulate a correction.
- Implement the correction.
- Test.
- Document the problem and the solution.
- Give feedback.

Every networking certification has outlined its own systematic outline for troubleshooting, and Network+ is no exception. This Network+ troubleshooting model has eight steps and is a fairly straightforward approach to troubleshooting.

Critical Information

Usually, when a network or network component has gone down, chaos can ensue. When this happens, it is best if you have a predetermined course of action. Learning the eight steps covered by this objective will save you some of the anxiety that sometimes happens when panic sets in during a network crisis. These eight steps are, in order:

1. Identify the exact issues
2. Re-create the problem

3. Isolate the cause

4. Formulate a correction

5. Implement the correct

6. Test the solution

7. Document the problem and the solution

8. Give feedback

Step 1: Identify the Exact Issue

The first step in troubleshooting a problem is to define exactly what the problem is, because if you can't define a problem you can't begin to solve it. Typically, to identify the exact issue, you may have to ask the person reporting the problem some questions for clarification. Based on the answers to these questions, you can state exactly what the problem is and then work toward solving it.

Step 2: Re-create the Problem

Computers and networks can work fine for months, experience a serious error, and then continue to work fine for several more months without experiencing the error again. When troubleshooting, therefore, it is important to be able to reproduce a given problem so you can witness the conditions under which it occurs.

Whenever you train end users, some of the best advice you can give them is to try to notice what isn't working when there is a problem. Users sometimes have knee-jerk reactions when they experience some problems, causing them to call user support immediately. This is not necessarily the best reaction because the person at user support will ask what they were doing. Users don't necessarily pay attention to all the things that are happening on their computers while they are working because they are busy doing their jobs. For this reason, if a user is trained to try to re-create a problem, they will more likely know the conditions under which the problem occurred.

Re-creating a problem is extremely important. If the problem doesn't occur again, you can't take immediate steps to cure it. Typically, it is best to have to users re-create problems themselves so they can show you the problems and explain why their workstations aren't working like they should be. In one possible example, whenever a particular user tries to access a Web site, they get the message shown in Figure 14.1. This problem can be re-created.

FIGURE 14.1: A sample error message

Step 3: Isolate the Cause

When you know that a problem is reproducible, you can try to determine its cause. To do this, you must draw upon your knowledge of networking. Considering the error message in Figure 14.1, you need to ask yourself (and possibly the user) some of the following questions.

- Were you ever able to do this?
- When did it stop doing this?
- Were any error messages displayed?
- Has anything changed since you were able to do this?
- Are other people experiencing this problem?
- Is the problem always the same?

These are just a few of the questions you can use to isolate what might be causing the problem.

As you may have noted, one of the questions is "Are other people experiencing this problem?" That is one question that you must also ask yourself—one way you can narrow the problem down to a specific item that may be causing the problem. It is a simple enough task to try and duplicate the problem yourself from your own workstation. If you can't duplicate the problem, it may only be related to one user or group of users (or possibly their workstations). If you are the network administrator and more than one user is experiencing this problem, you may know it because several people will be calling about the same problem.

Step 4: Formulate a Correction

Now that you have observed the problem and have isolated the cause, you can work on formulating a solution to the problem. Like the other steps of troubleshooting, this gets easier with time and experience.

In this step, you must come up with at least one possible solution to the problem, even though it may not be the correct one. You will come back to this step time and again until you come up with the correct solution. You personally don't have to think of a solution; someone else may already have the solution. You can check online sources and vendor documentation for possible corrections to the problem.

Step 5: Implement the Correction

The fifth step may seem rather obvious, but it must be done. In this step, you must implement your formulated correction. The particulars of this step differ depending on the problem and its solution.

Step 6: Test the Solution

Now that you have made the changes, you must test your solution to see if it solves the problem. Basically, to test the functionality of your solution, have the user try to repeat the problem. If they can't, great; the problem is solved! If they can, try the operation yourself. If the problem isn't solved, you may have to go back to step 4 again and formulate a new correction, performing steps 5 and 6 again. But it is important to make note of what worked and what didn't so you don't make the same mistakes twice.

Step 7: Document the Problem and the Solution

As mentioned in Chapter 6, it is very important to have network documentation. One item that you can include in your documentation is all the steps you took to troubleshoot a problem and arrive at a stated solution. This may seem like busy work, but if you don't do it you may come across a similar problem at some point and wonder what you did to fix it. With documented solutions to documented problems, you can assemble your own database of knowledge, or knowledge base, that you can use to troubleshoot other problems.

Your knowledge base could include information like what the conditions surrounding particular problems were (i.e., OS version, software version, type of computer, type of NIC), whether problems were reproducible, what possible solutions were tried, and what the ultimate solutions were. A postmortem conversation is most valuable in making sure that the problem does not reoccur.

Step 8: Give Feedback

Of all the steps in the troubleshooting model, this is probably the most important. You want to give feedback to the person experiencing the problem (and possibly the person reporting the problem) so they know that the problem is fixed.

Most service providers have some sort of work order tracking system that reports when a problem has been fixed, but nothing beats going the extra mile for someone than seeking them out and telling them directly what the problem and the solution were. It may be to your benefit to show the user exactly what happened. Fifteen minutes of training may go a long way toward preventing recurrences of the same problem. Additionally, you may find out how the problem happened in the first place.

During this feedback session, tell the person that you regret the time they were without the use of their computer. Then tell them what happened, why, and what you did to solve the problem. You should also tell them that you tested the solution. Above all, however, you must be able to gauge the knowledge level of the person you are talking to. You likely wouldn't use the same language when talking to a network administrator that you would when talking to a user with less knowledge of networking practices.

Exam Essentials

This objective is based on your recognition of and adherence to the eight steps to network troubleshooting.

Know how to identify specific network problems. Start by getting the full story from several different sources. Then, from the information the users provide you, determine the exact problem.

Know how to re-create reported problems. "Show me what not working looks like," is a great way to start your investigation with a user. If the problems cannot be re-created, then you cannot solve them.

Know how to isolate the causes of reported problems. Determine whether the problems are software or hardware related. See if they occur with other workstations in the same office or site.

Know how to formulate solutions. Based on your theory behind each problem, come up with a solution. If you think the network cable is bad, look into replacing it, for instance. If you think the TCP/IP configuration is wrong, look at what settings need to be changed.

Know how to implement solutions. You need to have the actual knowledge for facilitating the solution. For example, how do you change a network cable and TCP/IP settings?

Know how to test solutions. Once solutions are implemented, attempt to perform the activity that had been problematic. Prove that the problem is fixed to the satisfaction of the user.

Know how to document both problems and solutions. As you perform network troubleshooting, write everything down, including what you think the problems are, what steps you take to resolve them, and the results of your solutions. A searchable troubleshooting database is the best place to store your solutions.

Know how to give feedback to customers, clients, and system administrators. Be polite and understanding when dealing with upset users and co-workers. Utilize the appropriate level of details with both users and the IT staff.

Key Term and Concept

You should know the acronyms and terms that relate to trouble-shooting. A common term is listed below.

Feedback   Refers to supplying customers with information regarding a failure and explaining what steps have been taken to prevent future problems.

Sample Questions

1. What is it best to do when a network problem is resolved?

    A. Make everyone aware that there was a problem.

    B. Discuss the problem with your clients.

    C. Document the problem and its solution.

    D. Conduct a postmortem as soon as possible.

    Answer: D—Do a postmortem as soon as possible. While the event is still fresh, document what was done and what can be done to prevent future failures. (Selection A is not necessary since everyone was most probably aware that there was a problem. B and C would be part of your postmortem.)

2. After you formulate a solution, what is the next step in solving network problems?

    A. Test the solution.

    B. Implement a solution.

    C. Isolate the cause.

    D. Re-create the problem.

    E. Identify the exact issue.

    Answer: B—You must implement a solution once a solution is determined. (Testing a solution occurs in the later stages. Isolating the cause and recreating the problem are early steps in the troubleshooting process.)

Identify the following steps as a systematic approach to determining whether a problem is attributable to the operator or the system, and, given a problem scenario, select the appropriate next step based on this approach:

- Have a second operator perform the same task on an equivalent workstation.
- Have a second operator perform the same task on the original operator's workstation.
- See whether operators are following standard operating procedure.

This objective defines a few of the procedures you can follow to determine whether or not an apparent problem is due to a computer's operator. An apparent problem will often actually be the result of an operator performing an operation incorrectly. The Network+ exam will test you on your ability to determine whether the problem is operator or system related.

Critical Information

In many instances, operator error may cause what appears to be a network problem. One of the first things that you might do is to have the operator duplicate their task on a workstation known to be stable. If the problem persists, one might assume an operator error.

Operator or System Errors

An operator performing a task on a workstation may experience a task failure. Sometimes it is difficult to determine whether this is due to a hardware error, software error, or an operator error. You should use a set methodology to determine the cause. This methodology is described in the following sections.

Second Operator on Another Workstation

To start troubleshooting, you might ask a second operator in the same group to try running the task on a second workstation. If the task operates correctly, the problem could be linked to the first workstation or the first operator. This would eliminate a software problem on a shared application.

Second Operator on the Same Workstation

You would then ask the second operator to try the operation on the first workstation. If the operation is successful, then you have isolated the problem with the first operator, and they can perhaps be re-instructed on the correct use of the application.

Operator Following SOPs

If an operator is following established procedures proven to function normally on other workstations and the operation fails on the workstation in question, then you have isolated it to a workstation or a network problem.

Exam Essentials

This objective is based on your ability to determine the cause of an apparent workstation failure.

Know how to determine the cause of an operation failure on a workstation.   If a failure is limited to one workstation, it could be due to the workstation, the software, or operator error.

Key Term and Concept

Know the acronyms and terms that relate to questionable failures on a single workstation. A common term is listed below.

SOPs (standard operating procedures) Written procedures and methods to complete tasks in an organization.

Sample Questions

1. An operator comes to you and reports that a workstation is not operating correctly. They say they have completed the same operation on two different workstations. From this information, which of the following might be a good assumption?

   A. Operator has made a mistake

   B. Operator's primary workstation has failed

   C. Software is not functioning

   D. Network connection to that area is bad

   E. SOP is not being followed

   Answer: B—The most probable cause is that the workstation has failed. (A,C, D, and E would be ruled out since the operator successfully completed the operation on two other workstations.)

2. An operator tells you that their workstation has failed. Every other member of the workgroup is functioning normally. What is the first step you might have the operator take?

   A. Repeat the operation.

   B. Try it on another workstation.

   C. Try the operation on the workstation in question.

   D. Try the workstation in another port.

   Answer: A—Check both the workstation and whether or not the operator was performing the operation correctly. (B and D would be secondary steps in troubleshooting if C fails.)

Given a network troubleshooting scenario, demonstrate awareness of the need to check for physical and logical indicators of trouble, including:

- Link lights
- Power lights
- Error displays
- Error logs and displays
- Performance monitors

Hardware and software manufacturers have ensured that there are obvious indicators for problems that occur. The Network+ exam will test your knowledge of several of the most common problem indicators.

Critical Information

Modern network equipment can be very administrator friendly. Use your documentation to find out what assistance network equipment can provide for in diagnosing a problem. For instance, diagnostic lights can save you lots of time, and knowing how to use error logs and performance monitors can help you be proactive in the network environment.

Link Lights

An item that can be easily overlooked is the link light. The link light is a small, light-emitting diode (LED) that is found on both the NIC and the hub. It is typically green and is labeled "link" (or some abbreviation). A link light indicates that the NIC and hub (in the case of 10BaseT) are making a logical (Data Link layer) connection. It can usually be assumed, if the workstation's NIC and the connection on the hub for that workstation both have link lights on, that the workstation and hub can communicate.

NOTE Some NICs won't turn their link lights on until the operating system driver is loaded for that NIC. So, if the link light isn't on when the system is first turned on, you may have to wait until the operating system loads the NIC driver.

Power Lights

This simple item is probably the most common in troubleshooting manuals. Many people are sick of hearing about it. That's because it's the one that occurs most often and is the easiest to overlook. In order to function properly, of course all computer and network components must be turned on and powered up! It's not uncommon for a user to place a support call only to find out that their machine's power is off.

Most systems have indicators that tell when they are powered up. Additionally, the power switch typically has a designation like "1" or "On" to indicate when it is turned on. The power switch isn't the only consideration, however, when troubleshooting a "no power" situation. The power switch might be in the On position, but there could still be no power to the unit. You should check to see if all power cables are plugged in, including the power strip that the components are likely plugged into.

TIP Remember that every cable has two ends, and both must be plugged into something.

When troubleshooting power problems, start with the device you are troubleshooting and work your way back to the power service panel. There could be any number of power problems between the device and the service panel, including bad power cable, bad outlet, bad electrical wiring, tripped circuit breaker, or a blown fuse. Any of these items could cause power problems at the device.

NOTE This is only a partial list of "simple stuff." You'll come up with your own list over time as you troubleshoot more and more systems.

Error Displays

Servers typically have an LCD status display. When a hard drive fails, a light starts to flash or turns on. Switches, routers, and hubs have link lights, collision lights, and error lights. The color red commonly indicates that there is a problem. Do not merely look at the display from a distance. The display text is small and needs to be examined up close.

Error Logs

Log files can give you an indication of the general well-being of a server. Each log file format is different, but, generally speaking, the log files keep a running list of all errors and notices, the time and date they occurred, and any other pertinent information. The following paragraphs take a brief look at a couple of log files of the most commonly used network operating systems—NetWare 5 and Windows NT 4.

NetWare 5

NetWare 5 contains three log files that can help diagnose problems on a NetWare server. These three files are the console log file (CONSOLE .LOG), the abend log file (ABEND.LOG), and the server log file (SYS$LOG.ERR). Each file has different uses in troubleshooting processes.

CONSOLE.LOG File The console log file keeps a history of all errors and information that has been displayed to the server's console. It can be found in the SYS:\ETC directory on the server and is created and maintained by the utility CONLOG.NLM that comes with NetWare versions after 3.12. You must load this utility manually (or by placing the load commands in the AUTOEXEC.NCF so that it starts automatically) by typing the following at the console prompt:

```
LOAD CONLOG
```

Once this utility has loaded, it will erase whatever CONSOLE.LOG file currently exists and start logging in to the new file. Figure 14.2 (on the next page) shows a sample CONSOLE.LOG file. Note that from this log file you can tell that someone edited the AUTOEXEC.NCF file and then restarted the server. This would indicate that a major change took place on the server. If you were trying to troubleshoot a server that was starting to exhibit strange problems after a recent reboot, this might be a source to check.

FIGURE 14.2: A sample CONSOLE.LOG file

```
CONLOG-1.04-10: System console logging started Fri Feb 12 13:52:40 1999.
CONLOG-1.04-9: Logging system console to sys:etc\console.log.
S1:edit autoexec.ncf
Loading module EDIT.NLM
  NetWare Text Editor
  Version 4.15    March 23, 1998
  Copyright 1989-1998 Novell, Inc.  All rights reserved.
File OWL501F.DLL in use by user ADMIN on station 23
File NWCORE32.DLL in use by user ADMIN on station 23
File WANMAN.DLL in use by user ADMIN on station 23
File SLP-SP.ZIP in use by user ADMIN on station 23
*** WARNING *** There are active files open.
Down server? y
IPXRTR: IPX link state router down.
Java: Cleaning up resources, Please Wait.

Module JAVA.NLM unloaded
Notifying stations that file server is down
Dismounting volume DATA

2-12-1999   1:57:26 pm:    DS-7.9-23
    Bindery close requested by the SERVER

2-12-1999   1:57:26 pm:    DS-7.9-20
    Directory Services:  Local database has been closed

Dismounting volume SYS
```

WARNING The information contained in the CONSOLE.LOG file is lost every time the CONLOG.NLM is unloaded and reloaded. It doesn't keep a history of *every* command ever issued but only those issued since CONLOG.NLM was loaded.

ABEND.LOG File The ABEND.LOG file is the log file that registers all abends on a NetWare server. An abend (stands for ABnormal END) is an error condition that can halt the proper operation of the NetWare server. Abends can be serious enough to lock the server, or they may just cause an NLM to force quit. You can tell that an abend has occurred because an error message that contains the word

ABEND will display on the console. Additionally, the server command prompt will have a number in brackets (e.g., <1>) after it that indicates the number of times the server has abended since it was brought online.

Because the server may reboot after an abend, the error messages and what they mean can be lost. With versions of NetWare after and including 4.11, NetWare includes a routine to capture the output of the abend to both the console and to the ABEND.LOG file, which can be found in the SYS:SYSTEM directory on the server.

The ABEND.LOG file contains all of the information that is output to the console screen during an abend (a portion of which is shown in Figure 14.3), plus much more. The ABEND.LOG file also contains the exact flags and registers of the processor at the time the abend occurred. It also includes information like the NLMs that were in memory, their versions, their descriptions, their memory settings, the exact time and date the abend occurred, and relevant additional information. This information can be useful when determining the source of an abend. For example, any time you see the words "Page Fault" or "Stack" in the output of an abend, the abend happened because of something to do with memory. Usually, it means that a program or process tried to take memory that didn't belong to it (i.e., from another program). When NetWare detects that this is happening, it shuts down the offending process and issues an abend. To examine the entire version of the abend file that is shown below, go to www.sybex.com and perform a catalog search for *Network+ Exam Notes*.

FIGURE 14.3: An ABEND.LOG file

```
Server S1 halted Friday, February 12, 1999   2:37:03 pm
Abend 1 on P00: Server-5.00a: Page Fault Processor
Exception (Error code 00000002)

Registers:
    CS = 0008 DS = 0010 ES = 0010 FS = 0010 GS = 0010
SS = 0010
    EAX = 00000000 EBX = D0AC2238 ECX = 0697DEF0 EDX =
00000009
```

```
    ESI = D0C5C040 EDI = 00000000 EBP = 0697DED0 ESP =
0697DEC0
    EIP = D0AC2232 FLAGS = 00014246
    D0AC2232 C600CC        MOV     [EAX]=?,CC
    EIP in ABENDEMO.NLM at code start +00000232h
```

Running process: Abendemo Process
Created by: NetWare Application
Thread Owned by NLM: ABENDEMO.NLM
Stack pointer: 697DCE0
OS Stack limit: 697A000
Scheduling priority: 67371008
Wait state: 5050170 (Blocked on keyboard)
Stack: D0AC22C1 (ABENDEMO.NLM|MenuAction+89)
       D1FEA602 (NWSNUT.NLM|NWSShowPortalLine+3602)
       --00000008 ?
       --00000000 ?
       --0697DF20 ?
       --D0134080 ?
       --00000001 ?
       D1FEA949 (NWSNUT.NLM|NWSShowPortalLine+3949)
       --00000010 ?
       --0697DEF0 ?
       --0697DEF4 ?
       --0697DFAC ?
       --D0C2E100
(CONNMGR.NLM|WaitForBroadcastsToClear+C90C)
       --00000003 ?
       --00000008 ?
       --00000012 ?
       --00000000 ?
       --00000019 ?
       --00000050 ?
       --000000FF ?
       --00000001 ?
       --00000010 ?
       --00000001 ?

```
--00000000   ?
--00000011   ?
--0697DFDC   ?
--0000000B   ?
--00000000   ?
D1FEABD9   (NWSNUT.NLM|NWSShowPortalLine+3BD9)
--0000000B   ?
--00000000   ?
--00000000   ?
```

Additional Information:

The CPU encountered a problem executing code in
ABENDEMO.NLM. The problem may be in that module or in
data passed to that module by a process owned by
ABENDEMO.NLM.

```
Loaded Modules:
SERVER.NLM        NetWare Server Operating System
   Version 5.00     August 27, 1998
   Code Address: FC000000h  Length: 000A5000h
   Data Address: FC5A5000h  Length: 000C9000h
LOADER.EXE        NetWare OS Loader
   Code Address: 000133D0h  Length: 0001D000h
   Data Address: 000303D0h  Length: 00020C30h
CDBE.NLM          NetWare Configuration DB Engine
   Version 5.00     August 12, 1998
   Code Address: D087E000h  Length: 00007211h
   Data Address: D0887000h  Length: 0000684Ch
NWKCFG.NLM        NetWare Kernel Config NLM
   Version 1.02     August 21, 1998
   Code Address: D0921000h  Length: 000027C4h
   Data Address: D0925000h  Length: 00001B6Ch
CPUCHECK.NLM      NetWare Processor Checking Utility
   Version 1.00     July 23, 1998
   Code Address: D000F000h  Length: 0000097Eh
   Data Address: D092E000h  Length: 00003ECCh
DIAG500.NLM       Diagnostic/coredump utility for NW
v5.00 (980731)
```

```
Version 1.01    July 31, 1998
Code Address: D0928000h  Length: 00002015h
Data Address: D0011000h  Length: 00000E4Ch
NEB.NLM            Novell Event Bus
Version 1.01    August 28, 1998
Code Address: D093E000h  Length: 000037FCh
Data Address: D0013000h  Length: 0000071Ch
NBI.NLM            NetWare Bus Interface
Version 2.24    July 27, 1998
Code Address: D0955000h  Length: 000098A9h
Data Address: D0017000h  Length: 0000172Ch
MM.NLM             NetWare Media Manager
Version 2.00    August 19, 1998
Code Address: D0AD4000h  Length: 00024BBEh
Data Address: D0947000h  Length: 000084BCh
```

SYS$LOG.ERR File   The general server log file, found in the
SYS:SYSTEM directory, lists any errors that occur on the server,
including abends, NDS errors, and the time and date when they occur.
An error in the SYS$LOG.ERR file might look something like this:

```
1-07-1999 11:51:10 am:  DS-7.9-17
Severity = 1 Locus = 17 Class = 19
Directory Services: Could not open local database,
error: -723
```

Note the second line with the "Severity, Locus = and Class =" designations. These designations are used instead of a lengthy text description of the error, and they can help to give more information about
the error message displayed. Severity is simply answering the question
"How severe is the problem?" Locus indicates which component
system is affected by this message (i.e., memory, disk, LAN cards),
and class simply indicates what type of error it is. Tables 14.1, 14.2,
and 14.3 on the following pages explain the codes used for severity,
locus, and class, respectively. Based on the information found in these
tables, it can be determined that the severity of 1 indicates a warning
condition (so the problem isn't really serious), while a locus of 17

indicates that the error relates to the operating system (which would make sense because this is a directory services error). And the class of 19 indicates that the problem is a domain problem, meaning that the problem is defined by the OS but is not an OS problem. These designations mean that the reported error is related to NDS and that it's not a really serious error. In fact, this particular error might occur when you bring up the server and the database hasn't yet been opened by the OS.

T A B L E 14.1: SYS$LOG.ERR Severity Code Descriptions

Number	Description
0	**Informational** Used for non-threatening information, usually just to record some kind of entry into the SYS$LOG.ERR file.
1	**Warning** Indicates a potential problem that does not cause damage.
2	**Recoverable** An error condition has occurred that can be recovered by the operating system.
3	**Critical** Indicates a condition that should be taken care of soon and that might cause a server failure in the near future. (An example would be mirrored partitions out of sync or when the abend recovery routine is invoked.)
4	**Fatal** Something has occurred that will cause the imminent shutdown of the server, or it has already caused a shutdown. (This type of error might occur when a disk driver unloads because of a software failure.)
5	**Operation Aborted** An attempted operation could not be completed because of an error. (For example, a disk save could not be completed because the disk was full.)
6	**No NOS Unrecoverable** The operation could not be completed, but it will not affect the operating system. (For example, a compressed file is corrupt and unrecoverable.)

T A B L E 14.2: SYS$LOG.ERR Locus Code Descriptions

Number	Code
0	Unknown
1	Memory
2	File System
3	Disks
4	LAN Boards
5	COM Stacks (communication protocols)
6	No definition
7	TTS (transaction tracking system)
8	Bindery
9	Station
10	Router
11	Locks
12	Kernel
13	UPS
14	SFT_III
15	Resource Tracking
16	NLM
17	OS Information
18	Cache
19	Domain

TABLE 14.3: SYS$LOG.ERR Class Code Descriptions

Number	Code
0	Class Unknown
1	Out of Resources
2	Temporary Situation
3	Authorization Failure
4	Internal Error
5	Hardware Failure
6	System Failure
7	Request Error
8	Not Found
9	Bad Format
10	Locked
11	Media Failure
12	Item Exists
13	Station Failure
14	Limit Exceeded
15	Configuration Error
16	Limit Almost Exceeded
17	Security Audit Information
18	Disk Information
19	General Information
20	File Compressions
21	Protection Violation

Windows NT 4.0

Windows NT, like other network operating systems, has comprehensive error and informational logging routines. Theoretically, every program and process could have its own logging utility. But Microsoft has come up with a rather slick utility called Event Viewer. Event Viewer uses log files to keep track of all of the events that happen on a particular Windows NT computer. Normally, though, you must be an administrator or a member of the administrator's group.

The Event Viewer utility can be found under Start ➤ Programs ➤ Administrative Tools on the Windows NT desktop. When you first start the program, it will ask you which computer's log files you would like to view (Figure 14.4). It will present you with a list, or you can type in the UNC name of the computer whose events you want to view. Double-click the computer's name or type it in, and then click OK to view the events for that computer.

WARNING Even though Windows 9.x computers show up here, you cannot view log files on those computers because their logging systems aren't designed to interface with Event Viewer.

TIP If you are connected to a Windows NT network over a slower link, like a slow WAN link or a dial-up connection, choose Low Speed Connection so the event viewer will be optimized for running over the lower-speed connection.

TIP If you want to view a different computer's log files, you can get to this screen again in Event Viewer by going to the Log menu and choosing Select Computer.

F I G U R E 14.4: Selecting a Windows NT computer for which to view log files

Once you have selected a computer, you can use the Event Viewer utility to view the three main log files for Windows NT. These log files are:

- System log
- Security log
- Application

Each has a specific use and is briefly examined in the following paragraphs.

TIP If you want, you can view the log files of any Windows NT machine from your Windows 9.x client by copying the Server Tools located on the Windows NT Server CD-ROM to your hard disk, making shortcuts for them, and then running them. The server tools directory is located in the \CLIENTS\SRVTOOLS\ directory on the Windows NT Server Installation CD.

System Log The System log in Event Viewer is the log file that keeps track of just about every action that happens on that computer.

This log file is similar to the SYS$LOG.ERR file that NetWare uses. However, where the SYS$LOG.ERR file has many different categories of errors, the System log, only has three main types of events—information, warning, and error. An information event is a log entry to give you information that something has happened. The warning error type indicates that a specific event could cause problems. An example of a warning of that type would be a disk drive running out of space. And an error event means that something has failed and will need immediate attention if the server is to function normally. When viewing any log file in Event Viewer, there will be an icon next to each event that indicates the type of the event. The different icons correspond to the different types of events. Figure 14.5 shows the three types of events found in the System log and their associated icons.

NOTE   There are two other types of events (audit success and audit failure), but they normally appear on the Security log, which is discussed later.

FIGURE 14.5: System log event types and their associated icons

Information

Warning

Error

Figure 14.6 shows a sample system log and the listing of events it has noted. This list contains several categories of information, including the dates and times the events occurred, the sources of the events (which process the event came from), which users (if applicable) initiated the process, the name of the computers on which the events occurred, and the event ID numbers (in the Event column). This last item is the unique error type to which that particular event belongs.

To get an explanation of each event ID number, you can check the help file or go to http://www.microsoft.com/technet/.

FIGURE 14.6: A sample System log. Note the different error types and event IDs.

Date	Time	Source	Category	Event	User	Computer
Event Viewer - System Log on \\S1						
Log View Options Help						
1/7/99	12:53:09 PM	BROWSER	None	8015	N/A	S1
1/7/99	11:39:17 AM	BROWSER	None	8033	N/A	S1
1/7/99	11:39:17 AM	BROWSER	None	8033	N/A	S1
1/7/99	11:39:17 AM	BROWSER	None	8033	N/A	S1
1/7/99	11:37:14 AM	symc810	None	9	N/A	S1
1/7/99	11:36:50 AM	symc810	None	9	N/A	S1
1/7/99	11:36:05 AM	symc810	None	9	N/A	S1
1/7/99	11:35:21 AM	symc810	None	9	N/A	S1
1/7/99	11:33:15 AM	Disk	None	7	N/A	S1
1/7/99	11:33:11 AM	Disk	None	7	N/A	S1
1/7/99	11:33:07 AM	Disk	None	7	N/A	S1
1/7/99	11:33:04 AM	Disk	None	7	N/A	S1
1/7/99	11:33:00 AM	Disk	None	7	N/A	S1
1/7/99	11:32:56 AM	Disk	None	7	N/A	S1
1/7/99	11:32:52 AM	Disk	None	7	N/A	S1
1/7/99	11:32:48 AM	Disk	None	7	N/A	S1
1/7/99	11:32:44 AM	Disk	None	7	N/A	S1
1/7/99	11:32:40 AM	Disk	None	7	N/A	S1
1/6/99	7:04:41 PM	BROWSER	None	8015	N/A	S1
1/6/99	7:04:41 PM	BROWSER	None	8015	N/A	S1
1/6/99	7:02:59 PM	EventLog	None	6005	N/A	S1
1/6/99	7:04:41 PM	BROWSER	None	8015	N/A	S1
1/6/99	6:57:00 PM	Service Control M	None	7000	N/A	S1
1/6/99	6:56:54 PM	EventLog	None	6005	N/A	S1
1/6/99	6:57:00 PM	E100B	None	5007	N/A	S1
1/6/99	6:00:37 PM	Service Control M	None	7000	N/A	S1
1/6/99	6:00:32 PM	EventLog	None	6005	N/A	S1
1/6/99	6:00:37 PM	E100B	None	5007	N/A	S1

If you want more detail on a specific event, just double-click it. This will give you a much better explanation of the event as well as the actual data that was recorded with the event. Notice the error event shown previously in Figure 14.6, dated 1/7/99 at 11:33 a.m. with an event ID of 7. If you were to double-click this item, you would see an Event Detail screen like the one shown in Figure 14.7 (on the next page). From this screen, in the Description box, you can tell that this error indicates that Windows NT found a bad disk block. Even though this is an error event, it is not that serious. One bad block is not a problem unless several disk blocks started going bad at once. Below the description is the Data box that lists the exact data the Event Viewer received on the error condition. This may be useful to you in determining the source of the problem. More than likely, if you have a serious problem that you can't fix, this is the information that will get sent to the vendor (or Microsoft) to help troubleshoot the problem.

F I G U R E 14.7: The Event Detail screen for a particular event

```
┌─────────────────────────────────────────────────────────┐
│ Event Detail                                         [x] │
├─────────────────────────────────────────────────────────┤
│  Date:      1/7/99          Event ID:  7                 │
│  Time:      11:33:15 AM     Source:    Disk              │
│  User:      N/A             Type:      Error             │
│  Computer:  S1              Category:  None              │
│                                                          │
│  Description:                                            │
│  ┌────────────────────────────────────────────────────┐ │
│  │The device, \Device\Harddisk0\Partition2, has a bad │ │
│  │block.                                              │ │
│  │                                                    │ │
│  └────────────────────────────────────────────────────┘ │
│                                                          │
│  Data:   ⦿ Bytes   ○ Words                              │
│  ┌────────────────────────────────────────────────────┐ │
│  │0000:  0e 00 18 00 01 00 66 00   .....f.            │ │
│  │0008:  00 00 00 00 07 00 04 c0   ........À          │ │
│  │0010:  00 01 00 00 9c 00 00 c0   ....I..À           │ │
│  │0018:  00 00 00 00 14 00 07 00   ........           │ │
│  │0020:  00 cc 7b 8a 00 00 00 00   .Ì{I....           │ │
│  └────────────────────────────────────────────────────┘ │
│                                                          │
│   [  Close  ]  [ Previous ]  [  Next  ]  [  Help  ]     │
└─────────────────────────────────────────────────────────┘
```

Security Log The Security log is used to keep track of security event items specified by the domain's audit policy. The audit policy is set in the User Manager for Domains and controls what security items will be tracked in Event Viewer. To set the audit policy, open User Manager for Domains, go to the Policy menu, and select Audit. This will bring up a screen similar to the one shown in Figure 14.8. From here, you can indicate which items you want logged and whether you want the success or the failure of those items to be logged. Since these are security settings, most often you want to log the failure of someone to do any of these items. Once set, you can click OK to accept these changes, and they will be in effect for all users and systems in the domain.

FIGURE 14.8: Setting the audit policy for a Windows NT domain

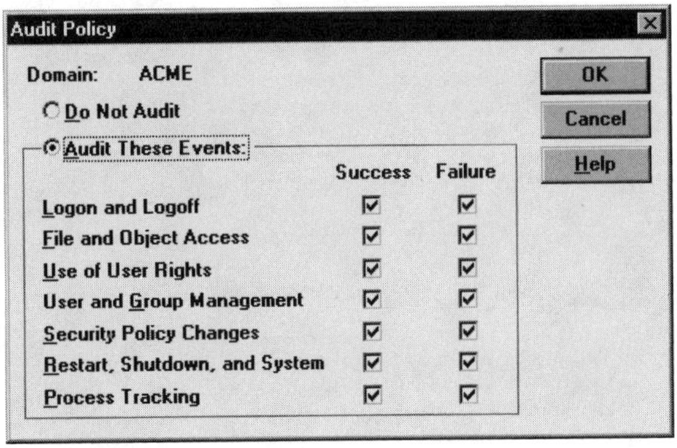

Once you have the audit policy set for a domain, you can view the Security log for any computer in that domain. To view the security log for a particular computer, start the Event Viewer, pick the computer whose security log you want to view, and then choose Security from the Log menu. This will bring up the security log in the Event Viewer (Figure 14.9 on the next page). As you can see, this log looks similar to the System log in most respects. The main items that are different are the icons and the types of events recorded here. You can still view the detail for an event by double-clicking it, as before.

There are two types of events shown in the Security log—success audit and failure audit. These two types of events show whether an item passed or failed the security audit. Figure 14.10 (also on the next page) shows the icons associated with each. When an item fails a security audit, it means that something security related has failed. For example, a common entry (assuming the Logon Failure checkbox is checked in the audit policy) is a failure audit in the category Logon/Logoff. This means that the user failed to log on. If you look at the log shown in Figure 14.9, you can see that one user failed to log on four times.

FIGURE 14.9: A sample Security log in the Event Viewer

Date	Time	Source	Category	Event	User	Computer
2/21/99	4:32:42 PM	Security	Object Access	562	SYSTEM	S1
2/21/99	4:32:42 PM	Security	Object Access	560	Administrator	S1
2/21/99	4:32:42 PM	Security	Privilege Use	578	Administrator	S1
2/21/99	4:32:42 PM	Security	Object Access	562	SYSTEM	S1
2/21/99	4:32:42 PM	Security	Object Access	560	Administrator	S1
2/21/99	4:32:42 PM	Security	Object Access	562	SYSTEM	S1
2/21/99	4:32:42 PM	Security	Object Access	560	Administrator	S1
2/21/99	4:32:42 PM	Security	Object Access	562	SYSTEM	S1
2/21/99	4:32:42 PM	Security	Object Access	560	Administrator	S1
2/21/99	4:32:42 PM	Security	Object Access	560	Administrator	S1
2/21/99	4:30:17 PM	Security	Privilege Use	576	Administrator	S1
2/21/99	4:30:17 PM	Security	Logon/Logoff	528	Administrator	S1
2/21/99	4:13:28 PM	Security	Logon/Logoff	538	Administrator	S1
2/21/99	4:06:11 PM	Security	Detailed Trackir	592	Administrator	S1
2/21/99	4:04:37 PM	Security	Detailed Trackir	593	Administrator	S1
2/21/99	4:04:25 PM	Security	Detailed Trackir	593	Administrator	S1
2/21/99	4:03:36 PM	Security	Detailed Trackir	593	Administrator	S1
2/21/99	4:03:34 PM	Security	Detailed Trackir	592	Administrator	S1
2/21/99	4:03:32 PM	Security	Detailed Trackir	592	Administrator	S1
2/21/99	4:03:32 PM	Security	Detailed Trackir	592	Administrator	S1
2/21/99	4:03:32 PM	Security	Detailed Trackir	593	Administrator	S1
2/21/99	4:03:32 PM	Security	Detailed Trackir	592	Administrator	S1
2/21/99	4:03:32 PM	Security	Detailed Trackir	592	Administrator	S1
2/21/99	4:03:27 PM	Security	Detailed Trackir	592	SYSTEM	S1
2/21/99	4:03:26 PM	Security	Detailed Trackir	593	Administrator	S1
2/21/99	4:03:26 PM	Security	Detailed Trackir	593	Administrator	S1
2/21/99	4:03:26 PM	Security	Detailed Trackir	593	Administrator	S1
2/21/99	4:03:26 PM	Security	Detailed Trackir	592	Administrator	S1
2/21/99	4:03:26 PM	Security	Detailed Trackir	592	Administrator	S1

FIGURE 14.10: Security log vent types and their associated icons

Success Audit

Failure Audit

From the screen shown in Figure 14.9, you can tell several security items have happened. There were four unsuccessful logon attempts and six successful logon attempts. There were also several instances of privilege (rights) use.

This log is especially useful in troubleshooting why someone can't access a resource. If your domain security policy has been set to log failures of Use of User Rights, you can see every time a user doesn't have enough rights to access a resource. Their username will appear in the user column of the failure audit event for the resource they are accessing.

Application Log   The Application log is similar in use to the other two logs except it is used to log events for network services and applications (like SQL Server and other BackOffice products). It uses the same event types and their associated icons as the System log. Figure 14.11 shows an example of an Application log.

F I G U R E 14.11: A sample Application event log

Date	Time	Source	Category	Event	User	Computer
2/13/99	7:00:10 PM	MSSQLServer	Server	17055	N/A	S1
2/13/99	7:00:10 PM	MSSQLServer	Server	17055	N/A	S1
2/13/99	7:00:08 PM	MSSQLServer	ODS	17056	N/A	S1
2/13/99	7:00:08 PM	MSSQLServer	ODS	17056	N/A	S1
2/13/99	7:00:08 PM	MSSQLServer	Kernel	17055	N/A	S1
2/13/99	7:00:08 PM	MSSQLServer	Kernel	17055	N/A	S1
2/13/99	7:00:08 PM	MSSQLServer	Kernel	17055	N/A	S1
2/13/99	7:00:03 PM	MSSQLServer	Server	17055	N/A	S1
2/13/99	7:00:02 PM	MSSQLServer	Server	17055	N/A	S1
2/13/99	7:00:01 PM	MSSQLServer	Kernel	17055	N/A	S1
2/13/99	7:00:00 PM	SQLExecutive	Service Control	101	N/A	S1
2/12/99	6:52:54 PM	MSSQLServer	ODS	17056	N/A	S1
2/12/99	6:52:46 PM	MSSQLServer	Server	17055	N/A	S1
2/12/99	6:52:46 PM	MSSQLServer	Server	17055	N/A	S1
2/12/99	6:52:44 PM	MSSQLServer	ODS	17056	N/A	S1
2/12/99	6:52:44 PM	MSSQLServer	ODS	17056	N/A	S1
2/12/99	6:52:44 PM	MSSQLServer	Kernel	17055	N/A	S1
2/12/99	6:52:44 PM	MSSQLServer	Kernel	17055	N/A	S1
2/12/99	6:52:43 PM	MSSQLServer	Server	17055	N/A	S1
2/12/99	6:52:43 PM	MSSQLServer	Server	17055	N/A	S1
2/12/99	6:52:43 PM	MSSQLServer	Kernel	17055	N/A	S1
2/12/99	5:49:52 PM	MSDTC	SVC	4104	N/A	S1
2/12/99	5:49:51 PM	MSDTC	SVC	4105	N/A	S1
2/12/99	5:46:37 PM	MSSQLServer	Server	17052	N/A	S1
2/12/99	5:46:37 PM	MSSQLServer	Server	17052	N/A	S1
2/12/99	5:46:37 PM	MSSQLServer	Server	17052	N/A	S1
2/12/99	5:46:23 PM	MSDTC	SVC	4105	N/A	S1

Event Viewer - Application Log on \\S1
Log View Options Help

You can access the Application log by going to the Log menu and choosing Application from the list of choices. Once there, you can tell which service logged the item by looking at the Source column. For example, in Figure 14.11, you can see that there are three error events that came from Microsoft SQL Server (the "MSSQL" entry under Source).

NOTE All of these log files together make it easy to check the general well-being of a Windows NT server. Generally speaking, if you get an error message, the first thing you should do is open the Event Viewer and check the System log. If the error message doesn't show up there, check the other two logs.

Performance Monitors

In addition to protocol analyzers, many network operating systems come with tools for monitoring network performance—including statistics like the number of packets sent and received, server processor utilization, amount of data going in and out of the server, and so on. NetWare 5 comes with the MONITOR.NLM utility, and Windows NT comes with the performance-monitoring utility known as Performance Monitor. Both of these utilities will monitor performance statistics, as previously mentioned. These utilities will also help you to diagnose problems where users complain that the network is slow. You can use the utilities to determine the source of the network performance bottleneck.

Exam Essentials

This objective is based on your ability to use diagnostic tools and logs to troubleshoot network problems and be proactive about preventing them.

Know how to use diagnostic lights on network equipment. Link lights, power lights, and diagnostic displays are used to analyze network problems.

Know how to use log files to help determine the causes of network failures.   When a portion of your network fails, log files, if they are accessible, can be an invaluable source of information to determine what caused the failure.

Know how to use system logs to monitor network performance and to prevent failures.   Use security, application, and performance logs to monitor system stability. You can do this by using the Event Monitor in Windows NT or the NetWare log files.

Sample Questions

1. What lights should you check on a hub?

   A. Link lights

   B. Power lights

   C. Collision lights

   D. Display lights

   Answer: All of the above are used in troubleshooting.

2. What error log is used with NetWare servers?

   A. Application log

   B. Performance monitor

   C. Abend log

   D. Security log

   E. Network monitor

   Answer: C—When a NetWare server crashes, the event is referred to as abending. The abend log file records what happened during the crash. (The Application and Security logs are used in Windows NT. The performance and network monitors are Windows NT utilities.)

Identify common network troubleshooting resources, including:

- Knowledge bases on the World Wide Web
- Telephone technical support
- Vendor CDs

This objective is designed to test your knowledge of the various technical support resources available to help you troubleshoot uncommon problems. These resources are designed to provide you, the troubleshooter, with all of the knowledge of a vendor's technical support personnel. The Network+ exam will test your knowledge of the different types of troubleshooting resources and the differences between them.

Critical Information

While being knowledgeable is good, technology changes at a rapid rate. And while a good network administrator tries to stay current with these changes, new problems, solutions, and advances happen every day. It is not so important that you need to know the answer to every question, but it is important to know where you can find the answers.

Knowledge Bases on the World Wide Web

When first introduced. technical support CDs were great, but people started to complain that they should get the information for free because it is vital to the health of their networks. Well, that is, in fact, what happened. The Internet proved to be the perfect medium for allowing many network support personnel access to the same information that is on technical support CD-ROMs. Additionally, Web sites could be instantly updated and accessed. They are one of the most up-to-date sources of network support information.

Searchable Web sites replaced search programs, and since Web sites are hosted on servers, which can store much more information than CD-ROMs, Web sites are more powerful than their CD-ROM counterparts. Because of their ease of access and use, plus their level of detail and currency of information, Web sites are now the most popular method for obtaining technical support information. Figure 14.12 shows Novell's technical support Web site (`http://support.novell.com/`), and Figure 14.13 (on page 373) shows Microsoft's technical support Web site, TechNet (`http://support.microsoft.com/service-desks/technet/`).

NOTE One of the great things about technical support Web sites is that they are dynamic, ever-changing entities. As such, the figures you see in this book and the actual look of the Web site when you visit it may be different. The figures shown are just examples of what technical support Web sites look like.

Telephone Technical Support

Telephone support is one option that people like. You actually get to talk to a human being—an employee of the software manufacturer—about the problem you are having. Most, if not all, software manufacturers have telephone support numbers. These phone numbers, which are typically toll-free, are used to provide anything from basic how-to advice to answers to complex, technical questions.

Unfortunately, because of their popularity, technical support phone lines are often busy, and callers, when they do get through, often find themselves in "voice mail hell." Most people don't want this and hang up. They would prefer to get a human being as soon as the phone is picked up. Thus, in the end, many telephone support users become frustrated.

Vendor CDs

With the development of the CD-ROM disk and drive, it was possible to put volumes of textual information on a readily accessible medium. On just one of the first CDs, you could access many books worth of information. Software vendors would put a copy of the technical support database of problems and resolutions on the CD in a searchable

F I G U R E 14.12: Novell technical support Web site

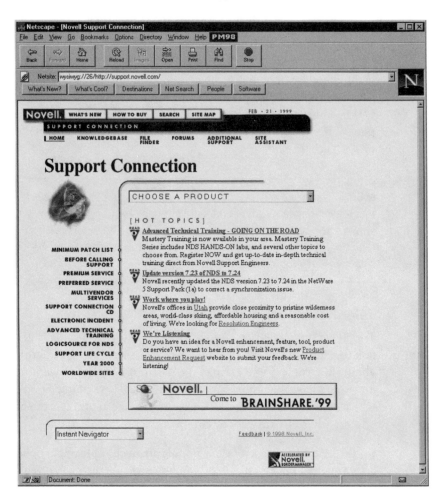

format and then distribute it to technicians in the field for little or no cost. Thus was born the technical support CD-ROM. You can carry it with you and have an entire searchable database of problems and answers. Plus, you don't have to wait on the phone to get the answer you need. Novell's Network Support Encyclopedia (NSE) CD-ROM was one of the first products of this kind, introduced in the early 1990s. Microsoft's Technical Support CD-ROM, called TechNet, came soon after. Figure 14.14 shows a screen from TechNet, which is released on a monthly basis to subscribers.

FIGURE 14.13: Microsoft technical support Web site

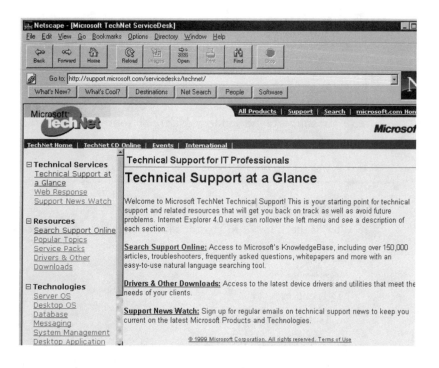

FIGURE 14.14: A sample screen from Microsoft's TechNet CD

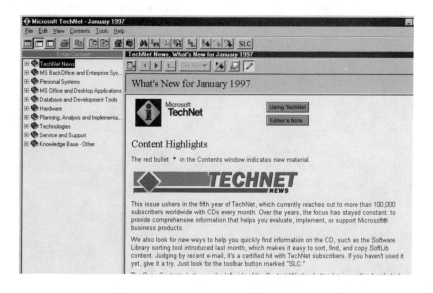

Exam Essentials

This objective is based on your ability to find help when you do not know the answer to a problem.

Know how to identify common network troubleshooting resources. Knowledge bases via the World Wide Web, telephone technical support, and vendor CDs are all sources of support when you are troubleshooting network problems.

Sample Question

1. What is the name of Microsoft's knowledge base that is accessible on CD and via their Web site?

   A. TechWeb

   B. TechNet

   C. Network Support Encyclopedia

   D. Network Support Web

   Answer: B—Microsoft's TechNet is available on CD, DVD, and via the Web. (TechWeb is Microsoft's Internet support site. The Network Support Encyclopedia is Novell's CD support product. D is a completely bogus answer.)

Given a network problem scenario, including symptoms, determine the most likely cause or causes of the problem based on the available information. Select the most appropriate course of action based on this inference. Issues that may be covered include:

- Recognizing abnormal physical conditions
- Isolating and correcting problems in cases where there is a fault in the physical media (patch cable)
- Checking the status of servers
- Checking for configuration problems with DNS, WINS, and HOSTS files
- Checking for viruses
- Checking the validity of the account name and password
- Rechecking operator logon procedures
- Selecting and running appropriate diagnostics

This objective is designed to help you "check the simple stuff" so you don't waste resources by looking for a difficult problem when the solution may be fairly straightforward. Any of the items listed in this objective can be checked without a great deal of effort and usually will solve apparent problems.

Critical Information

Network administrators can become absorbed in the virtual world of their network. The physical realm is just as important. Walk around your office. Check the server room. Actually walk into the wiring closets. Configuration issues can be as complicated as DNS and WINS configuration problems or as simple as a loose network cable.

When looking at possible network configuration problems, go beyond DNS, WINS, and HOSTS files. A user may misspell their username or password. A virus might corrupt the operating system. Look to using the appropriate software diagnostics tools when your troubleshooting skills are not enough.

Recognizing Abnormal Physical Conditions

You want to make sure that, from a network design standpoint, the physical environment for a server is optimized for placement, temperature, and humidity. When troubleshooting an obscure network problem, don't forget to check the physical conditions the network device is operating under. Check for problems like the following:

- Temperature too high
- Humidity too high (condensation)
- Humidity too low (leads to ESD problems)
- EMI/RFI problems
- ESD problems
- Power problems
- Cables unplugged

Isolating and Correcting Physical Media Faults

Cables, generally speaking, work fine once they are installed properly. Rarely is the cabling system the source of a problem, unless someone has made some change to it. If you suspect that the cabling system is the problem, first try replacing the patch cables at the workstation and hub. These are the easiest to get to and replace. If that solves the problem, you know it was related to the patch cable; it was either faulty or the wrong type.

If the patch cable isn't the problem, use a cable tester (*not* a tone generator and locator) to find the source of the problem. Wires that move can be prone to breakage or shorting. A short happens when the wire conductor comes in contact with another conductive surface, changing the path of the electrical signal. The signal will go somewhere instead of to the intended recipient. Cable testers can test for many types of problems, including the following:

- Broken cables

- Incorrect connections

- Interference levels

- Total cable length (for length restrictions)

- Cable shorts

- Connector problems

NOTE As a matter of fact, cable testers are so sophisticated that they can even indicate the exact location of a cable break (accurate to within 6 inches or less).

Checking the Status of Servers

Servers are key to your organization. When a workstation goes down, only one user is affected. When a server goes down, all users who access that server are impacted. When a user reports that a server is down, you must isolate the problem. Check to see if the TCP/IP stack on the server is working. And then you should ping the server, which will not tell you that the server is operating properly but will let you know whether a communication protocol is up or down.

Checking the Configuration of DNS, WINS, and HOSTS files

Network problems can often be traced to software configuration. Make sure that when you are checking the software for problems you don't leave out the software configuration. Some places to check for mis-configured items are:

- DNS configuration

- WINS configuration

- HOSTS file

- AUTOEXEC.BAT (DOS & Windows)

- CONFIG.SYS (DOS & Windows)

- AUTOEXEC.NCF (NetWare)

- Registry (Windows 9.*x* and NT)

Software configuration settings love to hide in places like these and can be notoriously hard to find.

Additionally, look for lines that have been "commented out" (either intentionally or accidentally). Most text configuration files use a command like REM (or REMARK), an asterisk, or a semicolon to place comment lines in a file.

TIP The HOSTS file is unique. It uses a # (pound sign) to indicate a comment line.

Checking for Viruses

Virus scanning is overlooked by many troubleshooters. Network administrators should not assume that network virus-checking software works automatically. Anti-virus software needs to have its virus definition files periodically updated.

Virus definition files need to be kept up-to-date in order to be effective. Vendors update their FTP sites periodically and when a major new virus is released. Update your anti-virus definitions on a monthly basis when everything is running normally. Also update the definition files right before tackling a virus outbreak; this is in addition to the monthly update.

If you are having unusual, irreproducible problems with a workstation, try scanning it with a *current,* up-to-date virus scan utility. You might be surprised at how many times people spend hours and hours troubleshooting a strange problem, only to run a virus scan and have the problem disappear.

Checking the Account Name and Password

In order to gain access to a network, users must follow the correct login procedure exactly. If they deviate from the norm, they will be denied access to the network. There are several items that can prevent a user from gaining access, and there is only one way to gain access.

The first, most basic thing a user must do in order to log in correctly is to enter the username and password correctly. As easy as this sounds, there are many incidents where usernames and passwords are entered incorrectly and the users wrongly interpret the resulting lack of access to mean that there is a problem with the network. As has already been discussed, one of the most common problems is when users don't remember that their usernames and passwords are case sensitive.

Selecting and Running Appropriate Diagnostics

Any software that can analyze and display the packets it receives can be considered to be a protocol analyzer. Protocol analyzers examine packets from protocols that operate at the lower four layers of the OSI model (including Transport, Network, Data Link, and Physical) and can display any errors they detect. Additionally, most protocol analyzers have the capability to capture packets and decode their contents. Capturing packets involves copying a series of packets from the network into memory and holding the copy so it can be analyzed.

You could, for example, capture a series of packets and decode their contents to figure out where each packet came from, where it was going, which protocol sent it, which protocol should receive it, and so on. This is useful in many areas, including analyzing the nature of the traffic sent across your network, determining which protocol is used the most often, ascertaining whether users are going to unauthorized sites, and son on. Protocol analyzers are also useful in determining whether a particular network card is "jabbering," or sending packets out even when there is no data to send. Software like the Network Associates Sniffer, Novell's LANalyzer, and Microsoft's Network Monitor are common protocol analyzers.

Exam Essentials

This objective is based on determining the most likely cause or causes of problems for given network problem scenarios.

Know how to recognize abnormal physical conditions and how to correct problems. Generally speaking, learn to notice any sight, sound, or smell that can indicate a malfunctioning component. Check the lights on your servers. Look for error lights and messages on LCD screens. Listen for abnormal sounds from your network equipment, including servers and workstations.

Know how to check configuration problems with DNS, WINS, and the HOSTS files. Look for duplicate entries and typographical errors in the server and workstation files.

Know how to check for viruses. Make sure that a passive virus protection program runs in the background on your computer. (A small anti-virus icon will appear on the system tray in Windows 9.*x* to indicate this.) Also run an active anti-virus program that requires a user to search an entire hard drive or a portion thereof.

Know how to check login procedures. Check that the user has the correct spelling of their account and password. Check to see that the Caps Lock key is off. Ensure that the proper account is being used for the specific workstation and network in question.

Know how to select and run diagnostics. A protocol analyzer can be used to look at the contents of packets. Depending on the results of your search, you will look at other areas (e.g., if a TCP/IP address is screwed up, you would look at DNS servers).

Key Terms and Concepts

Know the terms that relate to network troubleshooting and software tools. Many of the terms, such as DNS, WINS, and HOSTS files, are already defined in earlier chapters.

Protocol analyzer   A software tool that copies network packets to a log file or a real-time display. These copied packets are then dissected by the utility to aid in network troubleshooting.

Virus   A hidden program that copies itself and has a harmful payload. These programs can be copied through e-mail, downloading files, and sharing floppies between users. The harmful payloads can facilitate word processor and spreadsheet file manipulation, hard disk boot sector corruption, or damage to other programs on the computer.

Sample Questions

1. How often should you update virus definition files for your anti-virus software?

   A. Never

   B. Annually

   C. Quarterly

   D. Monthly

   E. Weekly

   F. Daily

   G. Just before you handle a virus outbreak

   H. Just after you handle a virus outbreak

   Answers: D, G—Update your definition files once per month, because most vendors release new files on a monthly basis. Also update your definition files right before handling a virus outbreak. (Interim updates are released by anti-virus vendors when particularly nasty viruses are discovered.)

Specify the tools that are commonly used to resolve network equipment problems. Identify the purpose and function of common network tools, including:

- Crossover cable
- Hardware loopback
- Tone generator
- Tone locator (fox and hound)

This objective will test your knowledge of four of the common network troubleshooting tools used to find cabling and other physical layer problems. The Network+ exam will test you on the use of each tool and the problems each can detect.

Critical Information

Network troubleshooting is also done with hardware tools. Four different tools are covered in the Network+ exam—crossover cable, tone locators and generators, and NICs. A crossover cable directly connects two computers or two hubs without intervening equipment. (Thousands of regular cables and crossover cables fill the ceilings, walls, and office spaces of a typical company.) Tone locators and generators are also helpful. And network interface cards are used to connect network cable to computers. These NICs are tested by using a hardware loopback device. Several of these devices are similar, so be sure not to confuse them.

Crossover Cable

As was just mentioned, one tool that is used in troubleshooting network cable problems is the crossover cable. Used only in Ethernet UTP installations, crossover cable is used to test communications between two stations, bypassing the hub. You can directly connect two workstations' (or a workstation's and a server's) NICs together by using a crossover cable (sometimes also called a cross cable).

A normal Ethernet (10BaseT) UTP cable uses four wires—two for transmitting, two for receiving. The cable is wired as shown in Figure 14.15, with all wires going from pins on one side directly to pins on the other side.

FIGURE 14.15: A standard Ethernet 10BaseT cable

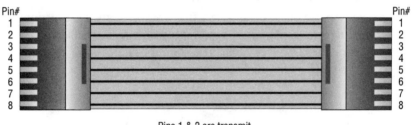

Pins 1 & 2 are transmit,
3 & 6 are receive

The transmitting and receiving wire pairs of a crossover cable, on the other hand, are crossed so that the transmitting set on one side (hooked to pins 1 and 2) are connected to the receiving set (pins 3 and 6) on the other side. Figure 14.16 illustrates this arrangement. Note that four of the wires are crossed, and compare this design to the standard 10BaseT UTP cable shown in Figure 14.15.

FIGURE 14.16: An Ethernet 10BaseT crossover cable

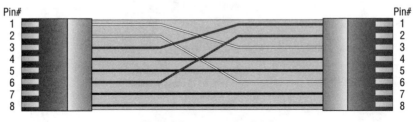

Pins 1 & 2 connect to pins 3 & 6
Pins 3 & 6 connect to pins 1 & 2

WARNING Make sure to label a crossover cable as such to ensure that no one will try to use it as a workstation patch cable. If it is used as a patch cable, the workstation won't be able to communicate with the hub and the rest of the network.

Crossover cables are typically used to connect two hubs together, but they can also be used to test communications between two stations directly. You can carry a crossover cable in a tool bag along with your laptop. If you want to ensure that a server's NIC's is functioning correctly, you can connect your laptop directly to the server's NIC by using the crossover cable. You should be able to log in to the server (assuming both NIC's are configured correctly).

Hardware Loopback

A hardware loopback is a special connector for Ethernet 10BaseT NICs that functions similarly to a crossover cable, except it connects the transmitting pins directly to the receiving pins (as shown in Figure 14.17). It is used by the NIC's software diagnostics to test transmission and reception capabilities. The NIC cannot be completely tested without one of these devices.

FIGURE 14.17: A hardware loopback and its connections

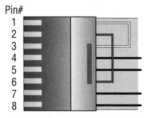

Pin#
1
2
3
4
5
6
7
8

In a loopback, pins 1 & 3 and
pins 2 & 6 are connected

Usually, the hardware loopback is no bigger than a single RJ-45 connector and has a few small wires on the back. If an NIC has hardware diagnostics that can use the loopback, the hardware loopback plug will be included with the NIC. To use it, simply plug the loopback into the RJ-45 connector on the back of the NIC and start the diagnostic software. Select the option in your NIC's diagnostic software that requires the loopback, and start the diagnostic routine. You will be able to tell if the NIC can send and receive data through the use of these diagnostics.

Tone Generator and Locator (Fox and Hound)

This combination of devices is used most often on telephone systems to help trace where cables are run. Since telephone systems use multiple pairs of UTP, it is nearly impossible to determine which set of wires goes where. Network documentation is extremely helpful in determining that. When documentation isn't available, a tone generator and locator can be used.

The tone generator is a small electronic device that sends an electrical signal down one set of UTP wires. The tone locator is another device that is designed to sense this signal and then emit a tone when the signal is detected in a particular set of wires. When you need to trace a cable, hook the generator (often called the fox) to the copper ends of the wire pair you want to find. Then move the locator (often called the hound because it "chases" the fox) over multiple sets of cables until you hear the tone. (You don't have to touch the copper part of the wire pairs; this tool works by induction.) When you hear a soft tone, you know that you are close to the right set of wires. Keep moving the tool until the tone gets loudest. Bingo! You have found the wire set. Figure 14.18 shows how a tone generator and locator are used.

NOTE   This tool should not be confused with a cable tester, which is used to test the many aspects of cable quality. The tone generator and locator should only be used to find which UTP cable is which.

FIGURE 14.18: Use of a common tone generator and locator

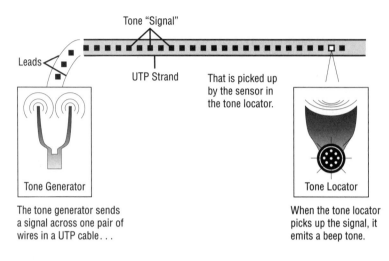

Tone "Signal"

Leads

UTP Strand

That is picked up
by the sensor in
the tone locator.

Tone Generator

Tone Locator

The tone generator sends
a signal across one pair of
wires in a UTP cable...

When the tone locator
picks up the signal, it
emits a beep tone.

WARNING NEVER HOOK A TONE GENERATOR TO A CABLE
THAT IS HOOKED UP TO EITHER AN NIC OR A HUB! Because the
tone generator sends electrical signals down the wire, it can blow an
NIC or a hub. That is why tone generators are not usually used on networks. Cable testers are used more often.

NOTE A time-domain reflectometer (TDR) is a hardware device that
tests cable continuity and distance. A TDR generates an electrical
signal. The signal is used to determine where in a cable there is physical damage.

Exam Essentials

This objective is based on your ability to specify the tools that are
commonly used to resolve network equipment problems. You will
need to identify the purpose and function of common network tools.

Know how to identify a crossover cable. A crossover cable is used
to directly connect two devices, such as two hubs or two PCs. The cable

consists of a minimum of four wires; two or more of the wires are crossed between each end. This allows two-way communications between each device without an intervening network hub or switch.

Know how to identify a hardware loopback device. A hardware loopback device connects to the port of a network interface card. This device is used to test the electrical signals that are sent and received through the physical port.

Know how to identify a tone generator and a tone locator. A tone generator, or fox, generates a signal over a network cable. The tone locator, or hound, can detect the signal sent by the fox.

Key Terms and Concepts

Know the terms that relate to hardware devices that are used in troubleshooting networks.

Crossover cable   A cable with several of the wires reordered in one of the jacks, allowing two nodes to communicate without an intervening network device.

Hardware locator   A device that connects to the port of a network interface card and helps to test the electrical signals coming out of the port.

TDR (time-domain reflectometer)   Used to check the continuity of a cable by sending electrical signals down the wire.

Tone generator (fox)   Creates an electrical signal on a cable so the cable can be located by using a tone locator.

Tone locator (hound)   Used to sweep over cables and find signals sent by a tone generator.

Sample Question

1. What device is used to check the actual electrical signals sent out of the port of an NIC?

   A. Crossover cable

   B. Fox

   C. Hound

   D. Tone generator

   E. Hardware loopback

   Answer: E—A hardware loopback actually receives electrical signals and sends them back to the port on the NIC to which it is attached. (A crossover cable is used to connect two network nodes. A fox— same as a tone generator—is used to select a cable by sending an electrical signal down the wires. The hound is the device that searches for the tone being generated on the wire by the fox.)

Given a network problem scenario, select appropriate tools to help resolve the problem.

This objective is kind of a summary objective. It asks, now that you know all the troubleshooting tricks of the trade, which you are going to use to solve a particular problem. The Network+ exam will present you with different scenarios and multiple-choice questions and then ask you to choose the best tool for the problem.

Critical Information

This last exam objective and chapter culminate the information learned for the entire Network+ exam. No specific skills or tools are looked for here. Rather, this exam section is more difficult because all of the skills and tools learned are tested here.

To prevent and locate network problems, remember to look at the physical world of your network. Patch cables can be disconnected or damaged. Link lights on NICs and hubs may not be on. Hubs, switches, and servers may not have their power cables plugged in. Space heaters can overheat network devices and PCs. Televisions, radios, and cordless phones generate EMI and RFI interference. Static electricity can damage circuit boards, floppies, hard drives, and chips. Water will short-circuit and ruin electrical equipment. Maintain the temperature and relative humidity in your computer areas. Your eyes and ears are the best tools for seeing these network problems.

Hardware problems warrant special tools. Hardware problems include bad NICs, lost cable ends, and faulty cables. The electrical impulses of an NIC are tested by using a hardware loopback device. This small block-like device returns electrical signals sent from the port of an NIC back to the NIC. Fox and hound tone generators and locators are used to isolate a single cable in a group, with tone locators finding the proverbial needle in a haystack. Faulty cables can be tested with time-domain reflectometers, which measure how long it takes a signal to bounce back on a wire. Simple line testers merely check to see if an electrical signal is on the wire.

Not every tool is hardware based. Much of your time will be spent in the software realm. Software tools are used to check connections based on protocols, performance, and packet content. Ping, tracert, NBTSTAT, NETSTAT, FTP, and Telnet are all used to check various aspects of TCP/IP and NetBIOS connections. Performance monitor and console programs in Windows NT and NetWare show the utilization of a server's RAM, hard disk, CPU, network card, and other hardware components. Protocol analyzers like Network Associate's

Sniffer and Microsoft's Network Monitor copy packets for dissection. As you can see, software tools comprise just one part of the network administrator's tool bag.

Good luck in your studies and exam endeavors. The Network+ exam is designed to help you show your multi-vendor skills in a heterogeneous environment. After passing the Network+ exam, the next step is to pursue advanced vendor-specific training and certification. Microsoft, Novel, and Unix vendors all offer engineering-level certifications.

Exam Essentials

This objective is based on a review of the tools available for network troubleshooting.

Know how to use the appropriate tools for physical problems.
Your eyes and ears are best used in finding physical problems. Also, use your knowledge of the various network troubleshooting methods and procedures discussed here to determine which method will work best to determine the solution to a problem.

Know how to use the appropriate tools for hardware problems.
A hardware loopback tests to see if you have a faulty NIC. After the NIC, cables are tested. A crossover cable directly connects two PCs. Tone generators are used to isolate a single cable out of a group of cables. TDRs are used to check the continuity of the wires in a cable.

Know how to use the appropriate tools for software problems.
Performance monitors can tell you when a server is overburdened. Protocol analyzers are used to check the contents of packets sent over the physical medium of the network.

Index

Note to the Reader: Throughout this index **boldfaced** page numbers indicate primary discussions of a topic. *Italicized* page numbers indicate illustrations.

NETWORK+™ CERTIFICATION FROM NETWORK PRESS™

The Network+ certification from the Computing Technology Industry Association (CompTIA) is a vendor- and product-neutral exam intended to test and confirm the knowledge of networking technicians with 18–24 months experience.

Each Network+ book:

* *Provides full coverage of every CompTIA exam objective*
* *Written by experts who participated in the development of the Network+ certification program*

Study!

NETWORK+
Study Guide

DAVID GROTH
WITH BEN BERGERSEN
AND TIM CATURA-HOUSER

EVERYTHING YOU NEED TO KNOW TO
PASS THE NETWORK+ EXAM

PROVIDES FULL COVERAGE OF ALL
COMPTIA NETWORK+ EXAM OBJECTIVES

INCLUDES HUNDREDS OF REVIEW
QUESTIONS

• NETWORK PRESS EDGE TEST
FOR NETWORK+

• 50 BONUS QUESTIONS

ISBN: 0-7821-2547-6
7.5"x 9" • 656pp • $49.99 U.S.

* Learn about networking technologies and network design concepts
* Includes hundreds of review questions
* CD includes exclusive Network Press Edge Test exam-preparation program

Practice!

Full
Network+
Coverage

NETWORK+
Test Success

DAVID GROTH
MATTHEW PERKINS

MAKE SURE YOU'RE READY FOR
COMPTIA'S NETWORK+ EXAM

REVIEW THE KEY MATERIAL FOR
EACH OBJECTIVE

IMPROVE YOUR TEST READINESS WITH
HUNDREDS OF REVIEW QUESTIONS AND
PRACTICE TEST QUESTIONS

ISBN: 0-7821-2548-4
7.5"x 9" • 480pp • $24.99 U.S.

* Reinforce your Network+ knowledge with detailed review questions
* Study summaries of all the information you need to know for the exam
* Gauge your test-readiness with tough practice questions

Review!

NETWORK+
Exam Notes

OBJECTIVE-BY-OBJECTIVE
COVERAGE OF COMPTIA'S
NETWORK+ EXAM

ESSENTIAL INFORMATION
ARRANGED FOR QUICK
LEARNING AND REVIEW

EXAM TIPS AND ADVICE
FROM EXPERT TRAINERS

ISBN: 0-7821-2546-8
5.875"x 8.25" • 432pp • $19.99 U.S.

* Quickly learn essential information for each exam objective
* Contains detailed analysis of the key issues
* Preview the types of questions found on the exam

NETWORK PRESS